inheriting the land

contemporary voices

from the midwest

Mark Vinz and Thom Tammaro

editors

University of Minnesota Press
Minneapolis
London

For copyright information see pages 331–35.

Published by the University of Minnesota Press
2037 University Avenue Southeast, Minneapolis, MN 55455-3092
Printed in the United States of America on acid-free paper

Library of Congress Cataloging-in-Publication Data

Inheriting the land: contemporary voices from the Midwest/edited by
    Mark Vinz and Thom Tammaro
        p.   cm.
    ISBN 0-8166-2303-1 (pbk.: alk. paper)
    1. American literature — Middle West.   2. Country life — Middle West — Literary collections.   3. American literature — 20th century.   4. Middle West — Literary collections.
I. Vinz, Mark, 1942-   . II. Tammaro, Thom, 1951-   .
PS563.I54   1993
810.8'0977-dc20   92-40561
                                                                                          CIP

Contents

The Presence of the Past

Town and Country

Gains and Losses

Introduction

In many ways, this anthology was begun a long time ago — back in the decade of the seventies when Mark Vinz edited the poetry journal *Dacotah Territory* in Moorhead, Minnesota, and first began exploring the idea of a literature of place, as Thom Tammaro was to do a few years later during his involvement with Barnwood Press in Muncie, Indiana. For each it has been a continuing dialogue, spurred not only by editing and teaching Midwestern literature, but also by meeting and talking with a number of Midwestern writers — Robert Bly, Tom McGrath, and William Stafford, to name but a few of the most important direct influences. In 1983, when Thom Tammaro had moved to Moorhead, a collaboration was begun that relaunched Dacotah Territory Press, culminating in a poetry chapbook series and the coedited anthology *Common Ground: A Gathering of Poems on Rural Life* (published in December of 1988), itself an outgrowth of Philip Dacey's Rural Writers Festival held at Southwest State University in Marshall, Minnesota, in 1986 (and again in 1989). It was after the second Marshall Festival that we began seriously putting together a new anthology — to include prose as well as poetry — first for Dacotah Territory Press, and then, as the manuscript grew beyond the limits of our original intentions, for a larger publisher.

What this dialogue and collaboration has meant for each of us has first of all been a confrontation of the idea of *regional,* and a continuing attempt to explore the extremes that term always seems to conjure up: provincialism and narrow remoteness on the one hand, but an exciting richness and connectedness on the other. If Tom McGrath has said that "North Dakota *is* everywhere," it is but a confirmation that in large part American literature has always been one of regions far more than nation—that the most positive and enduring sense of regional is indeed that link between particular and universal, local and international. If there is a beacon that has guided our thinking about the nature of region and place, it is William Stafford's often quoted statement "On Being Local," first published in the *Northwest Review* in 1973:

> All events and experiences are local, somewhere. And all human enhancements of events and experiences—all the arts—are regional in the sense that they derive from immediate relation to felt life. It is this immediacy that distinguishes art. And paradoxically the more local the feeling in art, the more all people can share it; for that vivid encounter with the stuff of the world is our common ground. Artists, knowing this mutual enrichment that extends everywhere, can act, and praise, and criticize, as insiders—the means of art is the life of all people. And that life grows and improves by being shared. Hence, it is good to welcome any region you live in or come to think of, for that is where life happens to be, right where you are.

In this spirit as editors, then, we have used the term *regional* more as a description than a valuation. For us, regional has meant individuals' responses to the particulars of their landscapes, using certain methods or techniques to create their worlds. These methods can be used in *any* region, and there are any number of books and anthologies and writers that make such exploration of the many regions of this country and the regions of other countries as well. This is indeed the spirit that has united and defined our efforts, and that has led us to a few important conclusions along the way, especially as Midwesterners who are more interested in exploring the region than in defining it, for definition—any definition—is by nature exclusionary. We are not so much interested in drawing or mapping the boundaries as we are in exploring the territory. If our boundaries expand or contract, if they seem fluid or arbitrary, so be it.

A starting point for our explorations has been this question: When we look specifically at the Midwest in terms of a literature of place, what do we discover? While it is perhaps impossible to define the identity of a region so large and diverse as the twelve states traditionally considered to be the Midwest (North Dakota, South Dakota, Nebraska, Kansas, Minnesota, Iowa, Missouri, Wisconsin, Illinois, Michigan, Indiana, and Ohio), certain themes and ideas tend to persist.

Having read hundreds of pieces of Midwestern writing over the years — as well as having used many of them in our classes on Midwestern literature, culture, and experience — we have independently and collaboratively arrived at some conclusions, which are reflected in the section divisions of this book. These divisions are to some degree arbitrary, in that there are other organizational principles by which to arrange the material — our choices are thus to be seen as a starting point rather than a closing point. But we have found that examining the tensions and oppositions that exist within climate, land, time, and change allows us to see with some resolution the forces at work in shaping the literatures and cultures of the American Midwest. These terms are plural because we believe there is indeed a plurality of literatures and cultures within the region, as in the nation as a whole, and it has often been their confluence that has produced the richness found therein.

First, as with the term *regionalism* itself, there are the familiar stereotypes, most of which are promoted — sometimes inadvertently — by the region's writers, both past and present. For example, if honesty, sincerity, and hard work are seen as important parts of the Midwestern ethic, so too are xenophobia and being out of the cultural "mainstream." The same may be said for the environment itself — the harshness and hardships of the extremes of weather versus the quiet and idyllic beauty of the rural. Indeed, these tensions have persisted since the beginning of Midwestern literature: the boundless Adamic optimism of Rølvaag's Per Hansa as opposed to Beret's terror of open spaces and the loss of the Old World; Cather's homage to the pioneer spirit and the bounty of rural life as opposed to the encroachment of "modern" mean-spirited towns (itself an echo of Twain and a forecast of Anderson and Lewis and the continuing rural-urban divisions of the Midwest); the loss of the Native American and pioneer past in an increasingly technological society (where farming has become "agribusiness"), which forms the basis of themes for writers as diverse as Erdrich, Hassler, and Gruchow. In many important ways, being a Midwestern writer today means being aware of those themes, as it means being aware of the landscape itself. Though a few eschew direct influences, most of us finally admit that contemporary Midwestern writing has much to do with the way one is rooted: not only one's sense of the past, but of a people, an idiom, and the power of the land itself. As Bill Holm has pointed out so well, it is a land by and large to be defined by its subtleties and understatements, not its picture-postcard scenery or outspokenness.

All of this, of course, comes down to the writer's particular attitudes and angle of vision. Indeed, the same landscape can be seen in so many different ways, from Cather's Romanticism to Lewis's cynicism, from McGrath's stark populist politics to Keillor's gentle satire and humor. And as John R. Milton so rightly emphasizes, in a region dominated by contradictions, the burden of the writer is to find new ways of seeing, of uniting the tensions between harshness and beauty, boosterism and cynicism, loving and hating—indeed, to give the reader new ways to *see.*

In putting together this anthology, these have been some of the ideas that have shaped our search for material. We indeed emphasized the rural Midwest, emphasized writing that is *grounded,* emphasized writing that seeks to find new ways to see and explore and unite the diversity and contrasts around us. We have sought writing, too, that in some way seems accessible to the general reader; and certainly, we must admit that while all the Midwestern states are represented in this collection, our emphasis has been on the Upper Midwest—Minnesota and the Dakotas, in particular—which, after all, remains our own most familiar frame of reference. As with any anthology, then, we realize that this one has its limits and incompletenesses, but we also hope it will provide both a useful introduction to contemporary writing about the rural Midwest and a spur to a continuation of the dialogue that is at the heart of Midwestern literature itself.

Finally, as editors, we want to discourage any urge to use this collection as a gauge or sociological survey. The work within is not data to be analyzed and massaged to gain some definitions or characteristics that will classify or define all that Midwestern writing is today. Rather, we think of the work within more as a literary sampler, offering poetry, fiction, and nonfiction by contemporary writers who have looked at their Midwestern landscapes and responded to them. And by no means are these writers the only ones to engage in such activities. Readers need only to look to their local libraries and bookstores and to readings given within their community to find other writers whose work may very well have been included in this anthology. Whatever generalizations can be drawn or inferences made from the particulars within must be done with a cautionary hand, for we have not attempted to be definitive or exclusive. Ultimately, what we have attempted is to offer the work of several writers who have spent much of their writing lives exploring their region. Many of the writers here have spent years—often with self-conscious commitments—imaginatively engaged with the particulars of their landscapes. It seems to us that "human imagination engaged with the world and expressed" is at the heart of the creative process and as close to a definition of "art" as we want to come. We ask our readers, then, to meet each work on its own terms: as an expression of one human's imaginative response to the particulars of his or her landscape. Reading, too, can—and should be—a creative act. It is in that spirit that we invite our readers to join us.

* * *

Special thanks are in order to several people who assisted us in various ways with this book: to Philip Dacey, organizer and director of two festivals of rural writers and writing held at Southwest State University in 1986 and 1989, and to Tom Sand, the angel of those conferences and of *Common Ground: A Gathering of Poems on Rural Life;* to Moorhead State University for continuing support and encouragement, including Release Time Awards for the editors; to Moorhead State University president Roland Dille and to English Department secretary Vicki Kirkhorn; to a number of Midwestern small presses and magazines and their editors, most notably David Pichaske and C. W. Truesdale, and to John R. Milton, who has given tireless support to Midwestern writing and writers as editor of *South Dakota Review* for more than twenty-five years (see, for example, his essay "The Dakota Image" in Volume VIII, no. 3, a brief excerpt of which appears in the "Climates" section of this book); to our many colleagues who shared their ideas about rural Midwestern writing with us, and especially to our students who participated in the many give-and-take classroom sessions in which we discussed Midwestern literature; to Robert Carothers, Sheila Coghill, Wayne Gudmundson, Thomas W. Koontz, Carl Malmstrom, Jay Meek, Joe Richardson, Rosemary Smith, Keith Tandy, Betsy Vinz, and Dave Williamson, whose friendships and intelligence were invaluable along the way; to Ron Gower and Norita Dittberner-Jax, who read the manuscript in its early form and offered valuable, constructive criticism and suggestions; to Beverly Kaemmer, our editor at the University of Minnesota Press, for her discipline, patience, guidance, and for returning all our calls; and finally, to all the writers who submitted work to this anthology during its three-year odyssey. As with any such project, length limitations and editorial collaborations necessitated sacrificing much good work from the final version, but *all* the work initially accepted indeed reaffirms our faith in the depth and breadth of talent to be found in contemporary writing in the Midwest.

M. V.

T. T.

Climates

You can be fooled into thinking [the Midwest is] not impressive because it lacks the topographical grandeur of the Far West . . . or the historic connectedness of the East Coast. What it offers, instead, is an atmospheric world—a world of light and distance and far horizon that is constantly changing with the seasons. In the course of a year it shows many different textures and colors and moods. You have to be patient to notice this. You can't just drive through the Midwest in two days and expect to understand it. Or fly over it and look down from thirty thousand feet and think you know what's going on. Being sensitive to these changes has a bearing on your ability to understand the literature coming out of that world, too. . . .

I think of the upper Missouri River watershed as a vast mirror for an amazing range of annual climatic changes. You can be struggling in two feet of snow in March, and by late May it will have turned into the most lush, green, leafy world imaginable. Follow that with a traditional summer full of sunlight and white thunderheads and semi-tropical evenings, and top it off with the kind of autumn that makes you want to go out with a friend and pass a football back and forth all afternoon, until it gets dark.

In the Midwest, the cycle of seasons is more pronounced—more beautiful, more invigorating, more challenging—than in any other place I have ever been. Which is probably why I came back to it, why I live there, why I write about it. . . .

—Jared Carter, from the *Yarrow* interview

. . . regional writers [need] to interpret and clarify their own land. The outsider cannot do it as well . . . it is the writers who establish the image, not the arguments of local chambers of commerce or any other kind of advertising. . . . It seems to me that our task lies in the tensions between the beautiful and the harsh. We have these extremes—perhaps they are our only real image. What we need to do now is understand and use *the materials of our land. We need to overcome the stereotype meaningfully, not in mere argument. For this we need writers and artists.*

—John R. Milton, from "The Dakota Image"

Summer Cloudburst

Candace Black

In the old days we fired the cannon
at the clouds. Those long
afternoons the sky filled, always
darker yet never spilling until all grew

quiet. The birds stopped singing.
Farmers stood squinting
in the fields. The women
eyed the lines of wash

hanging slack. Boys flung rocks
toward heaven. Soon we heard
the muffled thump from Gustave Haufman's
farm. If his aim was true, the charge

dry, the mottled screen tore,
releasing breeze that at first
stirred only the poplar. As the drops
fell, explosions of dust peppered

the yard. Children scurried
to save the laundry, chickens
ran from beneath the house, bug
hungry. The sky opened

and we knew Papa would come in
early, smelling of wet horse and corn.
The bowl filled with snapbeans
and Mama stoked the stove for supper.

Three Kinds of Pleasures

Robert Bly

I
Sometimes, riding in a car, in Wisconsin
Or Illinois, you notice those dark telephone poles
One by one lift themselves out of the fence line
And slowly leap on the gray sky—
And past them, the snowy fields.

II
The darkness drifts down like snow on the picked cornfields
In Wisconsin: and on these black trees
Scattered, one by one,
Through the winter fields—
We see stiff weeds and brownish stubble,
And white snow left now only in the wheeltracks of the combine.

III
It is a pleasure, also, to be driving
Toward Chicago, near dark,
And see the lights in the barns.
The bare trees more dignified than ever,
Like a fierce man on his deathbed,
And the ditches along the road half full of a private snow.

One Hundred Percent Chance of Snow, Accumulating Six to Eight Inches by Morning

David Citino

Snow billows over cracked blacktop
in parking lots of K Mart and Whirlpool plant,
plexiglass domed roof of Southland Mall
where young and old cluster and dissolve
in weekend conspiracies.

Snow blows over churches downtown,
each spire and arch shaped by antique disputes
concerning the shape or taste of God
obliterated now by tons of lovely nothing.

Here's my heaven: Ohio, bitter enough
to set teeth on edge and turn my face red
as litmus paper. Still, for all
our dirty profits, there's more love
than I can use, and more cold.

Near me beneath the ice run
the Olentangy and Scioto. So much
of our lives gets named by what's fallen.
I think of the ruddy women and men

whose teeth and bone lie arrayed in strata
beneath me, earth of their every fire dark
as obsidian. I step over burrows
where they weather forever's winter.
I'm coming soon, Grandparents.

My feet leave lines of script to mark
my progress, each step a fossil moment,

no two the same, lines that sing
my stride to anyone willing to follow

before this pure and ruthless beauty
disproves that I was ever here.

Eighty-four Days without Rain

Robert Dana

Each day, dawn—
and the scorched penny
of the sun coppery
already in the white
sky, fields
bitched and brown,
topsoil stone dry
ten inches down
under even the deepest
oaks. Two days
now, they've dragged
the river below
the old power-dam
for the body of the boy
who slipped away there
last Friday night
trying to keep cool.
Bindweed shrivels
in this heat. Late
morning markets rise
and fall. Pray
for an hour of shadow,
a thimbleful of rain.
We stunt and wither
and die upward from
the roots like gods.

Geraniums

Susan Strayer Deal

What does she
really feel,
digging in flowers?
Hands, knuckle deep
in soil. Putting
these tense blooms in.
What does she
really want? A spark
from the nerves of
living roots travelling
up the conduit of
fingers. The tingling
shock of fingers
stuck in a socket.
The pain and pleasure
of something tensely
living touching
something electrically
alive? Kneeling woman
entranced in a flower
bed who digs in the light,
in the current of her
pulsing red geraniums

June Walk

Alice Friman

I walk an old country road
that parts the flat fields not yet
sprung with corn or bean, and runs
straight and mean as an old man's mouth.
A car swooshes by. Dust leaps, hangs
in the air, then drops like an old coat.
It is Sunday in Indiana. Quiet.

On the side of the road beer cans and
chunks of green bottleglass fire dimly.
A child's necklace, broken yellow beads.
A plastic sack of trash,
orange peels, a dirty sock, papers.
I count six dead birds along the way.
Each, fluffy with dust, offers itself
up to the flies. The feet bent back
at the ankles, bent like knees.

In front of a farmhouse door
white peonies left over from May
still clutch, desperate as old brides,
lean back on their stalks, spread open
their petals, and as I pass, flash the
blood spot in their wedding dress
like an advertisement. Flies
buzz around in their little tight
tuxedos like 1930s chorus boys
flicking their canes.
One fat one shimmies her petals.
They drop like teeth. She leers
gap-toothed through the fence
palings of herself.

The flies break into a buck and wing
chanting litanies through their
buzzy throats and close in.

The sky is cloudless. Nothing interferes.
It is the order of things, hanging
from the sky, upside-down.

Rules for Winter

Joanne Hart

When it's time for sleepwalks to the cabin,
salute the stars and check the yeasty moon.
Listen for the owls. If you are lucky
there will be a row of holes
by morning where wolves walked.
Sleep cool in feathers.
Dream your lover moves to you through water.
Dress at dawn in cotton wool,
feed the children roses, buttered wheat,
raspberry tea. In autumn, only,
keep deer mice. When whiskey jacks
knock on the windows, wave
and watch them float. Set
fish for ermine in bird feeders
and expect squirrels to fly,
by night. Don't look
for heat from bleeding trees,
or sense from strangers rapping
at your door blind, deaf, and mainly dumb.
Serve laying hens fresh snow
and corn. Shovel wide,
for deep snow grow webbed feet,
and when the rain is freezing stay inside,
sniff a sweetgrass ring, sing poems.

Fishing with My Two Boys
at a Spring-fed Pond in Kansas

William Kloefkorn

Truth
like those sunfish
swimming under that overhang of willows
darts in and out among the shadows:
my boys are no longer
boys.

I sit on a campstool
trying my hand with a surface lure.
My sons meanwhile
circle the pond slowly,
looking for that perfect spot.
In their belief that such a place exists
they yet are boys, after all.
And with the luck that goes
with keeping the faith
they find it,
each landing a bass
sufficient for what lies ahead,
the multitude.

At dusk the girls, who are women,
arrive,
and by the time the first bullfrog
clears its ancient throat
we are eating the hot white flesh of the fish,
prepared and cooked by the boys
on the coals of a bonfire
tended by them,
and soon the lights in the tents
go on, then off,

and the men lie down with the women,
and their babes, who are children,
giggle until the moon drops into a cloud

and by feel I work a nightcrawler
onto a treble hook,
then spit in the general direction
of that wiggling bait,
hoping to hit it,
wanting what every lucky father wants,
more luck.

In Late Spring

Ted Kooser

One of the National Guard's F-4 jet fighters,
making a long approach to the Lincoln airfield,
comes howling in over the treetops, its shadow
flapping along behind it like the skin of a sheep,
setting the coyotes crying back in the woods,
and then the dogs, and then there is a sudden quiet

that rings a little, the way an empty pan
rings when you wipe it dry, and then it is
Sunday again, a summer Sunday afternoon,
and beyond my window, the Russian Olives
sigh foolishly into the air through the throats of their flowers,
and bluegills nibble the clouds afloat on the pond.

Under the windmill, a cluster of peonies huddles,
bald-headed now, and standing in piles of old papers.
Beneath its lipstick, the mouth of the tulip is twisted.
Spring moves on, on her run-down broken toe-shoes
into the summer, trailing green ribbons of silk.

I have been reading for hours, or intending to read,
but over the bee-song of the book I could faintly hear
my neighbor up the road a quarter mile
calling out to his daughter, and hear her calling back,
not in words but in musical notes, and now that they
have fallen quiet, and I have listened long into their absence,
I have forgotten my place in the world.

But the world knows my place, and stands and holds a chair
for me, here on these acres near Garland, Nebraska.
This April, in good health, I entered my fiftieth year.
The perfect porcelain bells of Lily-of-the-Valley

ring into the long, shy ears of the ferns,
and the horsefly sits in the sun and twirls his mustache
and brushes the dust from his satin sleeves.

Plowing

Orval Lund

Crawling steady at a slight slant,
smooth waves of sliced and shiny earth spiralling
behind, the engine droning, the floor-hum tickling
your feet, the big yellow Moline fenders
defining your cabin, you're much alone
on flat fields, not a tree in sight, seagulls,
a punctuation in the sky, hovering
for worms sliced and tossed atop.

At field's end, you jerk the frayed rope to raise
the plow. The shiny, scoured blades climb
out, the tractor takes its little step
up to sod, sighing from its upright pipe, and you turn
and steer your right wheel toward
the clean square trough, then jerk the cord to drop
the plow; the tractor grunts, hunkers
down, squares its shoulders, snorts and starts again.

Again, the engine's drone, the scrape
of stone on steel. You can feel
your back relax, the tingle in your feet, can smell
dark earth and remember a day
you prepared the field for growth,
the rolling sod streaming back and scouring
shares to a shine, the poetry
of straight black lines across a flat field.

Too Long Away from Small Things

Roger Pfingston

Behind the main street stores
of a small town in Illinois
I walked the snow-covered tracks
that take the boxcars to the canning
company, stopping now and then
for pictures. The only person
I saw that morning — a trash man
running his truck from can to can
between the tracks and the straight shot
of backyards — caught me, both knees
in the snow, focusing down on a tuft
of dead grass. As he heaved one can up
and banged it empty, he kept an eye
on me as if I'd found something
that should've been his that early
in the morning. I waved: he blew his nose,
pressing one nostril shut and snorting out
the other. I took one more of the grass,
then turned for a shot of my own footsteps
coming down the tracks, slowly filling with snow.

Finnish Women in the Summer Kitchen

Gail Rixen

They serve the fire.
Indifferently, it rolls steam
off the canner
by them through the screen.

But for the digital watches,
they could be their mothers.
Finnish or English,
the rhythm's the same,
rolls off like a hard boil.
They talk about the season,
measuring out spices with their hands.
Some gossip about a neighbor's microwave.
Someone's kid gone bad
or hanging out-of-season deer.

What they do not say
drips into the jars to wait
till cold January to whisper
in the quiet house.

Canoeing — the Lakes

George Roberts

when the lakes leap out before you
   shining in the morning sun
   like stepping stones across a brook
and you first risk the fragile surface
   of water,

when your shoulders have not yet found
   their rhythm
and early lakes drain
   the magic from your ribs,

then place your paddle across the thwarts,
feel the drift of the canoe
the insistent whispering of water
   under you,
and look for a while at your wet boots
   curled under you like squirrels
   sleeping in the rain
or at the sun glinting off water
   bright as a bluebottle fly.

choose your route to avoid
   people, roads near the shore,
   sudden noises.
look back occasionally to see
   how shoreline and skyline
   will look when you return.

remember, no two rocks along the shore
   have the same name, no slanting jackpine
   standing inland on a rise
   of rock and rotting deer shit
has a twin.

the easy stride of your paddle will grow
   like breathing,
your shoulders will remember
   the wing sounds of migrating ducks
and you will know each boat length
   of water and sun with delicious fear
   of entering a new country.

the necessary stretches of land
   between lakes,
the expected moments of deadfall and bog,
are reminders of the delicate balance
   you must maintain.
portage everything in one trip, throwing
   the canoe onto your shoulders
   like a tightrope artist
   shouldering his pole,
and pass over rock, deep mud and sloping weeds
memorizing their textures to keep your feet
   from wanting webs.

resume the water, each time, with simple
   amazement at finding your first self.

and when, near sunset, you begin to search
   the shore for a campsite,
look for wind to clear away the bugs,
   east shore for morning sun,
   and deepest moss
to give your sleep the floating echo
   of your day's travel.

Fishing with My Daughter in Miller's Meadow

Lucien Stryk

You follow, dress held high above
   the fresh manure,
missing your doll, scolding Miller's horses

for being no gentlemen where they graze
   in morning sun.
You want the river, quick, I promised you back there,

and all those fish. I point to trees where
   water rides low
banks, slopping over in the spring,

and pull you from barbed wire protecting corn
   the size of you
and gaining fast on me. To get you in the meadow

I hold the wire high, spanning a hand across
   your freckled back.
At last we make the river, skimmed with flies,

you help me scoop for bait. I give you time
   to run away,
then drop the hook. It's fish I think

I'm after, you I almost catch, in up to knees,
   sipping minnowy
water. Well, I hadn't hoped for more.

Going back, you heap the creel with phlox and marigolds.

Going West

Alan Davis

In a science-fiction story I read last year when Audrey and I were separated, an Earthling and a Martian meet in a time warp. Each believes the other's civilization is in ruins, or never existed. They stand perplexed in the Martian desert, sand swirling around them, and try finally to clasp hands in a gesture of goodwill. But their fingers slide through each other like the blades of a skate through ice.

Recently, we were housebound with the two kids in the dead of a blizzard for three days. I had the television, the kids their Lego blocks, Audrey her sewing. But how many reruns of *M*A*S*H* can you stomach, especially with the sound turned up to drown out Margaret's tantrums and Stevie's new obsession with percussion instruments? Legos were scattered over five rooms and Audrey was reduced to thumbing through magazines.

I raised the white flag. "Let's go find the sun," I announced, clicking off *The Dukes of Hazzard* and dropping on all fours to reach under the couch for Stevie's long-lost farm implement hat. He wouldn't travel without it. Otherwise, the world might find out about his cowlick. "Licked by a cow, licked by a cow," he repeated, clamping the tiny hat on his head, as though capping a geyser.

"How the hell does he know about cowlicks?" I asked Audrey. "Is that what he gets at nursery school?"

"Beats me," she said, still in her magazine. "The sun?"

"I figure we head south," I said. "I'll check the weather channel first." I pulled out the big suitcase.

"Hey," she said, Margaret half-stuffed into her snowsuit, "what's this? I thought we were going for a ride."

The plastic on the picture window had bubbled. Only an occasional pickup or four-wheel drive ventured past as a single plow worked its way down our street, wind swirling snowdust around it. Its driver had on a moonsuit of metallic silver. Long tubes as thick as a forearm led from his glass compartment to the plow's hot engine.

"I'll warm up the car and shovel the drive," I said. "Why don't you gather up some cassettes, make a thermos of coffee?"

On the road the kids fell asleep, Stevie cuddled against Margaret's carseat. Audrey loosened their seat belts and covered them with a plaid quilt. Every time I glanced in the rear-view mirror I thought of Scotland.

"We're not going to stop until we find it, you know."

The interstate was dry and plowed, with great dirty drifts tilting towards us on either side, snow swirling across in fine sandy layers. Everything was white.

"That so?" Audrey said, dreaming. "That means we never go back."

We went west. The weather channel had mentioned a warmer front in that direction. The temperature did rise a few degrees, but after three hours the sky was still slate-grey, the horizon still the color of dirty laundry.

At a gas station an attendant, stocky as a steer, grunted when I asked his advice. "Let me get this straight," he said, lips downturned, gruffness quick-frozen, shipped from the Scandinavian tundra. "You not going anywhere? You just looking for the sun?"

"You bet," I said, signing the credit slip. "Am I going to find it?"

He considered my question. "Not once it gets dark."

At the motel I pulled out the map and spread it on one of the two rumpled beds. For a few minutes I talked about routes, figuring mileage and driving time, leaning close to the unfolded crinkled paper to make out place names: Medina, Williston, Miles City, towns of mud engineers, farm implement manufacturers, owners of greasy diners.

"We don't have a marriage anymore," I remembered shouting. "We have a family."

I folded the map and jammed it into the slip pocket of the nylon suitcase. Stevie, twice Margaret's age, was teaching her how to turn the second bed into a trampoline. Audrey had her hair down, one arm outstretched like a guardrail near Margaret, who landed on her back and squealed.

"Maybe we ought to forget about it," I said.

Neither of us fell in love with anyone else. In some ways an affair would have made sense. But Audrey was busy with two kids and I wasn't interested. Instead, I rented an apartment near the plant where I worked.

"I have one baby crying for a bottle and another screaming for a bath," Audrey would say over the phone. "When the hell you coming home?" The line would go quiet. "You're deserting me, aren't you?"

"No," I would say, tapping the windowsill. "I've been working fourteen hours. Don't you appreciate that?"

I sat on the balcony, some nights, once it got warm, and drank, and watched the stars.

"I'm sorry," she said. "Did I disappear in the middle of your plans?"

"No, it's not that." I shrugged, running my fingers over the pasteboard cover of a Gideon Bible. I opened it at random: "Will you judge them?" I read. "Will you judge them, son of man? Then confront them with the detestable practices of their father and say to them. . . . "

Stevie took Margaret into one corner of the motel room. Beneath a picture of mountains, all rosy in the late afternoon, he tried to change her plastic diaper. She started crying when he snatched it and waved it like a flag. "Hey!" I shouted.

"Were you serious?" Audrey asked later, the kids asleep. She rested her chin on her knees, still steaming from the shower. "Because the trip is a good idea, Rod. The weather's okay now, not dangerous. What the hell."

The empty thermos floated in the basin. Water dripped from the faucet. "Thinking about it makes it weird," I said. "Going after the sun is something a kid might do."

She shifted on the bed. "So what? Weird is good. People up here, they're afraid to be weird. You start to think the Nazis won the war." She sipped the last of the day's hot coffee. "Let's move," she said. "Let's get back down South, maybe Louisiana, where people aren't so bored with their lives."

The next day we passed a couple of old missile silos, concrete slabs in the middle of nowhere surrounded by heavy-duty fences. We peered into the heavens now and then, beyond the snow and stubble, but the flat fields stretched for miles. We could hardly tell in the mist where ground stopped and sky began.

"Audrey?"

"Hmm?" A magazine jostled on her lap.

"What happened with us?"

One Sunday morning I had met her and the kids for breakfast, and afterwards I went home with the family. "My old flame," Audrey had said, leaning on my shoulder.

"You want an answer?" she asked.

Far ahead, on the road, someone flailed his arms, as though doing side-straddle hops. "What the heck is that?" Stevie wondered. "A midget?"

"He's just far away," I said, slowing down. A car had its hood up a half mile or so beyond the waving figure. And then I saw the hair falling from her knitted cap. "She's had a breakdown."

On the upper plains, you feel you've fallen off the edge of the world. Houses, grain silos, even people take on a two-dimensional tiltiness. The sight of a polar bear lumbering across desolate fields would be disorienting but not entirely unexpected, while the woman, snowsuited, waving her arms, shocked me to attention.

She ran towards our car. I snapped on the emergency lights and inched to the roadside. Shoulders slumped, she stopped several feet from us. "Wait here," I said absurdly, zipping up my coat.

We talked on the edge of the flat snowy fields, and I knew from her tone of voice, even before I made out the words, that her companion had left the car. It's the one thing you never do in such weather, not ever. You pack slow-burning candles, sleeping bags, high-energy grub in case of breakdown. But leaving the car is taboo. The cold makes you tired, sluggish; not even an arctic expedition would have better than even odds if the wind started up again.

The skin on her cheekbones was purple and raw, tears of frustration frozen beneath her eyes. Her old car could have been propped up with a pair of two-by-fours.

"Have you seen him?" she shouted.

He was dead. I found out next day. The two of them had a fight. He decided to cool off, fast, in his windbreaker, and got frozen against a fencepost. He looked alive in the picture—jeans snagged on barbed wire, one hand scratching at his scalp.

Over her shoulder a squad car U-turned across a strip of neutral ground. Lights flashing, it pulled beside her disabled vehicle. My eyes stung in the wind as I pointed to the officer. She turned to see the hooded bear-like figure walk to her car, peer inside, then spot us.

She squeezed my arm. "Thanks." She had pale determined features, lips indrawn, eyes hard-set.

We stared at each other. Under different circumstances, I might have found her quite lovely.

Before I could offer a lift, she was halfway to the squad car, running bow-legged for balance.

"The police are out on a day like this," I said, with authority, but Audrey and I exchanged glances.

Later we stopped again. In the distance we saw a mountain range. "We've gone far enough, haven't we?" Stevie asked.

"Besides," added Audrey, "I think I see the sun."

Huddled around the car, we argued. In the far distance, through a geometry of high-powered telephone lines and scaffolding, there was something, though it provided little heat or light, just the barest trace of a disk, something noticeable only because it was different from what had been there before. It was like the way you can tell in a dark room by heartbeat, or breathing, whether you're with people you care for or not.

The Undistinguished Poet
(from *Staggerford*)

Jon Hassler

Few could remember a time when Miss McGee — slight and splay-footed and quick as a bird — was not teaching at St. Isidore's. This was her forty-first year in the same classroom, her forty-first year of flitting and hovering up and down the aisles in the morning when she felt fresh, and perching behind her walnut desk in the afternoon when fatigue set in. In the minds of her former students, many of whom were now grandparents, she occupied a place somewhere between Moses and Emily Post, and when they met her on the street they guarded not only their speech but also their thoughts.

They knew of course — for she had been telling the story for over half a century — that when she was a girl she had met Joyce Kilmer, but who would have guessed the connection between that meeting many years ago and the fire alarm this afternoon? Standing in the garden among her cabbages, she decided that she would never tell a soul — not even Miles — about the cause of the fire alarm. She could not lie, but she could keep a secret.

Agatha McGee met Joyce Kilmer when she was six. She was a first grader at St. Isidore's. The year was 1916 and her teacher, Sister Rose of Lima, primed the first grade for months, leading them in a recitation of "Trees" every morning between the Apostles' Creed and the Pledge of Allegiance; and then on the last day of school before

Christmas break, Joyce Kilmer stepped through the classroom door at the appointed hour, casting Sister Rose of Lima into a state of stuttering foolishness and her students into ecstasy. Miss McGee remembered it like yesterday. Mr. Kilmer was handsome, cheery, and a bit plump. He wore a black suit and a red tie. With a playful sparkle in his eye he bowed to Sister Rose of Lima, saying he was delighted to meet her, and then he walked among her students, asking their names. The children's voices were suddenly undependable, and they told their names in tense whispers and unexpected shouts. Jesse Farnham momentarily forgot who he was, and the silence was thick while he thought. When he finally said, "Jesse," Mr. Kilmer told him that he had known a girl by that name, and the first grade exploded with more laughter than Sister Rose of Lima permitted on ordinary days. (Priests and poets melted her severity.) The laughter, ending as suddenly as it began, was followed by a comfortable chat, the poet telling stories, some without lessons. Before Mr. Kilmer left, his admirers recited "Trees" for him. For Agatha McGee his visit was, like Christmas in those years, a joy undiminished by anticipation.

But that was long ago. Nowadays poetry, among other things, wasn't what it used to be. Yesterday at St. Isidore's as Miss McGee sat at the faculty lunch table she overheard Sister Rosie tell Sister Judy in an excited whisper that Herschel Mancrief was coming to town. He was touring the Midwest on a federal grant, and would arrive at St. Isidore's at ten the next morning. The two sisters were huddled low over the Spanish rice, trying to keep the news from Miss McGee. She wasn't surprised. She was well aware that the new nuns, although pranked out in permanents and skirts up to their knees, were still a clandestine sorority. How like them to plan an interruption in the schoolday and not let her know.

"About whom are you speaking?" she asked.

"Oh, Miss McGee," said Sister Rosie, the lighthearted (and in Miss McGee's opinion, light-headed) principal of St. Isidore's. "We were discussing Herschel Mancrief, and we were not at all sure you would be interested." Sister Rosie was twenty-six and she had pierced earlobes.

"I will be the judge of my interests, if you please. Who is Herschel Mancrief?"

"He's a poet the younger generation is reading," said Sister Judy, blushing behind her acne. "We studied him in the novitiate."

"His credentials are super," said Sister Rosie.

"And he's coming to St. Isidore's? I might have been told. Will he visit classes or speak to an assembly?"

"He will visit classes. But of course no one is obliged to have him in. I know what a nuisance interruptions can be."

"Poets are important to children. I was visited by Mr. Joyce Kilmer when I was a girl, and I treasure the memory. Please show Mr. What's-his-name to my classroom when the time comes. What's his name?"

"Herschel Mancrief. He can give you twenty minutes at quarter to twelve."

So this morning Miss McGee announced to her sixth graders that they were about to meet Herschel Mancrief. They looked up from their reading assignment, a page headed "Goths and Visigoths," and as a sign of their undivided attention they closed their books. Divided attention was among the things Miss McGee did not permit. Slang and eye shadow were others.

"Meeting a poet is a memorable experience," she said. "When I was a girl, my class was visited by Mr. Joyce Kilmer, who wrote 'Trees,' the poem every child carries in his heart from the primary grades, and to this day I can recall what Mr. Kilmer said to us. He came to Staggerford a mere two years before giving his life for his country in World War One." She tilted her head forward, in order to read her twenty-four sixth graders through her bifocals—difficult reading these days, for they lurked, boys and girls alike, behind veils of hair.

"The poet, you understand, is a man with a message. His mission is to remind us of the beauty God has made. He writes of the good and lasting things of life. His business is beauty. Are there any questions?"

There was one, and several students raised their hands to ask it: "How does 'Trees' go?"

"Heavens, surely you remember."

But it was discovered that no one in the class had heard it. As Miss McGee began reciting, " 'I think that I shall never see,' " a frightening sensation crept up her spine and gripped her heart — an invisible tremor like the one she had felt in 1918 when her third-grade teacher said that Joyce Kilmer was dead in France. An imperceptible shudder that moved out along her nervous system and left her nauseous. Her name for it was the Dark Age dyspepsia, because it struck whenever she came upon a new piece of alarming evidence that pointed to the return of the Dark Ages.

Dark Age evidence had been accumulating. Last month at Parents' Night, Barbara Betka's father and mother told Miss McGee they would see her fired if she did not lift her prohibition against the wearing of nylons by sixth-grade girls. They were standing in the assembly room where coffee was to be served. Mr. Betka, fidgeting and averting his eyes, did most of the talking while Mrs. Betka, having called the tune, stood at his side and fingered his arm like a musical instrument. "Fired indeed!" said Miss McGee, turning on her heel and snatching up her purse in a single motion of amazing agility, like a move in hopscotch, and she flew from the assembly room before coffee was served. She was followed home by the Dark Age dyspepsia and scarcely slept that night, haunted by the specter of a man in his fifties sent out by his wife to do battle for nylons. "The craven ninny," she said to herself at dawn, rising to prepare the day's lessons.

And that was the day Dr. Murphy from the State Department of Education came to town to address a joint meeting of public and parochial school faculties. Both Miles and Miss McGee attended his lecture. "Never," Dr. Murphy said at the end of a tedious address on language arts, "never burden a child with a book written earlier than the child's date of birth. That way you can be confident that you and your students are in tune with each other, that you are moving with them on a contemporary plane." This harebrained proposal proved to Miss McGee that not even the State Department of Education was immune from the spreading plague of dark and crippling ignorance.

Nor were the sisters immune. More than once, for their spring picnic, Sister Judy had taken her fourth graders to a hippie farm. When Miss McGee first heard about that, she went to the pastor, Father Finn, and warned him about the return of the Dark Ages. Father Finn, ordinarily a man of understanding, did not understand Miss McGee's anxiety. If the Dark Ages were coming back, he had not yet caught sight of them. He told Miss McGee that she was an alarmist.

This morning as she concluded with the line, "But only God can make a tree," the door opened and Herschel Mancrief appeared. He was led into the classroom by Sister Rosie. He was untidy. That was Miss McGee's first impression of him. Under his wrinkled suitcoat he wore a T-shirt and under his nose a thicket of hair that curled around the corners of his mouth and ended in a stringy gray beard.

Miss McGee said, "I am pleased to meet you," and she gracefully offered her hand.

"Groovy," said the poet, tapping her palm with the tip of one finger. Up close she saw that his neck and his T-shirt were unmistakably unwashed. His asymmetrical sideburns held lint. She hopped silently backward and slipped into an empty desk halfway down an aisle, and Sister Rosie introduced the visitor, training a spit curl as she spoke.

"Mr. Mancrief has already been to three rooms and he has another one to visit after yours, class, and he has to leave by twelve thirty, so when his time is up please don't bug him to stay." On her way out the door, Sister Rosie added, "Room 102 is next, Herschel. It's just across the hall."

The sixth grade regarded the poet.

"I am here to make you childlike," he began, blinking as he spoke, as though his words gave off too much light. "I am here to save you from growing up." His voice was deep and wheezy, and his frown was fixed. "You see, grownups aren't sensitive. They get covered over with a kind of crust. They don't *feel*. It is only through constant effort that I am able to maintain the wonder, the joy, the capacity for feeling that I had as a child." He quit blinking and inserted a hand under his suitcoat to give his ribs a general and thoughtful scratching. "Do you understand what I am saying?"

The class looked at Miss McGee. She nodded and so did they.

"Good. Now here's a poem of mine called 'What I Envied.' It's an example of what I'm saying." He closed his eyes and spoke in an altered voice, a chant:

"I envied as a child
the clean manikins in store windows
because their underwear fit
their toes were buried in thick carpet
their happy smiles immutable,
until my father driving us home
past midnight after a day in the country
passed a window full of manikins
and then I knew
the trouble it must be
to smile all night!"

After a silent moment the poet opened his eyes signaling the end of the poem.

Miss McGee had heard worse. Except for the reference to underwear, it came as close to poetry as most of the verse she had read lately, and she set the class to nodding its approval.

Herschel Mancrief shed his suitcoat and revealed that his pants were held up by a knotted rope. It was not the white, carefully braided rope of the Franciscans, who were Miss McGee's teachers in college, but a dirty length of frazzled twine.

"Good," said the poet, laying his suitcoat across Miss McGee's walnut desk. "You remember how heroic those manikins used to seem when you were small and they were larger than life. You would see one in a store window and it was enough to make you salute. The pity is that you gradually lose your sense of wonder for things like that. Take toilets, for example. My poem 'So Tall' is about a toilet."

He recited with his eyes shut. Miss McGee shut hers as well.

"How tall I seem to be these days
and how much I am missing,
things at ground level escape my notice
wall plugs wastebaskets heat registers,
what do I care for them now I am so tall?

I was once acquainted with a toilet
when it and I were eye to eye,
it would roar and swallow and scare me half to death.
What do I care for that toilet now,
now I am so tall?"

There was the sound of a giggle, stifled.

"You are surprised I got a toilet into a poem?" He was asking Miss
McGee, who had not giggled. "But poetry takes all of life for her domain. The beautiful and the unbeautiful. Roses and toilets. Today's
poet seeks to represent the proportions of life. You don't very often
pick a rose, but you go to the bathroom several times a day."

Certain now that he had taken the measure of Miss McGee's toler-
ance for the unbeautiful (color was rising in her face) the poet announced his third selection, "In My End of Town."

"In my end of town
like a cathedral against the sky
stands the city sewage plant,
the direction of the wind
is important to us,
in my end of town
man disposes."

He opened his eyes to study Miss McGee's reaction, but the desk
she had been sitting in was empty. She was at his side, facing the class.

"Students, you will thank Mr. Mancrief."

"Thank you, Mr. Mancrief." They spoke the way they prayed, in
unison and without enthusiasm.

She handed the poet his coat and, not wishing to touch his hairy
arms, she steered him to the door as if by remote control. "There"—
she pointed—"is Room 102."

Nothing in his government-sponsored travels had prepared Herschel Mancrief for the brush-off. "Actually," he said, blinking as he
backed into the corridor, "I hadn't finished."

"I regret we can spare you no more time. We recite the Angelus at
twelve."

Looking more surprised than offended, he raised a hand as though
to speak, but then thought better of it and stepped across the corridor

and knocked on the door of 102. It opened instantly and Sister Judy put her head out.

Miss McGee, afraid now that her treatment of the man had been too delicate, said, "Another thing, Mr. Mancrief. Your poetry is . . . " She searched for the word. The poet and Sister Judy listened for it.

"Your poetry is undistinguished."

Sister Judy rolled her eyes and the poet chuckled into his hand. Miss McGee turned back to her class, pulling the door shut behind her. "Entirely undistinguished, class. You will rise now for the Angelus."

Later, entering the lunchroom, Miss McGee saw at the far end of the faculty table Herschel Mancrief and Sister Judy ignoring their beans and tuna and laughing like ninnies.

"I thought he was to have been on his way by this time."

"We asked him to stay for lunch," said Sister Rosie. "He has agreed to stay a while longer. Isn't he super?"

"He's horribly dated. He said 'groovy.' I haven't heard anyone say 'groovy' for at least three years."

"Oh, Miss McGee, he's super. Admit it."

"Pass the relish, if you please."

Two hours later, after putting her class to work on equilateral triangles, Miss McGee opened her door for a change of air. From behind the closed door of 102 she heard raucous laughter alternating with the excited voice of Herschel Mancrief. The man evidently could not bring himself to leave St. Isidore's. She stepped closer and listened through the door.

"Acquainted with a toilet," said the poet.

The fourth grade laughed.

"It would roar and swallow and scare me half to death."

More laughter.

"There, now you've caught the spirit of the poem. Now repeat it after me."

They did so, briskly, line by line.

"Now let's try another one—a poem I wrote just the other day called 'Be Careful Where You Grab Me.' "

Fierce laughter.

Miss McGee hurried to the nearest fire alarm and with a trembling hand she broke the seal and set off an ear-splitting jangle of horns and bells that emptied the building in forty-five seconds. Two ladder trucks pulled up to the front door and while the fire chief, a former student of Miss McGee's, gave the building a thorough inspection, Herschel Mancrief drove off in his rented car, the fourth grade throwing him kisses from the curb.

"A false alarm," declared the fire chief, emerging from the front door of the school in his yellow rubber coat.

"Someone set off the alarm near your room," he said to Miss McGee as she led her sixth grade up the steps and back into the building. "Did you notice anything suspicious, Miss McGee?"

"Goths and Visigoths," she said.

Strand of Wire

Dan O'Brien

Framed in the square lines of the farmhouse window Judith Nelson watches her husband walk. She notices the limp yet she can still see the strength. She can see the power that was important so long ago. She stands with her head up, in front of the kitchen sink. Her husband walks toward the growing bean field. The morning sky is pink and brightening in front of him. His stiff black boots push up tiny billowing clouds from the dusty lane. They are like the giant afternoon clouds that rise black in the west. Judith's hand dangles absently into the cooling dishwater. Two plates are beside the sink, the breakfast untouched, cold.

There is a numbness. Since Billy Knutson died she has known this morning would come, but she has never understood. She has listened to her husband, never saying what he meant but telling her just the same. Telling her he was afraid. Wishing he had the money to buy the Knutson place, wondering who would have it. And worry, a terrible worry about the fence and the people who would own its other side. There would be that awful awkwardness.

The fence had belonged to the two of them, Billy Knutson and her husband; they had mended it together. Now it would be according to the law. *Face the fence, standing on your land. The half of the fence to your right is your responsibility.* There would be strangers there. Not like before. Not the Knutsons, or the Olsens, or the Johnsons. They were all gone, dead, moved, gone away. Of the old times only the river remained. And she thinks of the river, there even before her parents, constant, chewing quietly at their back pasture.

Except for the oldness, the slowness, the walk is the same. She has known it since she was a child. He leans forward, into the walk, swinging the left hand, jerking it up almost to his chest. It is the way he used to run. The same as sixty years before, wide-eyed, speaking a different language, running to the schoolhouse, running to bring the cow, running to their own church, gone now. And thinking back she can see that even then the signs were there. This morning had been coming since then.

Billy Knutson had been the last. He would visit them, drink coffee, and talk to her husband of horses that wore size ten shoes and plowed without a line. They would laugh sometimes and the sound would be funny, like from a dream. And sometimes they would drink whiskey and speak, then, the old language and they would talk about the disappointments, shake their heads at their parents' choice of land, wonder at the ocean whose memory forced their parents to settle beside the river. The wild, fouled, fishless river that moved, not by tides but by the twisting power of the land itself.

And that talk would make them silent. They would grip each other's forearms and shoulders. But Billy Knutson was gone. Five years now. And his farm was owned by a man they did not know. Only that he was from the east, that he had new tractors and a combine that harvested six rows at a time, and that he squeezed the land for all it was worth. She did not know him to see him but she could feel him all around them. Except for the narrow right-of-way Billy had insisted that her husband accept, they had no access to the road. They were captive there, between the river and the rusting wire fence that they shared, now, with a stranger.

Their farm had been diminishing since before she could remember. Every spring the river would claim another section of crumbling bank, and even in dusty August handfuls of topsoil washed daily into its rolling belly. Judith had watched him walking the riverbank, gazing across its width. Walking the boundaries of his land and stopping to stare at a spot in the river, remembering when he had stood there and gazed even further out to where the river boiled brown, almost thick. Then he would look up stiffly and go on. Until he came to where the river turned and where the boundary fence began, appearing rusty, ghostlike, from the water. And he would turn and walk that boundary for two miles. Along the way he would pull up the sagging wires, twist the broken ends back together, make the fence stand if he could. But along its entire length, from where it appeared to where it descended again into the river, he knew that hungry cattle would be pushing at it from the other side, straining at his corn and beans and that, as always, it would give to their weight. And once, though he never said he had, she knew that somehow he had made himself go to the neighbor's house, according to the law, and asked to share the cost and labor of a new fence. She knew this because she had seen him return, sit in the pickup after the engine died, then slowly open the door, swing his feet to the graveled drive, and show her his chalk-rock face, dusted with years of disappointment and now the courage spent.

So it had been five years that he had raised a crop to feed to the neighbor's cattle, and each year the land growing smaller and the price of the crops he could glean from the fields getting lower and lower. Until she had told him that something must be done. She had never meant it to come out the way it did, it had come out hard and cold and when it was out he stared up at her from the table. His gray eyes were steady into hers and for an instant she thought that she had been wrong, that there was no trouble in his world. But she had been right, the eyes narrowed and he was forced to look away.

She lets some water out of the sink and warms what is left with hot from the spigot. Her husband is further down the lane, still sending up dust from around his feet, walking with his limp past the grown-up weeds of their grove. And hiding in those weeds is the story of the farm. Obscured from sight, laid in rows surrounded by waist-high weeds, are the rusted walking plows, the rotted harness, and the discarded corn knives. One row closer are the steel seats and boilers of the days of steam, and closest to where her husband is walking are the one- and two-row cultivators and plows. And gasoline engines from tiny tractors that stopped running years before. Even now she knows that in the machine shed there is nothing that can turn the ground, plant the seed, or harvest the crops more than three rows at a time. That, she decides, is part of the trouble. But a small part. The rest of the trouble goes deeper than even steel can penetrate. It has to do with flesh, with something inside that man walking away and with something that will die with him, would have died with Billy Knutson but didn't. It crawled from the cheap wooden casket that day in November and into her husband's chest. And when he stood up from where he'd sat alone all night he carried the trouble that Billy had gathered from this land, inherited from the others. Her husband was silent then, frightened and crippled by the burden.

Almost a year ago he brought home enough material to fix his share of the fence. Borrowed the money, she imagined, and unloaded the fifteen spools of wire and the bundles of fence posts beside the barn. The next morning he walked out to begin fixing his half of the fence. He walked the same direction that he is walking now but in a different way. He had made many trips, carried the posts and wire, struggled with them, and she had seen that the loads were too much for him. But last year she had been able to look down at the dishwater. This morning his load was lighter. The wooden butt of his rifle slapped against his lame leg with every step, and for the second time she notices that the water is going cold.

He had fixed his share of the fence, from the river to the center of the boundary. He worked alone, for three weeks, steady. When it was finished he waited for the spring which came that year, as always, overdue yet catching everyone unprepared. And when he went to the fields the neighbor's fence was still rusty, tumbled down. He said nothing. He plowed his land and planted it and watched his crops grow up as fast as the neighbor's pasture was grazed down.

He would stand at the end of the lane where he is standing now, watch across the field to where the cattle strained at the fence, stretching their bulky heads over and reaching for the pollinating bean plants. In the last days of September when it seemed the fence could hold them no more, he would wake up before light, stand in the kitchen, and stare into the darkness. Finally he would walk out to meet the morning and chase the cattle away from the fence, save his crops for another day.

And yesterday he stood out where he is standing now, watching the dusty pasture on the other side of the fence that could not feed the cattle for one day more. By morning they would be grazing in his beans as they had done every year since Billy Knutson died. And so that night the rifle came out from behind the door and at the kitchen table he sat wiping the barrel and sliding the oiled bolt in and out. But it was not the rifle that troubled Judith. It was the silence. All that evening and early, hours before sunrise this morning, there was silence. Not that it was different, there were never many words, but this morning in the darkened kitchen the old times lay thick on the counter and oozed out from around the cupboard doors.

When she awoke he was back at the kitchen table and she could hear that he was talking, a conversation. But when she came into the kitchen he was silent. And the bacon sizzled in the pan, moved to the table, and grew cast-iron cold on the plates in front of them. There were no words. Just the pale, brightening kitchen walls and her husband, slumped forward, pushing at the bacon with his fork.

When there was light enough to see he took the rifle from the corner where he had left it shining clean and slowly pushed shells into the magazine. They made a scraping sound, and Judith brought the dishes to where they are stacked now, beside the sink below the white-framed window. And from that window she watches the rifle come up to her husband's shoulder, sees the first puff of smoke, and the bellow and the crack from the rifle reach her ears at the same time. She feels frightened, helpless, and yet she holds her head up watching and listening to the deaths of the second and third cows and suddenly she knows what her husband has known since the beginning. She knows the coolness of his gray eyes, the steadiness of his hand in the half-light, sliding the cartridges into the rifle. She too is standing at the end of the lane, and she realizes what he would have said, had he spoken at all.

Horizontal Grandeur

Bill Holm

For years I carried on a not-so-jovial argument with several friends who are north-woods types. They carted me out into the forests of northern Wisconsin or Minnesota, expected me to exclaim enthusiastically on the splendid landscape. "Looks fine," I'd say, 'but there's too damn many trees, and they're all alike. If they'd cut down twenty miles or so on either side of the road, the flowers could grow, you could see the sky, and find out what the real scenery is like." Invariably, this provoked groans of disbelief that anyone could be insensitive enough to prefer dry, harsh, treeless prairies. There, a man is the tallest thing for miles around; a few lonesome cottonwoods stand with leaves shivering by a muddy creek; sky is large and readable as a Bible for the blind. The old farmers say you can see weather coming at you, not like woods, where it sneaks up and takes you by surprise.

I was raised in Minneota, true prairie country. When settlers arrived in the 1870s they found waist-high grass studded with wild flowers; the only trees were wavy lines of cottonwoods and willows along the crooked Yellow Medicine Creek. Farmers immigrated here not for scenery, but for topsoil; 160 flat acres without trees or boulders to break plows and cramp fields was beautiful to them. They left Norway, with its picturesque but small, poor, steep farms; or Iceland, where the beautiful backyard mountains frequently covered hay fields with lava and volcanic ash. Wives, described by Ole Rølvaag in *Giants in the Earth,* were not enamored with the beauty of black topsoil, and frequently went insane from loneliness, finding nowhere to hide on these blizzardy plains. But the beauty of this landscape existed in function, rather than form, not only for immigrant farmers, but for Indians who preceded them.

Blackfeet Indians live on the Rocky Mountains' east edge in northern Montana—next to Glacier National Park. Plains were home for men and buffalo, the source of Blackfeet life; mountains were for feasting and dancing, sacred visions and ceremonies, but home only for spirits and outlaws. It puzzles tourists winding up hairpin turns, looking down three thousand feet into dense forests on the McDonald Valley floor, that Blackfeet never lived there. It did not puzzle the old farmer from Minneota who, after living and farming on prairies most of his life, vacationed in the Rockies with his children after he retired. When they reached the big stone escarpment sticking up at the prairie's edge, one of his sons asked him how he liked the view. "These are stone," the old man said; "I have stones in the north eighty. These are bigger, and harder to plow around. Let's go home."

When my mother saw the Atlantic Ocean in Virginia, she commented that though saltier, noisier, and probably somewhat larger, it was no wetter or more picturesque than Dead Coon Lake or the Yellow Medicine River and surely a good deal more trouble to cross.

There are two eyes in the human head—the eye of mystery, and the eye of harsh truth—the hidden and the open—the woods eye and the prairie eye. The prairie eye looks for distance, clarity, and light; the woods eye for closeness, complexity, and darkness. The prairie eye looks for usefulness and plainness in art and architecture; the woods eye for the baroque and ornamental. Dark old brownstones on Summit Avenue were created by a woods eye; the square white farmhouse and red barn are prairie eye's work. Sherwood Anderson wrote his stories with a prairie eye, plain and awkward, told in the voice of a man almost embarrassed to be telling them, but bullheadedly persistent to get at the meaning of the events; Faulkner, whose endless complications of motive and language take the reader miles behind the simple facts of an event, sees the world with a woods eye. One eye is not superior to the other, but they are different. To some degree, like male and female, darkness and light, they exist in all human heads, but one or the other seems dominant. The Manicheans were not entirely wrong.

I have a prairie eye. Dense woods or mountain valleys make me nervous. After once visiting Burntside Lake north of Ely for a week, I felt a fierce longing to be out. Driving home in the middle of the night, I stopped the car south of Willmar, when woods finally fell away and plains opened up. It was a clear night, lit by a brilliant moon turning blowing grasses silver. I saw for miles—endless strings of yardlights, stars fallen into the grovetops. Alone, I began singing at the top of my voice. I hope neither neighborhood cows, nor the Kandiyohi County sheriff were disturbed by this unseemly behavior from a grown man. It was simply cataracts removed from the prairie eye with a joyful rush.

Keep two facts in mind if you do not have a prairie eye: magnitude and delicacy. The prairie is endless! After the South Dakota border, it goes west for over a thousand miles, flat, dry, empty, lit by brilliant sunsets and geometric beauty. Prairies, like mountains, stagger the imagination most not in detail, but size. As a mountain is high, a prairie is wide; horizontal grandeur, not vertical. People neglect prairies as scenery because they require time and patience to comprehend. You eye a mountain, even a range, at a glance. The ocean spits and foams at its edge. You see down into the Grand Canyon. But walking the whole prairie might require months. Even in a car at 60 miles an hour it takes three days or more. Like a long symphony by Bruckner or Mahler, prairie unfolds gradually, reveals itself a mile at a time, and only when you finish crossing it do you have any idea of what you've seen. Americans don't like prairies as scenery or for national parks and preserves because they require patience and effort. We want instant gratification in scenic splendor as in most things, and simply will not look at them seriously. Prairies are to Rockies what *Paradise Lost* is to haiku. Milton is cumulative; so are prairies. Bored for days, you are suddenly struck by the magnitude of what has been working on you. It's something like knowing a woman for years before realizing that you are in love with her after all.

If prairie size moves the imagination, delicacy moves the heart. West of Minneota, the prairies quickly rise several hundred feet and form the Coteau. This land looks more like the high plains of Wyoming. Rougher and stonier than land to the east, many sections have never been plowed. Past Hendricks, along the south and west lake shores, things open up—treeless hills with grazing cattle, gullies with a few trees sliding off toward the lake. Ditches and hillsides are a jumble of flowers, grasses, and thistles: purple, pink, white, yellow, blue. In deep woods, the eye misses these incredible delicate colors, washed in light and shadow by an oversized sky. In the monochromatic woods, light comes squiggling through onto a black green shadowy forest floor. My eye longs for a rose, even a sow thistle.

A woods man looks at twenty miles of prairie and sees nothing but grass, but a prairie man looks at a square foot and sees a universe; ten or twenty flowers and grasses, heights, heads, colors, shades, configurations, bearded, rough, smooth, simple, elegant. When a cloud passes over the sun, colors shift, like a child's kaleidoscope.

I stop by a roadside west of Hendricks, walk into the ditch, pick a prairie rose. This wild pink rose is far lovelier than hot-house roses wrapped in crinkly paper that teen-agers buy prom dates. The dusty car fills with its smell. I ignore it for a few minutes, go on talking. When I look again, it's dry, as if pressed in an immigrant Bible for a hundred years. These prairie flowers die quickly when you take them out of their own ground. They too are immigrants who can't transplant, and wither fast in their new world.

I didn't always love prairies. On my father's farm I dreamed of traveling, living by the sea and, most of all, close to mountains. As a boy, I lay head on a stone in the cow pasture east of the house, looking up at cloud rows in the west, imagining I saw all the way to the Rockies and that white tips on the clouds were snow on mountaintops or, better yet, white hair on sleeping blue elephant spines. Living in a flat landscape drove me to indulge in mountainous metaphor, then later discover that reality lived up to it. When I finally saw the Rockies years later, they looked like pasture clouds, phantasmagorias solider than stone.

The most astonished travelers do not come from the Swiss Alps, or the California coast. Only William Carlos Williams, who lived in the industrial prairies of New Jersey, would notice the Mexico of *Desert Music*. A southwest poet with a wood's eye would have seen saguaro cactus or medieval parapets. Trust a prairie eye to find beauty and understate it truthfully, no matter how violent the apparent exaggeration. Thoreau, though a woodsman, said it right: "I can never exaggerate enough."

Grace

Robert Schuler

"A man who is but a dream."
—W. B. Yeats, "The Fisherman"

The fly-line snakes white slow through gauzy blue air and a Parmachene Belle sinks a red and white feathered, tinselled whore into waterfall foam. When the brook trout struck-shocked his wrist, bones and nerves locked into a vision: he would set out from this creek, a tiny vein twisted through a willow-lined plain, and trace it, cast by cast, pool by stone, sandpath into tall grass, mazes of brush, until it branched into other veins, new capillaries, brooks, creeks, streams and the arteries, waterways through the heartland (in this county alone a network of forty trout streams crossed, re-crossed the ground). He would cast Gray Drake and Grey Fox, Pale Evening Dun and Cream Dun, match the hatches, freelance with Picket Pins, Bumble Puppies, Mickey Finns, land brook trout, suns bursting out of their seagreen flanks, and German Browns, lords of the slow pool, working his way from Mud Creek to Salley Ridge Break on down to the Coon, the Running Valley, the Sly, the Sinking. Maybe he'd wander the Swan, enter the vined-thickets of the Eighteen-Mile.

When he reached the Red Cedar, he'd scrape silver spinners against the reeds for smallmouth, their bronzed bodies cartwheeling through steaming mist, hurl bucktails, yellow arrows, into fast frothy runs for white bass, fullbacks that rammed shoulders against the current, bounced off boulders. At night, whirlwinds of mosquitoes in the watery moonlight, he'd feather streamers under waterfalls for walleyes.

Where farmpools gleamed out of cornrows and sand, he flicked poppers onto lily pads, teased them over the edges of broad raspy leaves until they plopped and fat sunfish and largemouth snatched them and ran. A granddad struck like a shark, wound his line around thick woody stems and broke off, his knees and arms shaking him into the cold, dangling sweat of a drug rush.

Weeks later, sidetracked into new veins, new synapses, he reached the Chippewa where he floated red and white hulapoppers, twitched pale green jitterbugs down shallow shady backwash pools, under curving cutbanks. Suddenly, the Mississippi spread swollen brown over the bottomlands, spined with limestone palisades. Lost in brushy backwaters, he cast behind every log, into cattail patches, under the waterfalls of small creeks he could trace to their sources. The Bloody Run looped round and down breaks in the bluffs. Rattlesnakes crawled out on the rocks to sun themselves. Rainbow and Brown rose to Gordon, Dark Red, and Pale Olive Quills, swallowed Wooly Worms, Witch Doctors, Grizzly Kings out of the sinewy silver and brown waters. He would live forever.

The Midwest

Herbert Scott

1.

No sense lying about the weather. Winter will soon be here. Haul the goose down comforter and the patchwork quilt out of the cupboard where they have remained since May and air them out. They smell a little sour from mildew, smell a little like linoleum or oilcloth.

The rabbits are fat, the deer are fat, the foxes are fat. In these parts pheasants are scarce. Pretty soon farmer fox will pull up stakes and move north and the pheasants will come back. It goes in cycles. During a hard winter, the county agent will tell you, be sure to keep the outhouse latched. Foraging skunks will leap down into the pit and eat for weeks and months until there is nothing left to eat. Unable to climb out they will starve to death, become a matted, picked-bone stench to be dealt with in the spring, in April, when the stars ding their little bells and the birds come back to the spiffy trees.

Now it is November. There is nothing much more satisfying than taking a leak at night beneath an open sky. The stars have never been closer. The trees by the river are loud with owls. A dog in the distance. Now, two dogs. I am reminded of my friend Virgil's description of a small midwestern town: "Three porchlights and a barking dog."

2.

I think a pragmatic honesty can be discerned among those whose lives have been lived in the midwest. I think interlopers, those who have come to the midwest lately for God-knows-what-reason, are more likely to put a false face on things. I give them credit, perhaps unfairly, for the new strip malls that seem to appear overnight at every inter-section in town. All are imitation art deco, and no matter how fast they open they close even faster, abandoned to the elements after some poor sucker has lost his life's savings on a doomed sandwich shop, or jiffy print, or bridal boutique, and so on, before the ink was dry on his twenty-year lease.

These newcomers are convinced that there is something here in the midwest that can be made into something else, that this is territory not sufficiently mined by the locals, that if a person with savvy and smoothness were to move in things would change, become market-able, profitable. But we who live here know that things do not change for the better. Life is difficult, but it builds character. One might as well face it honestly: one lives alone. One might as well live with an honest person.

This is not to say that I believe human nature changes from place to place. I'm simply suggesting that those who have lived their lives here have learned a hard lesson others may not have learned as well.

If life here were too easy we'd be even more suspicious of it than we already are. Drive north on a November day in Michigan. In marshes along the roadside, the cattails hang like limp, gray mice. The only green one sees seems almost tragic: the undone willow trees. Here and there, houses rise up out of the flatness like forgotten promises.

3.

If you were to come to the midwest during late spring among the first things you would notice are the greenness of the landscape and the plentitude of water. You would think there are fish in those lakes and streams and you would be correct. And almost any fruit or vegetable or grain will grow in the midwest without irrigation. People plant and cultivate and grow produce for the pure miracle of it.

We also have pests such as black flies that can raise a welt on your wrist, and mosquitoes so prosperous you can pull handfuls of them out of the air. And we are now being invaded by outside interests. We see in the paper that ticks bearing Lyme disease will soon cover the entire midwest, and that the tiger mosquitoes, hitching rides from Asia in freighter loads of used tire carcasses being brought to America for some brilliant financial scheme or another are expected to reach the midwest any day now. We understand that they have a mean disposition and will stir up our resident population. We also understand they do not rest during the daylight hours as local mosquitoes do.

In anticipation of their arrival we are already becoming sentimental about our own mosquitoes.

4.

We like the fall, perhaps best. The mosquitoes are lazy have eaten their fill. The mice come in from the fields as do the yellow jackets, to stay warm. Lift up the window shade, there they are, a dozen yellow jackets enjoying the late October sun. They want to live a little longer. They are polite and friendly though inclined to keep to themselves. Bats slip through the smallest cracks where screendoors and windows have warped a little. They want a cozy place to bear their young. We can hear them in the stove chimney, their wings beating up and down that narrow passageway.

We like the changing of the seasons, we say. We wouldn't live in Florida or California. We love the colors of Fall. Usually—not to lie—there are only a few glorious, clear days when the color has almost reached its most dizzying degree of variation that the sun lights up the countryside with unequalled beauty. Then the rains come and the first frost and it's over.

But every seven years or so Fall seems to last forever. The leaves stay brilliant on the trees into November. My wife has picked red raspberries the week before Thanksgiving, the bushes heavily laden, the berries "as large as your thumb," my grandmother would say. They fall from the branches, fill your hands, your hat, your mouth. This is why we live in the midwest.

The Spirit of Place

Larry Woiwode

. . . When you are actually *in* America, America hurts, because it has a powerful disintegrative influence upon the white psyche. It is full of grinning, unappeased aboriginal demons, too, ghosts, and it persecutes the white men like some Eumenides, until the white men give up their absolute whiteness. America is tense with latent violence and resistance. The very common sense of white Americans has a tinge of helplessness in it, and deep fear of what might be if they were not commonsensical.

Yet one day the demons of America must be placated, the ghosts must be appeased, the Spirit of Place atoned for. Then the true passionate love for American soil will appear . . .

— D. H. Lawrence, *Studies in Classic American Literature*

I suspect that there are some who view my work as regional, so perhaps the simplest solution would be to buy one of those T-shirts that Larry McMurtry used to claim he wore, before he donned the Pulitzer, which had "Minor Regional Writer" printed across it, and let it go at that. Certainly in our American universities the regional writer barely merits condescension—an underdeveloped tyke running around in a T-shirt of personal boosterism, bearing book titles such as "Welcome to the Bitter Winters of the Beautiful Badlands," or "Gnomes I Have Known in Northern Door County," and the like.

Writing of this kind is, of course, no more than glorified boosterism, appealing to commerce and the gullibility of tourists in T-shirts that read "I Am Free."

I agree with the excerpt from Lawrence on at least one important point: there is certainly something rampant in America that must be atoned for.

Americans tend to apply "minor" and its variations to whatever they wish to condescend to, as in "minority." Minorities are those others Americans wish to help out. This help is to arrive out of a superior view of what is right, even if the minority considers it wrong. It is generally conceded that it is right to live in New York City or Washington, D. C., for instance, and perhaps even San Francisco or Los Angeles, but not Peoria or Waco. A writer whose work is filled with the richness of a place that isn't quite right—I might mention Lois Phillips Hudson and Frederick Manfred in this regard—runs the risk of being looked upon as regional. Categories and labels enable us to pigeonhole, or set aside, a book or a strain of writing whose particularity might otherwise be difficult to classify. Blame, I believe, falls on both sides of the line I hope to be walking for the rest of these pages that lie like representations of the place where I live.

In my own writing, which I'm as familiar with as any, I've wondered more than once what region it is I write about: Michigan, Wisconsin, Illinois, North Dakota, New York City, or that gray expanse from Philadelphia to Las Vegas that New Yorkers call the Midwest. North Dakota, where my umbilical roots lie (probably literally, somewhere) has certain qualities other than those I associate with the Midwest. I can say with impunity that the North Dakota I will describe exists, since I moved to the state a decade ago, after trying to write about it in one of my first books. I had spent several years in North Dakota growing up, and had reached a point of needing to relearn its configurations, to find if these in any way coincided with what I was writing about.

When I arrived and the natives asked me what I did, and I told them I was a writer, they were impressed, because being a rodeo rider is a perfectly respectable and dangerous occupation—not nearly as dangerous as writing, I might have said, but then that wasn't respectable.

I didn't disabuse them of their notion of me but made a note to work on my enunciation. North Dakotans are precise. After living several years in the East, that was the first truth that was ground in on me: they use few words and the words they use are precise; they mean what they say. I had with me more than three hundred pages of a novel set partly in North Dakota, and within a matter of weeks I knew I had to scrap it or start over.

I came to understand that the North Dakota I would like to have appear in my writing is not a North Dakota of the mind, or a visitor's or Easterner's misconception of it, nor one you may encounter in a general book about the Great Plains, but a real place; a region, perhaps: now my home.

About 600,000 people live in the state, which is not many more than live in two metropolitan Peorias, for instance, yet the state covers an area about the size of Maine and Ohio put together, if you could accomplish that union; and the figure of 600,000 is in itself deceptive, since nearly 200,000 of its 600,000 inhabitants live in the five—can we call them metropolitan?—areas of Fargo, Grand Forks, Bismarck, Minot, and Jamestown, in descending order. Which leaves about 70,500 square miles empty of even the hint of urbia, or sets down approximately five people within every square mile.

Even this is deceptive, however, as most statistics and demographics are, because of the many other villages and towns, and the clusters of these three architectural phenomena: grain elevator, bar, and church—usually with a few houses in the vicinity, but not always. If you compared this population density with a European country, with Germany, say, where many North Dakotans emigrated from, you would find that there were only this few people in Germany at the time of Julius Caesar; now there are over 300 per square mile. And to compare this to New York City is revealing, since there are about 48,000 people per square mile in Manhattan, and these are actual residents, not the many others, perhaps another million, who work on the island over the day. These would elevate the total, for those New Yorkers interested, to approximately 80,000 per square mile.

So you see that when we look toward South Dakota, and notice not many more people there, or to our expansive neighbors to the west,

Montana or Wyoming, to mention two other states that contain in certain areas features of the plains states, and see that they are even more sparsely settled, as the stretches of Canada above us are, we wonder why it is that there is concern about "the population explosion." We've hardly heard a cork gun go off.

Statistics don't begin to give a picture of the open stretches here, where for miles you see nothing but grass, and perhaps cattle, or grain fields and summer fallow; few trees, no farms for long passages of time (travel here is measured in units of hours), and every second or third of these abandoned, it seems, due to yet another foreclosure.

Here, then, human contact and company are not taken for granted. It's an event out of the ordinary when a car, or more likely, a pickup, rolls up. Conversations, except in town, are rare, and then you have a whole week to replay and mull them over, fashioning the perfect replies for those moments when you were dull as nails, if not literally tongue-tied. So every Dakotan is his own dramatist and latent writer—Dakotan, I say, because much of this is applicable to South Dakota, also. A wry and often hearty sense of humor, though generally controlled (so you don't upset your neighbors) isn't uncommon, either, in order to keep from the pitfalls that the replaying of those conversations can bring.

Living essentially alone, usually a good distance from any place that only in generosity could be called a city, people here are of necessity self-reliant.

They must be their own mechanics, psychologists, teachers, meteorologists, historians, chefs, entertainers, doctors, accountants, storytellers—and on and on into nearly every occupation that can occur to you, because people here manage to exist largely by their imaginations; the only limit under this sky is the reach of the individual mind in its ability to pile one potential on top of yet another. And, as is the case when people tend to rely on their own resources, Dakotans are knowledgeable about their faults and shortcomings. If not, they wouldn't last long on this frontier, through the situations that can overtake one at the edge of possibility. Which makes Dakotans even more conscious of their dependence on others, and on the working of Providence in their lives. The family is the center of dedicated life and activity, or it was before television. Dakotans have so often depended upon their wives, and wives on their husbands, that for nearly a century there has been no need for any false mode of politically imposed equality; here it actually exists.

There is a diffidence, a humility, a tendency toward self-effacement in most Dakotans — surely partly due to looking over these unpeopled miles every day, under this dazing vault of blue — an abiding sense that man, here in bib overalls baggy at the butt, or in Levis and peewee boots, which he notices need scraping again, is, after all, rather insignificant. This Dakotan, no matter how the conversations, both real and imaginary, have gone, tends to brood, slowly turning over every fugitive thought that enters the imagination. One of the matters he might brood about is why other regions of the country imagine he lives in the Midwest. Surely the Dakotas, and especially those areas of the Dakotas west of the Missouri, on through the Badlands into the Missouri breaks and down to the Black Hills, are as much the West as anywhere — a blue frontier.

When Pennsylvania was the West, and Lewis and Clark set out for the opposite coast, they found their guide, Sakakawea, near Bismarck; Custer left on his long, last, ill-fated ride from Fort Lincoln, not far from Bismarck, and the man at least partly responsible for his defeat, Sitting Bull, surrendered to the white cavalry at Fort Buford, North Dakota, and was killed trying to escape, or was executed, or shot in the back — however you historically see it — in the same state, by another Indian, who was perhaps urged on by a white man. It is this Indian's profile, not Sitting Bull's, which is engraved on all of the state road signs — a Dakotan's daily reminder of how history will exalt the sneaky above the noble.

So there is history, which I hope this sketchy reprise at least partially suggests, behind a Dakotan's thinking of his home as the West. The distinctive characteristic of the West, other than being close to the coast where the sun sets, is the relative undeveloped youth of the land, where history lies close to the surface or, indeed, is being made with every footstep taken forward by a man with a pencil and a piece of paper in hand. The major portions of the Dakotas stand today as they did on the day their creation was finished, untouched by bulldozers, blasting, dredging, or even tractors — though to say this I have to discount a few open pit mines, Mount Rushmore, and the Garrison Dam. Major portions of both states weren't settled until the turn of the century. But I believe it goes further than this for the Dakotan; I believe that more than other Americans, the Dakotan has developed a sense of the sort that Richard Wilbur attributes to Americans in general in his essay "A Sense of Place" — "a liking for the rough and unpruned — a liking for the wild which goes far beyond that picturesque aesthetic still visible in so much English parkland. It is a taste with political overtones, having to do with freedom and self-realization, and it also entails an atavistic gesture toward the frontier."

Our grandfathers, or great or great-great grandfathers, are gesturing within us toward that frontier once present here, or that they travelled over oceans to reach. There are some here who feel these outward gestures in themselves each day. That frontier, though barely visible at times, and at other times only raggedly visible, is perhaps more present in the Dakotas than in any other region of the United States. This is one of the reasons I moved back to North Dakota. I want to spend as much time in this area as I'm able to, while a frontier still exists, because it's daily being eroded. I will return to this.

One element that affects every person and every aspect of life here is, as many Dakotans plainly put it, weather. The wind can shift to almost every point of the compass within an hour. Storms and blizzards sometimes blow up so fast there's no preparing for them. It can get down to nearly a hundred below with the wind-chill factor. "Cold?" the upper half of a bumper sticker reads: "Keeps the Riffraff Out." There are tornadoes.

The Dakotan lives by his crops or cattle, or both, or the business he runs is dependent upon the farmers' crops and cattle. Both of these can be wiped out by this kind of weather, or a least greatly damaged by it, as man himself may be, which this man well knows. Dakotans are aware of their helplessness against the natural elements, and this enforces the feeling of insignificance I've mentioned — which is less a puny feeling, I believe, than an awe, a hint of what the Indians once lived with, and what other ancestors felt when they crossed an ocean to find themselves at the edge of another: plains rolling away in waves under their feet like buffalo robes, or like herds of buffalo in motion, as Willa Cather has described it in *My Ántonia.*

So then, many Dakotans tend, for whatever motives you wish now to attach to it, to believe in God. No matter how small the village here, it seems to have a church or two in it. Approximately seventy percent of the rural population calls itself Christian, and a fair amount of that percentage appears at least once a Sunday in a church. Here we move somewhat closer to the center of our representative Dakotan, and begin to see why it is that he's often classified as a Midwesterner, or I believe I do. And now I want to draw into focus some of the things I've been hoping to reveal about him, and perhaps in an ancillary way cast some light on a region I'm concerned with in my own writing, the materials I find myself using, and what my rationale is when I sit down to make use of those materials.

In an interview from the late seventies, I am quoted as saying, "Living in Illinois"—which goes as well for North Dakota, or more so; I lived in Illinois on and off from the time I was eight until I moved to New York City in the early sixties—"Living in Illinois, on the prairie, I came to appreciate the soundness of the people and their basic values. There's a discernible ethic that creates depth in the Midwestern character—a sense of responsibility for personal action; a lack of superficiality. Midwesterners are multi-dimensional, colored by the shadings of the careful choices they make."

The basis of these values, or the ethic out of which the choices are made, I might well have gone on to say (and probably did, to my interviewer's consternation) is the Bible. In Western culture, and our Westernized version of that culture, Scripture is the source of our laws and the standard by which we measure behavior—whatever our present beliefs or lack of them, or our stand vis-à-vis biblical authority and content.

I once heard Thomas McGrath, the poet laureate of our region, describe his vision of the arrival of both sides of our ancestors. The folks from Europe appear in covered wagons, he said, and suddenly see a band of Indians after them. They whip up their horses but the Indians keep gaining. Finally they realize they have to lighten the load, so they throw out the grandfather clock: boomp, time and its entanglements no longer exist for them. But the Indians are gaining. They throw out their books and then the Bible and, wham, there goes knowledge and religion. And at last, as the Indians pull closer, they throw out grandma, and with her goes family tradition—along with life, of course, at the center of which are the covenantal promises that travel from generation to generation.

It was a dark vision McGrath was recounting that chilly afternoon in western North Dakota, but it is near the heart of the truth. What was once at the center of the lives of many North Dakotans is going under or overboard. That discernible ethic is disappearing; we're losing our distinctiveness; we want to be like everybody else. Dakotans, like others, even make accommodations to gain friends: a pickup regularly pulling up. This is the front edge of the erosion, mentioned earlier, of the frontier.

I leave it to you to define, in our wise poet's metaphor, exactly what it is the Indians represent.

When I moved with my family to North Dakota, that long decade ago, I recognized here and there some of the rough-and-tumble individuality, even crankiness, in people, that I remembered from my childhood. There was a decided difference, my wife and I noticed, between the young people in this region and young people in other parts of the United States. In the years that we have lived here, we've seen change and accommodation and homogenization occur that has almost entirely wiped out those distinctions, except in the elderly.

This has largely occurred through one of the most powerful forces operating in America today—television. Television has raptured Dakotans out of the reality of their actual lives and convinced them they must become indebted consumers like the rest of the citizens of the U.S. in order to maintain their identity. Dakotans are dressing and acting more and more like people everywhere else, and the medium that keeps us all *au courant,* if you wish to see it so (or else the same), is television.

It's as if the Eumenides that Lawrence saw pursuing Americans had taken on visible form and were being projected into every living room. How can these one-dimensional ghosts be appeased? How can the Spirit, not only of Place, but of individual distinctiveness that place partly defines, ever be atoned for, once entirely lost?

In the *The Dean's December* by Saul Bellow, Dean Corde thinks, as he talks with his boyhood friend, Dewey Spangler, of the phenomenon of always-arriving information:

> In the American moral crisis, the first requirement was to experience what was happening and to see what must be seen. The *facts* were covered from our perception. More than they had been in the past? Yes, because the changes, especially the increase in consciousness — and also in false consciousness — was accompanied by a peculiar kind of confusion. The increase of theories and discourse, itself a cause of new strange forms of blindness, the false representation of "communication," led to horrible distortions of public consciousness. Therefore the first act of morality was to disinter the reality, retrieve reality, dig it out from the trash, represent it anew as art would represent it.

We are easily swayed by the false communication Bellow mentions. We believe newsmen so much we quote them line and verse; they are our patriarchs. We see a program or observe a trend on TV, and decide, That's it! Then start trying to live that way. The next week we read an article in a magazine that seems more valid, because of the angle at which it strikes us, and decide, Aha, I'm going to live *this* way now. And then next week, a new program debuts . . . And so on. Nothing is fixed. We have become actors and participants in somebody else's false drama, at the mercy of a media storm.

It is both a truth and an irony that intellectuals, who should be able to stand firm in what they believe, are generally the most susceptible to the pull of each current and wave of every new theory and concept, as though the ability to be receptive to a broad spectrum of thought has crippled their powers of discernment. This wasn't true of our ancestors, who were often looked upon as overly suspicious, if not xenophobic. And perhaps this is partly the reason our representative Dakotan broods in silence. Those atavistic gestures within might be saying, This *was* the frontier.

Part of the problem is that we, unlike our ancestors, have come to believe there is no longer any distinct truth or standard, only different shades of grayness. We assume this to be so not only in religion but in writing. We are reluctant to hold to truths and ideas that are unpopular, or not à la mode with the published majority this season. Or perhaps we're fairly sure of our own grasp on the truth, and hope to stand fairly firm in it, but on the other hand we don't want to offend others with views that might to them seem strange. We can imagine the implications of such an attitude, and the problems that would arise, if we were lawmakers, or, even more pertinent, enforcers of the law. And, actually, many educators are asked, within the legal codes of their states and the institutions they serve, to be exactly that: enforcers of laws.

In education, the realm of concepts and ideas, what one is dealing with is the entire person, his or her consciousness and well-being — even the larger, extended consciousness. One is fostering or promoting ideals and attitudes that can eventually work down to actual life-and-death decisions for an individual, a young person — a student, I mean. Intellectuals and educators seem more willing to promote the valueless homogenization in our present-day world, also known as socialism, than accept responsibility for their effects on the young people they teach each week.

This is one of the reasons why Dakotans must resist the diminishment of the frontier. Its openness permits originality of every stripe. We residents at its edge have learned of the inexorable laws, such as weather, that govern it, and are self-reliant not out of fear of *not* being commonsensical, but in order to save our lives and the lives of our children. The faith and the hope of our ancestors, acknowledged or not, is also within us; we persevere on its momentum.

We must learn to lean on these ancestors to the extent that they are solid, and to trust in the truth as we have received and understand it, rather than tending toward the popular, or looking for confirmation of our individual truth in others. And if our views seem crotchety to some in the East, well, that's as it should be. Theirs seem at least as much so to us. Let us preserve, each of us, East and West, the integrity of our convictions. Permit us that in this region. We are a minority.

Some years ago when I was teaching a seminar in the novel to graduate students who hope someday to be novelists, we looked at novels we felt communicated something quintessential and primal about the American novel and, beneath that, something about place itself in the novel and in America. We read *The Assistant, Seize the Day, Pnin, So Long, See You Tomorrow,* and *My Antonia,* and were struck to notice that Morris Bober of *The Assistant* doesn't move out of the square block of his New York neighborhood until near the end of the book; and that a good part of *Seize the Day* takes place in a New York hotel. Now this is truly regional writing, no? Provincially, parochially, regional, no? Yet it's in the cities that writers are moving into another frontier. I'll return to this.

There are several ways a writer can handle the place of his or her origins. He can go to New York, say, or another urban area, and sever those connections, which is usually about as successful as a lobotomy. She can report on a remembered place as accurately as she's able; use it as the grid against which to measure all future experience, as Hemingway did; and as Eliot, in London, discovered his "still point of the turning world . . . " Or he or she can try to find in it some common denominator that relates to more than just a geographical region.

When I began to write seriously (and I'm the only writer I feel entirely qualified to report on, and sometimes question those qualifications) — when I began to write seriously, that is, willing to give up my life for it, I was in a room in New York that I rented for nine dollars a week. It was 1964. I was experimenting with alterations in time and the grotesque in my writing — influenced by Beckett, Joyce, Babel, Kafka, and a new discovery, who would soon ascend in popularity, Nabokov. I was involved in what was modishly experimental, on the cusp of Postmodernism, moving into metafiction, delighted by my nearly impenetrable complexity.

Then, on an early fall afternoon, my maternal grandmother entered my mind with such force it occurred to me that she had influenced me more than any of these writers. I felt that if I didn't admit this I wouldn't be telling the truth; I'd be a liar; and if I didn't record this truth with as much care as I could summon, then her life, and a skein of other lives interconnected with hers, including mine, might be lost without a trace, as a name is wiped off a blackboard. In the case of my grandmother, I felt the loss would be monumental. She had not only helped rear me but had raised me up, after my mother died, from the point of such depressed speechlessness it was as if she had taught me to talk; she coaxed me out of myself to her level, which seemed grander even than the level where my mother once stood, since I was old enough to understand that she had given actual birth to my mother.

I put aside a pile of what I was doing and began to write about my grandmother, and the story turned out to be the first finished piece of *Beyond the Bedroom Wall.* It was also, as these things turn out, the first story of mine accepted by *The New Yorker* — actual truth always stands out crisp — and now rests near the center of that novel under the title "The Way You Do Her." Implicit in the story is gratitude to this grandmother, and before I move from her I want to further affirm that she was indeed the person who in a sense taught me to speak, since it was through her that I found the voice that enabled me to enter my own material and to say whatever I have said since in the twenty-five years I've been writing.

I would like to be able to report that I can recapture my exact emotions at the moment when she reentered my life, my tensions and expectations that afternoon, along with the angle of the sun coming through the window of my rented room, but I can't. I find it a terrific struggle backward, overlaid by false starts built up before that story and by thousands of printed pages since. So I turn rather to a similar moment that another writer, John Updike, has recorded in "The Blessed Man of Boston, My Grandmother's Thimble, and Fanning Island" — a story about non-stories which we know, from some of the brave paragraphs in *Hugging the Shore,* came out of a period of great self-doubt and depression.

The narrator picks up his grandmother's thimble, which rolls out of a sewing basket he has kicked over on the stairs one night, and at first he doesn't know what the object is, standing in the darkness of the stairwell, and then he says, "Then I knew, and the valves of time parted, and after an interval of years my grandmother was upon me again, and it seemed incumbent upon me, necessary and holy, to tell how once there had been a woman who now was no more, how she had been born and lived in a world that had ceased to exist . . . ”

What particularly catches at me here, though the whole passage goes through me like lightning, piercing that moment of mine and perhaps burning it away for good in Updike's agile eloquence, is this: *necessary* and *holy.* These words apply exactly to my experience.

Now I want to put forward provisionally and in such a tentative manner that I'm nearly prepared to withdraw the statement (but I won't) this: the essence of what I'm examining in *What I'm Going to Do, I Think* and *Beyond the Bedroom Wall* and my other books is the working, or lack of it, in the hearts of men, of God. This isn't always apparent in them, certainly, page by page, or as apparent as it is in *Born Brothers* or *Poppa John*—the very reason, it seems to me, for the misreading and lack of popularity of these books.

And now I will set forth another proposition, no more popular, I suspect, by a colleague of Bellow's and another of America's living Nobel laureates, Isaac Singer, as recorded in *The New York Times* of June 17, 1984: "We are still at the very beginning of learning both in science and in the arts. I foresee a time when many of the ideas we have rejected so lightmindedly may come back into science and art; such as the existence of God, Providence, the soul, a plan and a purpose to Creation, reward and punishment, free will and other such obsolete and refuted notions."

Cities represent a frontier in their literary activity and reportage of it, and I'm grateful for this confirmation of a mutuality between writers from such opposite regions. Writers in cities often participate in this literary activity, viewed as the politics of the profession, or they enter the monolith of the media and either perpetuate its standards or try to alter them. How long since you last saw a program about the Midwest, much less North Dakota, on national TV? Is it any wonder young people feel disenfranchised, or abhor their homeplace? Better that writers in the city submit so entirely to the anonymity of its overpopulation that they're forced to retreat, for spiritual sustenance, to their own centers: home.

Words are a witness to our thought and work. It's in the application of the words of our writing that we should trust to the truth as we receive it, or as it's imprinted in us by a spirit greater than the spirit of place: the Holy Spirit. I don't presume to understand the ways of God, and wouldn't presume, like Milton, to explain those ways to you, gentle reader, wherever you are, if I could. But I will continue to examine the areas, dark and light, at the center of a particular character, and examine his relationship to her, and the effect that the creation, in its local particulars, has had on him and her; and examine each character's relationship to time, which includes the past, the particular present a person is bound within, and whether those flashes we experience of a gap in time, or of a rent opening in time while a wholly other element pours through with stilled density—eternal moments, as they've been called (is reality eternal, or eternality real?)—whether these aren't of the actual essence of reality.

Included here would be aging, and the worry about whether age will bring change, regenerative or not, along with that inevitable confrontation that time eventually will take each of us up against: death—whatever form it might take in reality or our imaginations, as it awaits us beyond the bedroom wall. What is our stand in the face of it?

"There are those to whom place is unimportant," Theodore Roethke writes in "The Rose," and in the poem's third section says

What do they tell us, sound and silence?
I think of American sounds in this silence:
On the banks of the Tombstone, the wind-harps having their say,
The thrush singing alone, that easy bird,
The killdeer whistling away from me,
The bobolink skirring from a broken fence-post,
The bluebird, lover of holes in old wood, lifting its light song,
And that thin cry, like a needle piercing the ear, the insistent cicada,
And the ticking of snow around oil drums in the Dakotas . . .

To that man near those oil drums, place is important. I believe there is a reason why we were born where we were, not to mention the reasons for our particular births; and though I don't believe that environment is the inflexible molder of character that some do, I know that a writer can write with authority only about those landscapes that have become entirely internal. One might skim over areas of America one has visited, like a bird touching down here and there, as Roethke does; one might, like Updike, be able to seize up a place he has visited, seemingly whole, and set it down, wadis and all, within the spiky grass of living print, as Willa Cather did with every region where her foot set down; or as Italo Svevo says in *Confessions of Zeno*, "Where I halt, there I take root."

I write about an infinitely smaller region than North Dakota; actually about the size of a fist: the heart. In the midst of it is that person slightly-to-the-west-of-Midwestern man, who, like all Westerners, tends to think of himself as a pioneer. And as that person, I will step forward now and say that I believe there are areas of the heart and spirit that remain unexplored, the true frontier; entire landscapes that haven't fallen under the scrutiny of the most rigorous analyst, although writing has taught psychiatry that the psyche and the dislocations in it, such as the Oedipal conflict, exist.

I believe that American writing now stands at the threshold of being able to speak of the habitations of spirituality, or the lack of them, within the human heart as in no other period in history. And if those of us at the center of America can retain what we presently possess or, even better, turn farther inward toward what we've inherited, clearing away the falseness and superficiality that is constantly and electronically being beamed into us from either coast, as if by its repetitiveness it could become the truth, and approach the land and the people who live on it as our ancestors did, with the cautious reverence of mutual regard, then I believe that a new form of expression, if not a new manner of literature, could, by the grace of God, be created for any generations who might come historically after us and wish to listen to our voices speak the truth to them about the places we have inhabited and that inhabit us through the unmerited gift of particular love.

The Presence of the Past

As a young girl, I was always observing things: ice formations in tractor tire ruts, rough cows' tongues going after sweet grain, green silage being elevated into the silo. I watched my folks shovel manure, chop off chickens' heads, castrate pigs, and extract honey. I listened for the John Deere in the lane, to milk hitting the rim of the pail, roosters crowing at dawn and our wringer washer at work in the cellar.

How anything in a person's life influences her writing is, of course, a mystery. I like to think that being a Midwesterner has given me a set of sensibilities, a solid foundation, if you will, from which to work. At an impressionable age I lived and breathed hay bales and clover blossoms and topsoil. Because there were few distractions, I looked at things closely and let my imagination go wild.

Being rooted in the Midwest gives me great freedom as a writer. I live now in the city, but at times I find myself walking down that old dirt farm lane, watching the heat shimmer up from Hoegemeyer's cornfield on a bright August afternoon.

—Twyla Hansen, from "Rooted in the Midwest"

I have come to the belief that if I can examine the function of recollection as it operates for me, if I can capture with proper resonance and vividness certain elements of my personal and family history, then I have accomplished one of my main tasks as a writer. We live in an era during which even this simple goal is an act of subversion. To strive to live a rich personal life and to articulate the meaning of that life is to do something which neither the government, the media, nor the McDonald's Corporation particularly wants for any of us. . . .

Only if we define regionalism as a way of writing about time am I able to claim myself as a regionalist writer, and the region of time and memory is one that I will continue to explore.

—David Wojahn, from "The Grammar of Memory"

Tornado

Leo Dangel

Aunt Cordelia was a tough old lady.
We could hardly believe
she was ever a little girl.
She told this story:

We stood on the porch and watched
the gray finger come down from clouds
in the west and dirt swirling up.
Mamma said, "It's over Milo's place."
"No," Papa said, "it's farther south."
My little sister knew
that Mamma and Papa were afraid.
Papa opened the outside cellar door
and herded us in. We stood crowded
on the top steps, watching that thing
in the west. Papa wasn't one to touch
us often, but now his hands hopped
like sparrows from one shoulder
to the next, making sure
we were all there. Even smarty pants
Benny kept his mouth shut.

The tail snaked out and swung around
to the south. Papa became his old self.
The next day, we piled in the car
to go see how bad the Knutson place
was wrecked. Papa said they were lucky
and all got into the cellar.
Benny said, "Pooh, if I got caught
outside in a tornado, I would just grab
a hold around a tree."
Papa smiled, but his face was fierce

and helpless too.
We turned into Knutson's driveway
and saw big trees broken, twisted and torn
out by the roots. Papa said, "Which tree
would you have hung on to?"

Elwood Collins: Summer of 1932

Dave Etter

On sticky summer Sunday afternoons
there would be lots of people
standing around in the yard,
mostly relatives and neighbors
in cotton dresses and white shirts.
They would come and go until dusk,
talking, talking, talking, talking
about jobs, bread lines, foreclosures,
about Hoover and Roosevelt,
about the latest layoff or suicide.
Someone, usually my father
or one of my unemployed uncles,
would be scratching in the dirt
with half a hoe or ragged rake,
not to plant, not to cultivate,
but to do something, to be busy,
as if idleness was some kind of dark shame
or red pimple of embarrassment.
I was there, too, a silent child
with my blue wagon and blue spade,
making little mountains of dirt
and patting them down with my fist.
When the lemonade ran out,
my mother or a maiden aunt
would bring out a pitcher of water
and someone would always say,
"You can't beat good old water
when you have a terrible thirst."
The Ford in the driveway was ours.
It was leaking oil, drop by drop,
and the battery was dead.
We were obviously going nowhere.

Varna Snow

Roland Flint

I hadn't seen snow in summer
In the forty-three years it's been
Since, early that morning, in North Dakota,
It snowed for an hour on the fourth of July.
It melted into the season's usual weather,
Into the day's parades, fireworks, and speeches,
So that by evening the snow, like the morning itself,
Was no more than a small boy's dream.
Gone away as that sounds, I can still see snow
Whitely silting the green fields of the farm.
Later, every summer, the tall cottonwoods
Would let fall their snow,
Softer than flakes, more finely formed,
Stuff that moves both up and down
With the lightest breath of moving air,
A snow of dreaming, or the dream itself.
I haven't been back to my hometown
When the cottonwood releases snow
But in June I've come around the world to Varna
And trees here are snowing down
The same fleecy letting go
Of an early harvest in Bulgarian cottonwoods.
The women sweep it up each day,
As we shoveled December walks at home.
I gathered up three big handfuls
And stuffed the open knot of a tree with it—
I don't know why, some wooly evanescence
Returning snow to the hard tree of ourselves—
As if I were standing here in my own yard
Holding in my open hands this blessing of my journey,
A dry little foam of where I come from,
Where I am today, and where I'm headed in the snow.

High School Boyfriend

Margaret Hasse

You are home town.
You are all my favorite places
the last summer I grew up.
Every once in a while
I write you
in my head
to ask how Viet Nam
and a big name college
came between us.
We tried to stay in touch
through the long distance,
the hum and fleck of phone calls.

It was inevitable
that I should return
to the small prairie town
and find you
pumping gas, driving a truck, measuring lumber,
and we'd exchange weather talk,
never be able to break through words
and time to say simply:
"Are you as happy
as I wanted you to be?"

And still I am stirred
by musky cigarette smoke
on a man's brown suede jacket.
Never having admitted the tenderness
of your hands, I feel them now
through my skin.
Parking on breezy nights,

in cars, floating passageways,
we are tongue and tongue like warm cucumbers.

I would walk backwards
along far country roads
through late evenings, cool as moving water,
heavy as red beer,
to climb into that August.

In the dark lovers' lanes,
you touched my face
and found me here.

Who Made Such Good Pies

Jim Heynen

It was always good to visit that lady because she made such good pies. What was so good about them was the little waves on the edge of the crusts. The boys could tell how big a piece they were getting by counting those little waves. A piece of her pie looked like this.

perfect little waves

Eight waves was a big piece.

How does she do it? the other ladies asked. No one knew.

The boys walked over to her house early one day before everyone was going over there for pie. They stood outside her kitchen window and watched her making her pies. This is what they saw.

When the lady had the pie crust rolled out in the pie pan, she reached into her mouth and pulled out her false teeth. Then she took them and pushed them down on the pie crust all the way around. The spaces between her false teeth made all those nice little waves that everybody liked so much.

Pretty soon everyone came for fresh pie.

What beautiful pies! all the ladies said.

The boys got eight-wave pieces that day.

Every now and then, between bites of that good pie, the boys looked at the lady. She was watching everyone eat and grinning a big grin.

Sacrifice of a Gunnysack of Cats

Joseph Langland

The quick small bubbles popping from the gunnysack,
Hooked by a pitchfork braced in the cattle tank,
Almost unhinged my heart and made me drop
The stick with which I forced the young cats down.

A population explosion, that's what it was.
With twelve mother cats and a year of visiting toms
We met September with the wildest host
Of squinting eyes behind our milking cows.

We divvied them up among the brothers and sisters,
And each had only six. But since we were nine
My father thought things were getting out of hand.
Next day I received my melancholy orders.

"You'll have to catch the most of them and drown them.
Just tidy up the place and make it normal.
Fifty-four cats! Why, that's an infernal nuisance.
Think what would happen next year!" What could I tell him?

So there I was dashing with my gunnysack
Into the bins and under the stalls and mangers.
The wild ones scratched me, but I thrust them in.
The tame ones? Oh, I brushed them with my cheek,

Sighed and kissed them, then I thrust them in.
I climbed the ladders to the highest mows,
Ran through the orchard under the heavy apples
And crept among the tall weeds by the granary,

Until I thought I could not bear that cross.
I dropped it once; that made it twice as hard
To lure them once again into that womb
And bear it backward to the spermal waters.

But there I was: filthy, bleeding, and sick,
Tired and thirsty, my cord pulled at its neck,
The undulating coffin on my wagon,
Trudging down to the sea, my cross upon me.

The thorny dissonance of dying song
Over the squealing of the wagon wheels
Ran up a cloud of dust that nearly drowned me.
It is one thing to think, and one to do.

I wanted to avoid the thinking in the doing
And, quick, be done with it and off to play.
But you can see this didn't work too well . . .
Thirty-three years to get that cord untied.

I stood in the dust, manure at my feet,
The green scum in the corners of the tank
Eyeing my smothering conscience toward a size
My body could not hold. Good God, I seized

That squirming sepulchre, that crying tomb,
That leaping heart familiar as myself,
And heaved it from my homemade hearse and plunged
It back to evolution. Hooking the fork,

I ticked five awful minutes by the hours,
Damned by the furious bubbles where they broke
Among my unwashed hands. And then I went
Up to the barn to find my mother cat.

We sat in a beam of sunlight on the floor
Petting and purring, while out of a knothole eye
Hung in the roof of God the motes of dust
Sang of our comforts and our curious loves.

In Early Autumn

Thomas McGrath

On a day when the trees are exchanging the cured gold of the sun,
And the heavy oils of darkness in the rivers of their circular hearts
thicken;
    when desperation has entered the song of the locust;
    When, in abandoned farmsites, the dark stays longer
    In the closed parlor;
                          a day when exhausted back-country roads,
Those barges loaded with sunlight and the bodies of dead animals,
Disappear into the Sand Hills under a swollen sun;
A day, too, when the sizzling flies are fingering their rosaries of
    blood
In the furry cathedrals of spent flesh, the left-over
Gone-green goners from the golden summer—

THEN I know a place with three dead dogs and two dead deer in
    one ditch.
I feel the displacement of minerals,
The stone grown fossils,
Under this hill of bones that calls my flesh its home.

Hockey on the River

Michael Moos

I am walking south on the frozen river,
along the dark hollowed banks and gnarled roots,
past the beaver lodge and the young willows
gnawed through last summer in the moonlight,
a cemetery of stumps turning gray in the snow.
I turn and look back around the bend,
through the stinging white wind and see
dark figures flying across the ice,
skating hard in faded jeans and sweatshirts,
young bodies leaning into bitter air,
arms and legs pumping blood and ghosts
of breath, taped sticks slapping,
dribbling, lifting the hard black puck,
like a period spinning through space
and time . . . For a minute I am with them,
shouting my curses, whispering my defeats,
calling their names — Charlie, Gene, Spots, Goody . . .
cutting a figure eight into the river's glass
so clear I can see into another world,
where shapes destined to become human,
in a billion years, swim below the surface.
I don't want to forget where I came from,
or let go of those who helped me stand alone,
those now grown up and lost out there
in offices and bars and marriages gone bad;
those who helped me let go of fear and fly
across this ice that may break at any moment.

Migrant Mother, 1936

David Ray

She was drawn as if by "instinct,
not reason," had seen the sign,
PEA PICKERS CAMP, had driven on,
the road slick, but something
called her back. She had
to turn around, to find the woman
sitting on a box, huddled
in a tarp as if waiting
always for Dorothea Lange.
"I drove into that wet and soggy
camp and parked my car
like a homing pigeon." She asked
no questions, moved in silence
with the lens. The woman told her
she was thirty-two, had come
from the Dust Bowl. She and the children
had been living on frozen vegetables
from the field and wild birds
caught with hands. They had sold
all that would buy food, their tires,
did not know if they could ever leave.
She nursed the baby at her breast,
revealed the madonna, lover, mother,
pale half-moon pressed against the head.
The hungry lens looked equally upon
the lantern, tin pie-pan, hacked pole
that held the half-tent up.
The dirty baby lay as if he'd drunk
the milk of death. The older two
leaned sadly on their mother,
their clothing made of gunnysacks

or else the linen of Christ's shroud.
Dorothea took no names, and said no thanks,
nor handed bread across,
nor joked until those ancient children laughed.
But she put her ten eternal minutes in
and called it work, before the dark rain fell.

Midwest Sex Education — 1965

CarolAnn Russell

1.
After the filmstrips where body parts
become cartoon characters
with a life of their own,
the boys were asked to leave the room
and go to the gym for a special
presentation on "the male organ."
We were awarded
pale pink pamphlets
embossed with magenta roses
on long stems.

2.
The teacher brought in a box
covered with gold stars and bows
like the ones we made in grade school
for valentines. For questions,
she said, anything we dreamed: petting,
tornadoes, marriage
and we filled it
because it was there
and each of us was
a white glove
waiting to be inched on
to a strange hand
in the heat.

3.
Weeks tracing the elaborate cloverleaf
of the fallopian tube, first one
then the other, in its exit from the womb's
strawberry mosque,

the word, "intercourse," emerged
like a runaway car
in concert with props:
a see-through lavender nightie,
some pink pills,
the dome of a diaphragm,
and a concertina of prophylactics
in silvery blue foil.

4.
But she couldn't really say
she said, except that we were young
and our bodies were questions.
Then she called us Miss-so-and-so,
passed around a rubber doll
and said things
would never be the same.

One Home

William Stafford

Mine was a Midwest home—you can keep your world.
Plain black hats rode the thoughts that made our code.
We sang hymns in the house; the roof was near God.

The light bulb that hung in the pantry made a wan light,
but we could read by it the names of preserves—
outside, the buffalo grass, and the wind in the night.

A wildcat sprang at Grandpa on the Fourth of July
when he was cutting plum bushes for fuel,
before Indians pulled the West over the edge of the sky.

To anyone who looked at us we said, "My friend";
liking the cut of a thought, we could say Hello.
(But plain black hats rode the thoughts that made our code.)

The sun was over our town; it was like a blade.
Kicking cottonwood leaves we ran toward storms.
Wherever we looked the land would hold us up.

Breaking Silence

Cary Waterman

It has taken us forever
to get this far—
Mitchell, South Dakota,
the Corn Palace,
that parched Russian mosque
held together with corn cobs,
corn silk hair, corn honey,
the sexual tassels sweating
down on the sweaty tourists.

We are too tired to assault
any more of plains and sky,
any more of the anonymous farms,
the predictable signs—
tennis court,
swimming pool,
vacancy.
There is a vacancy inside our bodies.
It is July, 98 degrees,
and the heat rolls through us
like quicksilver.
We take what we can get.

But everything is broken,
or nearly broken—
door latches,
promises, a man's work,
and the tile in the bathroom
curls off like old skin.
We carry towels to the pool,
my daughter and I,
our pubic hair singing

inside our suits like corn silk,
yellow and red and gold.
And we ride the slippery aquamarine slide
with a curve halfway down
like a badman's heart
that shoots us off into a deepness
where we must know how to swim,
because in Sioux country
this is the Mariana Trench.
But we can swim and do,
dog-paddling, kicking,
getting our breath,
filling our lungs with corn dust.

Tomorrow we will go on,
through Mission, a rebel enclave,
past the white-crossed cemeteries
missionaries built,
past Russell Means going to jail
for inciting to freedom,
for teaching children how
not to sink,
their black hair flowing out
around them like cilia.

We will cross into Nebraska,
drive through Valentine
where the highway plunges down,
a bloodline into the Sand Hills,
where the telephone poles rock
like ghosts in the wind.
We will arrive finally at McCook
in time for the 90th birthday
of Winona Metheny, great-grandmother,
girl child of homesteaders, and
survivor of silences

who has a story to tell
as long as the long wind rushing
across these plains.

Star Quilt

Roberta Hill Whiteman

These are notes to lightning in my bedroom.
A star forged from linen thread and patches.
Purple, yellow, red like diamond suckers, children

of the star gleam on sweaty nights. The quilt unfolds
against sheets, moving, warm clouds of Chinook.
It covers my cuts, my red birch clusters under pine.

Under it your mouth begins a legend,
and wide as the plain, I hope Wisconsin marshes
promise your caress. The candle locks

us in forest smells, your cheek tattered
by shadow. Sweetened by wings, my mothlike heart
flies nightly among geraniums.

We know of land that looks lonely,
but isn't, of beef with hides of velveteen,
of sorrow, an eddy in blood.

Star quilt, sewn from dawn light by fingers
of flint, take away those touches
meant for noisier skins,

anoint us with grass and twilight air,
so we may embrace, two bitter roots
pushing back into the dust.

Star Quilt — Plains Indian women make quilts with a central star for their children and grandchildren. A young man seeking a vision may take one to use during that time. Some are also used as blankets. In either case, a star quilt is a valued possession, connecting the generations to one another and to the earth.

Visiting the Graves—February

Patricia Zontelli

Everyone here sleeps:
as spring sleeps still
in hard centers
of these midwestern hills,
as sawdust hearts sleep
in beeches. No last leaves
trickle down.

Beneath the ground,
bones of those who came
before me.

Their voices return:
those I knew throb
in my own voice,

those I did not
still circle the earth
spilling their song. Snow

begins,
falling heavily. Sky
generous as my Norwegian
grandmothers, Anna and Anna,
their bowls of thick white
cream for pale coffee.

The day darkens.
All around
lights in the houses
come on one by one.

      I walk through
shadow cross-hatching

this cemetery, away
from bones of those
for whom I hold such
tenderness in my heart

for having been there first
for having left first
for having left me
   here
under these brief, unfinished stars.

Bloodsuckers

Stephen Dunning

To help us settle in, Father drove his Packard, me riding with him, and Mother took Rosie in the Ford. It's ninety-four miles from Cannon Falls to Rose Lake. With both cars loaded to the gills, and with stops, it took three hours. After that weekend, Father was in and out, every other weekend or so. What he and Mother had worked out.

In August he didn't come up at all.

It was no secret. Things between them were bad.

Luckily, my friend Robert Enquist visited most of the summer. He and I became famous bloodsucker hunters, at least in our own eyes.

Anyway, what can an eleven-year-old do to make parents act right? If I tried to break into one of their arguments, they'd say, "Stay out of this." Actually Father would say, "Stay *the hell* out of this."

If I tried to put something true into their argument, one of them might say, "You don't know what you're talking about." But I saw Mother making her phone calls at Twig, and I knew Father's drinking first-hand.

"God dammit." Father's voice angry and low. "I'm *not* drinking too much."

I don't think he knew how much. His argument was that he needed to relax at the lake. Business was terrible, the Depression was terrible, and Roosevelt was crazy. "Gotta forget my woes," he'd say. But when he took a bottle and quarts of beer outside—the beer "just to wash it down, son"—he'd get drunk. One Friday night in late June, for example, he drank at least six drinks of Old Grand-Dad and three quarts of beer. "Just a little nip for the late innings," he'd say, no matter what time it was.

These are facts. I was the one picked up the empties next day.

My idea was that he should only drink inside. I told him that, a couple of times. He never heard. If he knew how much he was drinking, he never admitted it in front of me.

He and I played catch that Friday night until the swallows and bats swooped and dived. Robert was on the porch, unable to run enough to play catch very well. I liked catch a lot, but in sixth grade I'd started having trouble with my eyes. One of life's mysteries. For a while things blurred and everyone was worried. Then around Easter, hiding eggs for Rose, I realized I could see fine again. Still, they made me wear glasses and I wasn't supposed to play any sport that had a ball or a puck or a stick. Robert had had polio. So the two of us were thrown together during recess, phys. ed., and after school.

After school we'd play catch, using a softball. Safe enough for me. But mostly we just hung around the playground, killing time. We weren't especially popular, but nobody teased us. Naturally we became best friends.

This night anyway Robert stayed on the porch listening to Mother read aloud to Rose. The kerosene lamp threw a cloud of light out where Father and I were playing. "Isn't it too dark, you boys?" called Mother from the porch. "Consider his glasses, Keith."

"Never too dark for a little kitch-catch," Father said.

"Well, too dark for Philip?" She really worried about my glasses.

"Let the boy speak for himself."

What happened next was predictable. Mother took the lamp inside, and we could hear her putting Rose to bed. Robert went by himself, so it was just Father and me in the dark, night growing deeper until I couldn't see the ball even right in my face.

"Pop up!" Father yelled, tossing one underhand.

"Where? Where?" I yelled as the ball disappeared into the dark. "Can't see it!" And about then the ball would drop from nowhere.

Once I got it right on the nose, but I wouldn't of told Mother for anything. Usually I'd grab for it, sometimes missing altogether, more often touching it, a few times making the catch. Father had played ball, and sober or not, he threw the ball good. He caught almost everything I threw, too.

So now Mother was inside, irritated, and we were outside, Father taking an occasional drink. "Wanna go down to the dock?" he said. "Lie down, look at the stars? Wanna see a few stars, Philsey?"

He knew the names of stars. But he'd been drinking too much. I said No thanks, as friendly as I could, and went inside. Robert had taken the top bunk and was asleep. Mother and Rose were in the other bedroom. I read in the main room and went to bed around ten thirty. Father didn't come in.

He probably slept on the dock.

The next morning Mother hissed into my ear. "Wake up, Philip! Philip!" Somehow she'd got Father into his car. She wanted me up. She was going to drive him down the road, and leave him to sleep it off. "Robert shouldn't have to see this. And keep an eye on Rose. Oh Philip, pick up the bottles, too. Please. Put them out back."

No wonder it became a summer of great voyages. Robert hadn't been there three days before we knew that bloodsuckers and us shared a destiny. If you imagine those little wormy ones, when I say bloodsuckers, dark brown or black, stretching out to maybe two inches, well think again. Those small ones suck blood, but they're hard to take seriously.

Ours at Rose Lake ran three to five inches. They were flat. They were cobras, ready to strike. Their backs were brown-black, speckled with orange-red. Their bellies were all orange-red, with brown-black speckles. The red that would have looked gorgeous in a flower or butterfly looked awful on a bloodsucker's belly.

Those red-bellied ones I remember well. I still shrug involuntarily, recalling them. But half our bloodsuckers were plain, brown-black. We kept the two colors separate when we captured them.

"What's the difference?" I asked Mother.

What she said was, "Well, males and females?" She didn't know.

Now believe this. At age eleven I'd never spoken the word *sex*. Adults used it among themselves, but Mother would never say it in front of Robert.

Dissatisfied with her answer, we created a myth of our own. Brown-blacks were good: They would not attack swimmers, at least *us* swimmers; nor were they poisonous, like red-bellies. Best of all, brown-blacks could be taught to go where the evil red-bellies were and lure them into ambush.

We were ready. We emptied every peanut-butter, jelly, and jam jar Mother brought from the Twig general store. Storage tanks. We had one genuine strainer, with a steel-mesh bowl, and one Robert and I created out of a two-pound MJB coffee can. I remember it felt good pounding nail holes into the bottom of that can, then flattening the bottom by jamming it from the inside with a stone. Dangerous work. We collected salt, sticks to move our victims with, and Mercurochrome, in case a red-belly got us.

We captured our first martyrs by lying on our stomachs at the end of the dock. Robert could lie still forever. We'd wait, still as posts, until we sighted one coming our way. When it was within range, we'd plunge like eagles, scooping with our strainers.

One stormy day, no suckers in view for what seemed hours, we tried to get Rosie to take a swim. She had blood.

"I can't swim by myself." She wasn't quite five.

"Just wade," Robert said. "You can splash us."

"Yeah," I said. "Or Rosie, show how you put your face in the water. Robert would like to see that." She hung around him as if he were a god.

"Yeah, let me see that," Robert said.

Not yet five, but wise enough not to be a sucker for us.

We got most of our victims from *Titanic*.

Robert had been there a week and Father came back for a weekend. He arrived before lunch and found Robert and me lying in wait on the dock.

"You need a raft," he said, without asking what we were doing. Even before lunch we started one.

He was the main builder, of course. We helped, finding good logs. He rounded up boards, hammers, huge nails, standing behind his car and taking a nip now and then. "Hair of the dog," he said, and winked.

But he knew how to treat boys.

Mother called us for lunch. "Just a minute, June," he yelled, using her name so she wouldn't get angry. He started a spike, then handed the hammer to Robert. "Think you can finish that spike for me, Bob?"

"Want to ride the other end of the saw, son?" he asked me.

When we went in, lunch was very pleasant, full of raft talk. Then we charged out behind the cabin, where we'd begun our raft.

"What do you think, Philsey? Finish her here or down near shore?"

If he hadn't asked, of course, the raft, gaining weight with each board and log, would have sat forever behind the cabin.

My happiest day at Rose Lake.

Sunday morning Father and everyone helped with the launch.

"Father! It floats!" I yelled as our craft wobbled into Rose Lake.

"It's a *she*," he said, smiling. "We built her to float."

Rose and Mother clapped as Robert and I proved we could paddle her. We took her out a few feet, then docked her. Before he left for Cannon Falls, Father suggested that we christen her *Titanic.* Mother suggested *Snark,* I didn't know why, although I liked that it sounded like *shark.*

"What name do you think?" Father asked Rose.

Rosie hemmed and hawed, making faces, and suggested *Log Boat.*

That night in bed, we thought of others, but Robert and I chose *Titanic,* knowing that name was famous, but not why.

Titanic was just the best sounding.

As long as Robert stayed, we hunted bloodsuckers every day there wasn't rain or too much wind. A good summer, with a few bad times thrown in. Father visited a few times; more and more Mother left us alone. I couldn't do anything about my parents' problems anyway, and bloodsucker hunting took my mind off them. Exactly what split them apart? That Rose Lake was Mother's didn't help. Father'd call it "your cabin" when they were fighting. Nor was it only his drinking.

Included in there were how he acted with other women, including Mother's sister Daisy, and the phone calls Mother was making to someone. But it was beyond me, I concentrated on wiping out Rose Lake's bloodsuckers.

Don't think that just because they were our allies that the brown-blacks escaped with their lives.

Titanic was seven feet long and nine logs wide. The middle log was shorter than the others, so she had an endearing imperfection. Nobody would confuse her with the real *Titanic*. We nailed boards of different widths across the logs, bottomside, topside. At the front we rigged a frame like a Christmas tree holder, and in it inserted our sturdy mast—the split oar we'd scavenged from D'Autremonts' junk pile.

Our sail was a patched sheet. We doubled an inch or so and nailed it along the height of the mast. The top far corner we doubled down and pinned into a triangle of sorts. We borrowed the paddles from our canoe, and with them came Mother's warnings not to lose or break them.

Why would we? Paddles were life or death. We had neither tiller nor centerboard; we knew nothing of sailing nor of those desperate seas we would roam. *Titanic* and her crew were at the mercy of the wind.

Where it blew, we went.

On journeys out we'd push into Rose Lake, set sail, and once we knew for sure where the wind was blowing us, steer as best we could. On journeys home, we furled the sail and paddled, accusing each other of malingering. Once the wind took us due south, toward Dodo Lake. The little rise that separated the lakes was thinly treed and hummed with mosquitos. A gravel road ran between the lakes. Local lore had it that gypsies and hoboes walked in from Highway 49 and camped there. They might have. It was level enough, there was fresh water and a good view of Rose Lake.

Robert and I ate lunch and walked along a marsh, trying to capture a frog. Did we think that a frog might battle the bloodsuckers? By midafternoon the wind had shifted miraculously so the breeze that took us to the beach later returned us close to home.

Standing at the south end of Rose Lake, we could just see the two cabins at the north end, a thousand yards away. Thirteen other cabins, including ours, lay along the west shore. Ours sat between the Garrys and Rose Lake's one rental cabin. Just past that, to the north, was D'Autremonts', the one fancy place.

As if they were stars, we steered on D'Autremonts' second-floor windows. I was captaining the voyage home, Robert up front scouting for bloodsuckers. Eventually I saw the reflector Father had nailed to the end of our dock and called out, "Land ho."

"Land ho!" Robert yelled back.

"Lower the mainsail," I yelled, all of three feet from his ear. Other salty terms peppered our trips. "Avast there" meant "Watch out." "Frigates to the starboard" or "port" meant bloodsuckers right or left. What a crew we were, ready to go anywhere to escape Rose and my parents' fights.

More, we were doing something everyone approved of. Who wanted to save bloodsuckers? Still, people not fond of bloodsuckers weren't automatically allies. Even though we kept our catch in jars, for example, the bloodsuckers scared Rose. Mother complained about the clutter on the dock, and was really miffed the day Mrs. Garry came for a swim; our gear was spread all over. And berthed alongside the dock, perhaps less beautiful to others than to us, was *Titanic*. Even Father once told us to clean up our act. We did, but things got cluttery again.

Still, on balance, bloodsucker hunting gave Robert and me a perfect mix of adventure—danger and reward. We were free of the tensions of the cabin, and from my tag-along sister, and were making big money. We'd conned Mother into paying a penny for each dead sucker, and earned many a Snicker and Oh! Henry from those bounties. Our daily goal was twenty suckers. Twenty suckers, twenty cents. Mother could afford it. And on a good day, *after* the candy bars, a dime for the match-box bank we'd buried in the pines. By summer's end we had two dollars plus.

Imagine. Two dollars. "What should we buy?" Robert asked. "Knives? Our own sieves?"

Delicious talk, contemplating the equipment we'd need to rid other lakes, Dodo and Leora to start, of their enemies. "What if . . . " Robert began. "What if they gave us two cents for every sucker?"

Lord, lord. "Or a nickel?" I asked.

Mind-boggling!

Once, coming home with our catch, Robert sieved up four suckers in a single scoop. Suckers swim with a vertical S wiggle, not flat S's like snakes. We'd sailed into a bunch. Apparently unaware that the planet's most-feared bounty-hunters were nigh, the whole herd continued on in the direction they were swimming. Paddling hard, we overtook them; with one long, not-too-fast swoop, Robert netted his record quarry.

That great moment, though, became our first disaster. Robert leaned out after an escaping sucker. I was turned from him, but heard the splash.

"Philip!" he yelled. "Help, Philip, help!"

He was within easy oar-reach. "Grab it," I yelled. "Hold on." I pulled him alongside *Titanic,* and he clambered up in milliseconds.

"Get 'em off me!" he yelled, brushing his arms, legs, and torso.

One had indeed fastened onto his thin leg. I scraped at it, taking three swipes to break it loose.

Another disaster happened after a long day. We were twenty yards from shore when the open jar holding our catch rolled off and sank into Rose Lake. Fifteen prime suckers wriggled out. They get a second lease on life, I thought blackly, suspecting Robert of having kicked the jar and also suddenly sad about Father—wriggling away from us all.

Most days, however, we brought home the bacon. Our storage jars were full of dead and dying bloodsuckers.

"Do you feel sorry for them?" Robert asked.

"No," I said. "Well, not really. Who wants bloodsuckers?"

Early on we faced the problem of what to do with their corpses, once they died. We took to lifting the dead ones from the jars and carrying them in a coffee-can into the pine grove out back. Why there? Maybe to keep Mother and Rose away from our money. They wouldn't go near the dead bloodsuckers — would they? But worried that *someone* might rob us, we camouflaged our trips into the stand of pines with zig-zag routes and fanciful talk. No gypsy or hobo would find our match-box of gold.

We also took to killing our catch immediately, impatient with the pace of their natural deaths, and eager to add to our loot. We'd lift live ones from their jars, lay them on the dock, and salt them. They wriggled and writhed most satisfactorily, curling into shrimp-like shapes.

No qualms. At the risk of sounding awful, I confess that I enjoyed killing them. Probably Robert enjoyed it less than me. But capturing and killing never got dull. Nights, in our bunk, we'd talk about making a living at bloodsuckers, later on. Adults liked our work. We liked the adventure and pay. And when we mentioned our money, we whispered.

Nobody stole it. Robert and I split it the morning his mother surprised us by coming after him. No warning at all. She just drove up, got out of her car, and said, "I've come to pick up Robert."

Mother's reaction was soft. "But he's fine with us, here?"

Mrs. Enquist was firm. She had Robert get his things, and for a minute it looked as if she wouldn't even wait until we divvied the money. But while Robert, cowed, gathered his stuff, I fetched the match-box. Mrs. Enquist waited while we counted it out. A dollar twenty something each.

"Fifty-fifty," I said. Robert nodded, and without a decent goodbye, off they went. Robert waved from his window until pines swallowed their car.

Mother took Rose inside, and they lay down. I heard Mother cry. I felt lousy too, Robert's being taken away. But everyone in Cannon Falls seemed to know about my parents; probably Mrs. Enquist suddenly didn't want her little boy "exposed." I myself was practicing "being a little man," not crying. I went to the dock and sat, trying not to think of my worries.

* * *

It's a fact, things disappear. Car keys, now, and lists of things. Gloves, an occasional friend. But things disappeared back then, too. When I was eight or nine, somebody took my chamois marble sack, with forty-five emmies and a cat's-eye shooter. I loved that shooter, and I remember the number of emmies exactly. When I was thirteen someone swiped my first Scout knife, although I might have left it sticking in a tree one rare time I was alone with Maxine Williams, cutting across the college campus on our way home from Ramsey School. And did not pickpockets roam the school hallways, lifting lunch-money dimes and quarters from me? Mother said it was my carelessness, that I'd lost the money wrestling or fooling around. Maybe she was right. Still, when I was fourteen, a thief took my twenty-inch bike from the front porch: on *that* one Mother called the cops.

But this was Rose Lake, and I was eleven, and I was losing people. Father was hardly ever around, and when he was, he and Mother would fight. Also, two or three times a week, Mother'd drive to Twig and be gone a couple of hours. We weren't supposed to know she was meeting someone, but it was obvious — her dressing up, putting on makeup. She could simply have gone, but she chose to say something lame: "We need bread" or "fresh fruit." No matter how full the ice box, she'd take off. I had to watch Rose when she was gone, and that cut into hunting time with Robert.

Worse, at the end of summer, I missed Robert. I considered him a kidnap victim. And as if his leaving were a signal of some sort, a few days later a man drove right up to our cabin in an Auburn. That was one kind of car I knew.

Mother got flustered. "I have to talk to someone," she said, and told me to watch Rose. She and the stranger drove off. The following day, slam bang, August first, Mother drove us home to Cannon Falls. "I have to talk to your father" is all she said about why.

That day we closed the cabin early and drove home. Mother had made an appointment for me to have my teeth checked, and she took Rose to her friend Obie's who, coincidently, was having a birthday party.

I waited in Dr. Hooper's office for more than an hour. We left Cannon Falls mid-afternoon and drove all the way back to the cabin.

We got there at sunset. "Ma," I'd said at least five times on the trip back, "let's get some ice cream, or something." She was in another world. I kept asking because it wasn't like her to ignore me altogether. I was dying by the time we got to the cabin.

"Put peanut butter on one slice of bread," she said. "*One.* I'll fix something soon as I can."

I spread the peanut butter thick and took my one slice out to savor as long as possible. I'd walked out onto the dock before I realized *Titanic* was gone. I looked left, then right, shielding my eyes from the setting sun.

Nothing.

"Ma!" I yelled, the half-eaten bread a forgotten weight. "Ma!"

Apparently she didn't hear me, back in the kitchen. What could she have done, anyway? I walked toward D'Autremonts', looking for signs. Not that any D'Autremont would steal a raft. Then I walked past our dock all the way to where Rose Lake drains into a little creek. No sign. By now the slice of bread was long gone.

It was getting dark. I was hungry. "Where have you been? Why don't you ever tell me when you're going?" Mother said the moment I walked in.

"*Titanic*'s gone," I said, gloomily. "Someone stole her."

The news neither surprised nor pacified her. "The raft will turn up," she said coldly. "It probably got loose and drifted off. Everyone knows whose it is." What she said next made me feel worse. "If it's lost, your father or someone will help build a new one."

Or someone! The man in the Auburn. He didn't look like he could build anything. To top it off, at supper Mother told Rose and me— again!—that Father wouldn't be coming to Rose Lake again.

Rose starts right in: "When will I see Daddy? Where's Daddy?"

After eating I go back to the dock. The bats and swallows are out, reminding me of catch with Father. This time I cried. I loved Father. He wanted to be a good father. He was better than Mother's new friend, whoever he was.

* * *

Days seemed slow. A couple of times I searched for *Titanic,* thinking off and on about Robert and Father and Mother. I could see why Mother would yell at Father, but why didn't she give credit for his good traits? Their fight had cost me Robert, and that made me angry.

Most of the time I read and hiked in the woods. I caught a few suckers off the end of the dock, and one day, wading, Rose got one on her leg and came screaming out of the water. She wouldn't let me take it off, although I easily could have. She went yelping to Mother on the porch.

The next day I waded around and swam a little, hoping a sucker would latch onto me. I couldn't even get one that way. Talk about feeling blue.

One day when the black flies were thick I found *Titanic,* or what was left of her. Somebody'd taken her to Dodo Lake beach and used her for firewood. They'd burned half the logs, and I saw charred ends of the boards we'd used to build her. The mast was gone, and the sail.

Titanic gone. Robert gone. Father not coming to the lake any more, and Mother distracted by this new man, a Mr. Claypool. You read about kids committing suicide, you can see why. I was surprised when we got back to Cannon Falls that Father was still living at home. But within a few minutes of that good news, I took another blow. I called and asked for Robert, disguising my voice when his mother answered. Robert said he was moving. Minneapolis. His father's company was closing down in Cannon Falls. I knew Mrs. Enquist wouldn't let us play after school, but I'd counted on seeing Robert at school.

Robert called a couple of days later, to say goodbye, and asked for my street address. We wrote a couple of times that Fall, always saying something about our great bloodsucker hunts, but that began sounding childish pretty fast.

Around my twelfth birthday, in October, knowing I missed Robert a lot, Mother said I could invite him to visit over Christmas. But she and Father were still battling, and Mr. Claypool was hanging around, so it didn't work.

By Spring, Robert and I weren't in touch. Father was almost a stranger.

Gopher Hunting

Lois Phillips Hudson

It is where there are the fewest distinctions between men and women that there can be the most bitterness between them. If a woman's major function in life is to contribute additional muscles and energy to her husband's physical battle for survival, then her usefulness will be judged by the same criteria that determine the usefulness of males. Such habits of thinking result in constant comparisons, usually to the disadvantage of females, so that women are seldom allotted any niche to dominate.

Even in the kitchen of a North Dakota home less than a generation ago, men had the feeling that women must be somehow inferior. There, the average farm wife, like my mother, still baked her own bread, churned her own butter, rendered out the lard for the crust of her pies, cultivated and harvested the family's vegetables, and nurtured, then executed, the chickens fried for the Sunday table. But still, as my father would often observe, "It's just *practice.* I can cook better than *any* woman if I put my mind to it. Of course, there may be some things a woman is born to be better at. Like bathing a baby, for instance. But I reckon I could even do a pretty fair job at that, too, if I ever had to."

North Dakota men didn't bathe babies, so the question never came up. On the other hand, the question of women and the important tasks of life came up all the time, and since women were judged by how much wheat they could shock or how many cows they could milk, they were almost always doomed to inferiority. Once in a great while a woman made a good showing, and my father would sound honestly admiring when he said something like, "You ought to have seen Hilda Jensen out there helping Aaron dehorn those calves. Why, she's as tough as a man! Quite a gal!"

When beauty and graciousness appear in such an existence, they are irrelevant, and they perish like any other delicate untended thing. Beauty fades into a dusty sun squint, and graciousness dies in exhaustion.

As a small girl on a North Dakota farm some thirty years ago, I probably resented the fate that made me female no more than did most of my contemporaries. There seemed to be nothing for us to look forward to except spending our lives as poor seconds to men. We could learn to live with that prospect or we could smolder hopelessly. Some of my friends achieved a resentful peace—that is, they openly, if grudgingly, admitted boys were superior. Some of them, like me, smoldered and fought. Our obsession with our inferiority we kept secret, and we courted opportunities to demonstrate our superiority. The boys, amused by our fanaticism, patronized and mocked us with ridiculous dares, not one of which we failed to accept. I remember the time when one of my second-grade classmates dared me to shinny up the iron pole that supported the top landing of the fire escape on the schoolhouse. I went all the way, of course, two and a half stories above the cement sidewalk.

But the efforts I made to impress the boys I went to school with were nothing compared to the efforts I made to impress my father. By the time I was seven years old, I was driving a team of horses up and down a hayfield while he worked in the back of the hayrack, pitching the hay forward to make room for more, piling it on the revolving teeth of the hayloader. When we transferred the load to the loft or the haystack, I tramped it down as he forked it up to me. As I floundered back and forth, sidestepping the flashing tines of the hayfork, reeling from the heat, choking in the swarming dust and chaff, lifting my dead legs over and over again with the false energy of my mania, I would tell myself that no boy could keep up with a man who pitched hay as fast as my father.

I fed calves, herded cattle, weeded the garden, husked corn, and hauled buckets of water up the long hill to the house, always wondering what more a boy could do to please my father. In winter when he hunted jack rabbits over miles of snow-covered prairie, I plodded after him, keeping my tracks straight like an Indian's and trying to stretch my stride as long as his.

"I swan, that child walks exactly like her father," my grandmother would say disapprovingly. Her tone didn't bother me at all; I was proud of what she had said.

But there was one thing all boys could do that I couldn't. I couldn't kill a gopher—or any other living thing, for that matter. This I knew was the failing that betrayed all my other efforts to become as useful and as admirable as a boy. My cousin, who was four years older than I, earned nearly fifteen dollars a summer by trapping gophers. Two cents a tail could add up remarkably, especially if you cut the big tails in half. My father would keep pointing out that if I were only like Warren I could earn some money too. Finally, the summer that I was going on eight, I decided that I would simply have to start trapping gophers. My father was very pleased. He located a gopher hole behind the chickenhouse and said, "Now here's some easy money right here. I'll fetch you a trap and you'll have him in an hour or so."

As we approached the hole I felt sicker and sicker, and the sicker I got the more I hated myself for being female. He showed me how to set the trap, but he wouldn't put it in the hole. He wanted me to think that I was earning this money myself. I pried the serrated jaws apart and laid the trap in the freshly dug earth. Then I took a big rock and pounded the stake on the trap chain deep into the ground, so that if the teeth caught the gopher's foot he couldn't drag the whole thing away before I got there to finish him off.

My father went whistling off to the fields and I slunk into the grove and sat in my swing. But I didn't swing, because I felt that somebody who was doing what I was doing ought not to be playing. I tried to imagine taking a rock in my hand and bringing it down on the head of a tiny frantic animal whose foot bled around a trap. I wanted to pray that God would make him stick his head squarely into the death I had set out for him, but that crunching snap was not the sort of thing one could pray for. Besides, every night I prayed that God would turn me into a boy while I slept, and I thought that if He was anything like parents, I was more likely to get one big favor from Him if I was careful not to ask for too many little ones.

I have no idea how long I sat in the swing before sneaking back around the chickenhouse to the trap; perhaps, measured by the clock (of all inventions the most irrelevant to human misery), it was no more than five minutes. The brainless levity of the hens and roosters in the chicken yard revolted me. It did not matter to them that a charming creature from the fields had to die for stealing a bit of the corn we showered upon them in return for a few eggs. I picked up the big rock I had pounded the stake with, to prove to myself that I could use it if I had to.

The trap was empty. I stood over it a moment until I realized that the gopher might come up and be caught before my eyes. I rushed back to the swing and began all over again the wretched process of hardening myself. After another five minutes I visited the trap again, and once more retreated, trembling with relief.

I made two or three more trips before I broke. Once I had made my resolution, I leaped from the swing, distraught at the possibility of being too late. The trap was still empty. I flung a stone on the trigger and jumped when it sprang shut. Then I wrenched the stake out of the ground and dragged the trap back to the barn, where I hung it on its peg. It clanked against the wall a couple of times, calling "Coward" after me.

Had I been craftier, I would have sprung the trap and allowed my father to think that a twig had fallen into it, or that the gopher had managed to spring it without being caught, as they sometimes did. That would have shown that I had done my best but that the gopher was too smart for me and knew how to hang on to his two-cent tail. But I was not crafty, and I spent the rest of the morning steeling myself against the pain of my father's disgust.

He was angry as well as disgusted. Gophers were one of the main irritations of his life. They robbed the fields and riddled the pastures with holes so that horses and cows would stumble into them and break their legs. Not only had I once again demonstrated my foolish weakness, I had also betrayed him. He stamped out to the chicken-house and set the trap himself. The next morning he came in from milking and said, "Well, I got your gopher for you. If you want the tail, go get it. Otherwise, throw him out in the pasture somewheres, so he don't stink up the yard."

I wouldn't have dreamed of taking the tail in for that two cents; I knew the sneer that would sit on my father's face all the way to town. Not that I didn't want the two cents, which was more money than I might see in two or three weeks. I stopped thinking about how much candy the two pennies would buy when I saw the dead gopher, his disheveled head bleeding and his pert little jaws askew, with the curved white teeth pointing out at chaotic angles. I picked him up tenderly by his valuable tail and walked out to the pasture. There I took a stick and scooped a grave for him, covering it with blades of grass and the indifferent faces of dandelions.

Neither my father nor I had forgotten my failure on the day Peter Liljeqvist, one of the town boys, walked out to our farm to ask my father if he could spend a few hours trapping gophers on our property. He was a year older than I, and from the dark tan of his staunch face to the lithe vigor of his slim legs, he was compellingly masculine. I could see that my father longed for a son like him, but though I resented him for being a boy, still I felt an unwilling attraction to him. As boys went, he was one of the nicer ones in school. Perhaps he had some sort of special feeling for me, too, for it occurs to me now that he surely didn't need to go three miles from town to find more gophers than he could catch in six months.

It was routine, in a male-dominated world, for him to nod toward me and ask my father, "O.K. if she goes along?"

My father hooted. "Sure, she can go along. Sure. Big help she'll be to you."

My mother interrupted him. "Just a minute and I'll pack you a lunch," she said.

"Nice stand of wheat you got out there along the road," Peter remarked easily but respectfully to my father. Good man talk. It would have done me no good at all to say the same thing.

My mother came to the door with the lunch in a gallon pail. The last thing my father said was, "Can't count on her for any help, Pete. You know what girls are like."

With a chivalry that nearly quenched my jealousy of him, Peter said, "Oh, she can carry the lunch. That's enough help."

We headed for the pasture, walking into the sun, with our shadows diverging at a squat angle to the left behind us. Peter's only equipment was a long cord, one end of which he made into a noose, and a knife for cutting off tails. When we came to what looked like a recently made hole, he arranged the noose around the mouth of it. Then he tested the breeze with a wet finger and we moved downwind. He knelt and sat back on his heels, clutching the end of the cord, prepared to yank it up tight the instant a head emerged.

My stomach felt the same way it had that day in the swing, but I was determined to prove to Peter that I could be as quiet and purposeful as any male. For a while we sat absorbed in anticipation—he in eagerness, I in dread. But Peter was not a very patient hunter, or perhaps he preferred exploring to hunting. He never wanted to stay at one place very long, and we wandered farther and farther, pausing to sit by a burrow now and then as much for rest as for trapping. We were having an argument about which holidays were the best— Christmas, birthdays, the Fourth of July, or Halloween—when a small striped head darted up through Peter's noose and startled us both. Before he could jerk the noose, the gopher was nearly out of the hole and he caught only its hind legs. It flopped on its back, twisted up its head, and raked Peter's fist with its long front teeth. "Ow!" he yelled, and in his shock he smashed down the rock he held in his other hand. It was a mangling blow to the gopher's little belly, but it did not die. It lay writhing at our feet.

"Go get a bigger rock!" Peter screamed.

Even if he had dared let go of the string, he couldn't have moved. I knew that we had to end the gopher's agony, but I also knew that I could never do it. I found a rock I could barely lift and lugged it back to Peter. He dropped it on the gopher's head, and the legs in the noose kicked once and were still.

We stood there for a minute and then Peter said, "Let's eat our lunch." The vacancy in my stomach was not caused by hunger, but I agreed. We moved a few yards away, turned our backs on the gopher, and opened the pail. "Boy, homemade bread!" Peter exclaimed. "My mother hardly ever makes it."

"Mine always does," I said. "My father doesn't like store bread. But I do," I added. It always seemed to me that store bread was much more aristocratic than homemade, but it made me happy to have Peter think the large thick slices with their heavy crusts were a treat. I was so cheered by his enthusiasm that I found the dry sandwiches going down with unwonted smoothness. We finished off our bottle of water and stuck it back in the pail. Our dread of the gopher was gone. I felt terribly sorry for him but I wasn't afraid to look at him any more. After all, I wasn't the guilty one; it was all Peter's doing. Peter drew his knife from his pocket with his old aplomb, snapped out the blade, and severed the bushy little tail. The great red ants had arrived and were at their task. He brushed them away and freed his noose.

We had no luck with the holes we tried after that, but our ramblings between burrows netted us a hoard of the natural litter that children feel compelled to save and store away — three discarded snakeskins, an abandoned bird's nest, the empty blue shell of a robin's egg, inexplicably far from the nearest trees, the thin, loose-toothed skull of a rabbit, and a delicate forest of toadstools pushing up from a dried heap of cow dung. We were skirting the edge of a wide slough a mile or so from our farm when we noticed a hawk circling persistently right over us. With his eyes on the hawk, Peter stumbled over the moist mound at the edge of a new gopher hole and we both remembered that we were supposed to be collecting tails.

"Hey, I bet the old hawk is just up there waiting for this gopher to come out. I bet he saw him go in this hole," Peter said, and his reasoning seemed to be corroborated as the hawk's shadow swept viciously over the mound at our feet. "Let's drown him out!" Peter cried. He found a rock and settled his noose in place while I poured the water down the hole. After the fourth or fifth pailful I ceased to worry about the little creature down there shuddering in the dark while an erratic flood gushed in upon him. I was sure he wasn't there. It seemed to me that the other end of the tunnel must empty back into the slough.

I began to regard the circulation of water, a gallon at a time, as a useful activity in itself, and I was not at all prepared when my pail of water erupted in a muddy backwash that boiled out of the hole over my feet and foamed about the sleek dripping head of a half-dead gopher.

At the sight of the flashing tin pail above him, the gopher dived back into his instinctive refuge, but he came clawing out again. Peter yanked his noose, but it had floated harmlessly to one side of the hole, and the gopher hauled himself weakly onto the sloppy ground.

Once again the sudden materializing of our long-sought quarry transfixed us, and we watched stupidly while the gopher's heaving sides pumped air into his collapsing lungs. Finally Peter snatched up his rock and dropped it. It slammed into the mud splattering us both up to our waists, and missing the gopher entirely. He made a wild plunge between our legs and disappeared into an old burrow just behind us.

"Phooey!" Peter spat. "Let him go! I hope that old hawk gets him the first time he comes out!"

He looked at our muddy legs. "Let's go down to the slough and wash," he said.

We took off our shoes and started sloshing the murky water up our shins. "I hear a frog!" Peter said. "Let's catch him."

"Aw, you can't tell where a frog is by the sound he makes," I said. I ought to have known; I had squandered hours leaping after a wily croak that switched direction while I was still in mid-air.

"I bet I can," he said, and he made a spectacular jump to the nearest hummock sticking out of the water. He wavered a little and dug his toes into the mud and said, "See, he was right here, just like I said. He just jumped into the water when he seen me coming."

It seemed to me that if the frogs were going to jump every time we jumped, our chances of catching one were pretty slim, but I didn't want Peter to think he was the only one who could make it from the shore to that hummock, so I said, "Get out of the way. Here I come."

He stepped to the next hummock and I took a little run and landed squarely in his oozing footprints.

"Jeez, I didn't think you could do it," he said.

"I can do a six-foot standing broad jump," I said. "My father took me out and measured it one day. He said if I was only a boy he could make a champion out of me."

Peter was distant and crestfallen. "I bet I can make it to that one over there," he said.

"I bet *I* can *too*," I said.

He gave himself a shove and lit with one bare heel slanting back into the slough. Then he stepped over on a teetering rock and slapped it back and forth against the water, trying to heckle me into missing my mark. But I didn't miss it. We jumped about for a while, daring each other, and then we began looking for frogs again.

The slough was probably not more than two feet deep at its center, but it covered a couple of acres or so, and my mother had warned me to stay away from it. Even if the water wasn't dangerously deep, there was a chance of getting stuck in the mud and drowning. Tall spiky reeds cast shadows so dark that the slough appeared to be bottomless, and frothy blotches of gleaming slime ringed the shores of our little hummocks like a green disease, while long ribbons of the stuff trailed through the water.

It was a place best suited for frogs, blackbirds, and mosquitoes, and the more clearly we saw that nothing human could prevail over such a wilderness, the more determined we became to make that wilderness yield us a trophy. Each of us must have known that the hunt was utterly hopeless. Yet we went on, leaping farther and farther into the tangle of weeds and scum, bruising our feet on hidden rocks and scratching our legs and arms against the stiff blades of the reeds. The more guilty I felt for disobeying my mother, the more I believed that capturing a frog would justify me. The more foolish our quest became, the more necessary it was to go on with it.

Hordes of red-winged blackbirds began settling in the rushes around us, and when we hopped too near a tribe of them, they would whir away before us, bold and angry. For every frog we sent splashing into the water, at least five frogs added their ventriloquy to the mounting bedlam. Mosquitoes fastened themselves on us in such exuberant numbers that the only ones we tried to brush away were those feeding upon our mouths and eyelids. And then, before it had even occurred to us to consider such remote and ordinary things as the revolving of the sun, night fell upon us and our madness.

We looked at each other in the dusk and then we looked for the shore we had left so far behind, but all we could see was the thicket of reeds around us.

The birds had gone to roost and the only sound they made was a startling rush of wings into the twilight whenever we came near their roosting places. The frogs became hideously loud; night had given them triumphant and undisputed possession of the slough. The eyes of snakes and hawks slept, and the eyes of the floundering human invaders were blurred and harmless. As soon as a hunter becomes harmless, he feels vulnerable to harm. It is part of the hunting instinct to believe that the savage balance is always maintained; those who do not hunt are hunted. And so as the din of our erstwhile quarry buffeted and surrounded us, we began to have an apprehension of retribution. The noise shaped itself into an invisible menace.

I became aware that the mud around my feet was cold. Peter must have had the same sensation, for he remembered our shoes. Our shoes! How would we ever find them? How would we ever even get back to them?

Prairie children usually have an almost infallible sense of direction, but panic and darkness confused us. Everything looked the same—as hopeless one way as another. We hopped aimlessly to two or three more hummocks. The darkness began to interfere with our accuracy. I mistook the green stuff lapping against a hummock for the solid earth itself and slid to my knees in muck.

The reluctance of that slimy mouth to give back my leg forced a female scream from me, and in that instant I became female. All day long the only thing my sex had meant was that I was inferior, but then in a flash of desperate insight I understood, for the first time in my life, the advantages that logically accrued to females if males were to deny them equality. If boys were smarter, bolder, stronger, and steadier than girls, then Peter was responsible for getting us into this mess and he was supposed to be able to get us out. It was his fault that I had not minded my mother. For once the world was all on my side.

"I don't know which way to go, Peter," I said. "Do you think we'll have to stay here all night?"

I would never have imagined that a show of female weakness could have such an effect on a male. In the society I knew, women never *showed* weakness.

"Of course not!" he declared stoutly. "Come on, let's go this way. You just jump right behind me." All right, I thought, if he gets us lost it'll just be up to him to get us found again. I felt that with him responsible I couldn't get too cold, too hungry, too tired, or too scared. It was the reward of his birthright to suffer for both of us.

And that night his reward was unenviable. *He* was the one who fell in when he thought the slime or a slippery rock was a safe hummock. Profiting by his mistakes, I managed to avoid immersing myself in green scum. Having surrendered myself to femininity, I shrieked each time he fell, but he always struggled up again, cursing in a brave masculine way, and assuring me through mouthfuls of stagnant mud that we were going to be all right.

When we finally could see the shoreline, he grabbed my hand and we ran through the last few feet of water, heedless of hummocks, reeds, or slime.

"You go that way and I'll go this way," he ordered.

We started around the banks of the slough, looking for our shoes. In a few minutes I caught the dull gleam of our lunch pail, and there, unbelievably, were the shoes. By that time we had our bearings and we headed for home, running barefoot over the dewy grass because our feet were too dirty to put back into our shoes.

About a quarter of a mile from home I began to hear my father's voice echoing over the prairie, and I could tell by its direction and rhythm that he was somewhere near the house, berating my mother about something. As we came through the barnyard I heard him say, "Oh, that kid is just an irresponsible nitwit—just another town nitwit. He's probably got them lost ten miles from here." He stopped and I saw the light of a lantern flare up. "I'll hang this out in the south grove and then I'll go get Liljeqvist and round up some men."

"Here we are!" I yelled.

My parents ran toward us. "Where the Sam Hill have you been?" my father shouted furiously. "I ought to lick you with the razor strop."

But he couldn't lick me because he would have had to lick Peter, too, and he didn't dare do that.

My mother made Peter come in the house, filthy as he was, and gave him an old towel to wipe his face and arms with. Then she fed us, while my father sat fuming behind an outdated *Country Gentleman.*

We put an old blanket on the car seat so Peter wouldn't get slime all over it, and he climbed in meekly beside my father. He looked much smaller than when I was following him out of the slough, but still I could never forget that he was the one who had taken the responsibility.

I felt sorry for him, having to sit so small and dirty and sheepish in the scorching heat of my father's fury all the way to town. It was the first time I had ever felt sorry for a boy, and I began to sense that perhaps the war wasn't so much between male and female as it was between generations.

Free
(from *Green Earth*)

Frederick Manfred

While Pa and Uncle John slopped the hogs and fed the fatteners hay by the cattle barn and spilled grain for Ma's white chickens, Free explored the strange new hills on the yard. The great snowbank had made the whole yard over. Some of the littler snowbanks had hoarfrost on them, and it made them so slippery he could slide down them like they'd been greased. He yelled and showed off in front of the kitchen window so Everett could see him.

Free's tumbling down the snowbanks finally brought him near the pump in front of the chicken house.

The black iron pump handle was covered with hoarfrost too. It looked like a sugar-coated stick of licorice.

Free couldn't resist it. He pulled down his shawl and leaned down to lick the frosted pump handle.

His tongue stuck to the pump handle. He was tied to it.

He tried to pull free. He pulled hard enough to feel his tongue all the way back to its root. Yow. He eased up a little, only to find that more of his wet tongue became stuck to the frosted iron. Now what.

He stood absolutely still. He didn't dare shift his feet. He looked past his nose to see if he could make out the edge of where his tongue was stuck to the iron, crossing his eyes until they hurt in the corners.

"Ulll!" he uttered as loud as he could.

Silence in the yard. The men and the dog were in the barn.

Free peered sideways across the yard to the kitchen window to see if Ma or Aunt Matilda might not be looking out. But there was no pale face at the window. Not even Everett.

"Ulll." It hurt to call. The surface of his tongue tore a little along the edge.

He could feel his tongue beginning to freeze. If someone didn't come quick his tongue would freeze into a solid lump. Suppose they had to cut it off to get him free? He'd never be able to taste dark rye bread with sugar sprinkled on.

"Ulll!"

Suppose nobody saw him in time. Why the whole of him could freeze into an icicle, not just his tongue. Into a statue like the one in the courthouse in Rock Falls.

"Ulll!"

Then his lower lip became stuck, just a tiny edge of it. With an effort, trembling. he managed to draw the lip in enough to free it. Wow. If his whole mouth got stuck they'd have to cut off half of his face to free him.

A barn door cracked open.

"Ulll!"

"Hey, what's the matter there, boy?"

Thank God. Free couldn't see Pa because he didn't dare swivel his eyes that way. He didn't even dare wave for fear of ripping his tongue.

Pa came stepping over. Behind him came Uncle John. Both stopped.

Free could feel them staring.

"Gotske."

"Yeh." Uncle John said, "here's one time you won't have to tell him to freeze to it and not let go."

"Yeh." Pa leaned down for a closer look. "Man, he's really stuck to it all right. Below zero like it is, he's going to have a frozen tongue in a minute."

Uncle John couldn't resist being jokey some more. "Maybe we should tickle him and then he'll jerk himself free. Ha, Free?"

Free waited, bent over. He didn't even dare shiver. If Pa wanted to give him a licking now there was nothing he could do about it. Couldn't dodge or anything. Certainly couldn't quick put a board in his pants.

Pa said, "Wal, the only thing for it is to disconnect the handle from the pump and carry both him and it to the stove in the kitchen. Got a plier handy in that plier pocket of yours?"

"You bet. Coming up," Uncle John said.

Pa took the plier, pulled out the cotter pin, and removed the bolt. Carefully he lifted the handle away from the pump.

"Ulll."

Uncle John said, "Better let the kid hold the handle. He'll know just how much stretching his tongue can take. He can hold it to the rhythm of his own step too."

"Good idee," Pa said. "Think you're strong enough to carry it your-self, boy?"

Free carefully took hold of the frosted handle, a hand to either end.

"Okay. Now walk slowly toward the house. One easy step at a time. Uncle John will walk on one side of you and I'll walk on the other side, in case you stumble."

Free walked very carefully. He could see past the pump handle just enough to make out where he should step next. The frosted handle was so bitter cold he could feel it through his wool-lined leather mittens. As he approached the stoop of the kitchen, he could see out of the corner of his eye that the womenfolk were staring at him through the kitchen window.

Pa opened the door.

Free edged the handle in sideways.

"Over to the stove now, boy. I'll open the oven."

Free headed carefully for the hot oven.

Ma said, "What in God's name . . . ?"

"Yeh," Pa said, "some people's kids stick their fingers into things and some stick their tongues onto it."

"Better call the doctor."

"What for? It'll thaw off in a minute."

"How do you know?"

"I did this too once when I was a kid."

"The things you men don't get into as kids."

Pa and Uncle John helped Free hold the heavy pump handle, each at an end and Free in the middle. The frost got thicker at first. But pretty soon it began to melt off. Then all of a sudden Free's tongue came free.

"What do you have to say for yourself now?" Uncle John asked.

"Mmm." Free's tongue felt like it had been starched. He couldn't form words right away.

PLAINSONG

Marilyn Coffey

I drink the wind like wine.
　　　—Hamlin Garland

The Great Plains region of the United States, where I was born and raised, is part of an enormous strip of flatland that stretches alongside the Rocky Mountain chain for more than three thousand miles, from the plateaus of northern Mexico to the Mackenzie River in subarctic Canada. In sheer extent, this North American grassland has no equal on earth, although similar areas exist on other continents: the steppes of Siberia, the pampas of South America, the veldts of Africa. Shaped roughly like the crescent of the waxing moon, the Great Plains swells to its maximum in the central United States, tapers to near points at its termini. Once, not much more than a hundred years ago, this plain was nothing but meadow, a tangled profusion of grasses and wild flowers that was broken only by an occasional tree-lined river or stream meandering slowly downslope or by buffalo and Indian trails which crisscrossed each other in an intricate but delicate network that led from waterway to waterway.

As a child, my keenest pleasure was to ride unhindered, bareback on my Indian pony, across this great sweep of meadowland, a fantasy that required only the window seat of our family car as it sped down the straightaway that nearly every Great Plains road provides. The view through the windshield would not do; it was time-fixed. Through the windshield, one saw the Great Plains split in two by a ribbon of asphalt rimmed with roadside ditches and decorated with telegraph poles, stuck in the earth like candles in a cake, holding a wire which strung from coast to coast. But through the side window at sixty miles an hour, instead of a blur of neatly furrowed fields or monochrome squares of golden wheat bounded by barbed wire, I could see, by merely squinting my eyes, the prairie as it must have looked unfolding beneath Coronado's visor or over the bow of Father Marquette's birchbark canoe, its variegated grasses and blooms interwoven into a canvas of the richest tweed, subtle colors blending with one another, shifting under the welter of the wind, shaded by the play of clouds casting shadows from the sky. Here, content, I could ride alone for hours, my hair streaming behind me like my mustang's mane and tail, my left hand cupping the rein that stretched out like a rawhide nerve between me and my steed's velvet mouth, my right hand waving wild and free. On and on we would ride, on and on and on, flying as the car sped, due east or west, following those paths that once were ruts cut by wagon wheels that followed earlier paths pounded deep by the thundering hooves of countless buffalo, through what Shimek in 1911 called the "monotonous magnitude." Monotonous? Such a thought never occurred to me. It was the thought of an outsider, one who is passing through. A native would never think such a thing, not here, by the side window in the back seat, the tires singing in her ears, here where every moment of time and movement of self changed one's relationship to the infinite space, here where one intuitively knew how to watch the shifting of the wind as, later, one would be taught to watch one's meditating breath, here where the earliest lesson learned from the land was that beauty and subtlety were inexorably intertwined.

I never actually laid eyes on virgin prairie when I was young. Except for scattered fragments of it, some of which can still be seen today, virtually all of the native grassland of the central plains had been plowed under long before I was born. In fact, my great-grandfathers James Thomas Coffey and Isaac Matts Smith were two of the hundreds of small farmers who resolutely overturned the sod, Smith in 1883 and Coffey in 1885, burying the last generation of native meadow deep in the Tertiary soil out of which its ancestors had sprung millions of years ago. But that didn't matter to me. I knew how the prairie must have been, not because I had been told, but because some vestige of it seemed to cling to me with the stubbornness of the afterlife of a recently amputated limb, as though knowledge of what the land had once been entered me through my very pores, carried, perhaps, by the ceaseless wind. It was, paradoxically, the most beautiful land I had ever seen.

Reports of the virgin prairie's beauty, written by early explorers and naturalists, confirm my childhood intuition. Journal entry after entry describes the vast meadows that were profusely decorated — gilded with myriad flowers. The fields of Quivira, in central Kansas, were "covered with flowers of a thousand different kinds, so thick that they choked the pasture," wrote the Spanish explorer Onate in 1601. "A thousand young flowers gemmed the grassy plains," wrote Thomas J. Farnham some two hundred years later. There were the sky-blue flowers of spiderwort and the light red phlox, the showy yellow sunflowers and purple asters, fields full of white flowers and long garlands of wild roses whose single corolla of pale pink petals surrounded a chunky golden stamen and whose fragrance lay heavy in the early spring air. "These vast plains, beautiful almost as the fancied Elysium, were enamelled with innumerable flowers," wrote English botanist Thomas Nuttall in 1819, "an uncommon variety of flowers of vivid tints, possessing all the brilliancy of tropical productions."

As profuse and varied as the flowers, although less spectacular, were the grasses which ranged in height from the short stubby buffalo and gramma grasses of the semiarid western prairie through the thick luxuriant mixed grasses of the subhumid central prairie, about ten inches high, to the great swaying blades of bluestem and Indian grass in the humid eastern prairie, blades that rose eight feet high. These heights were directly proportional to the rainfall, which tapers off from east to west, as can be seen today by the commercial grasses that have replaced the native strains. In the east, our corn, a grass, rustles higher than a man's head, while the less humid central region is renowned for another, shorter, grass: winter wheat. The semiarid western prairie, then as now, was good primarily for grazing, its clumps of short grass mixing with the prickly pear and with the sunflower, a tiny wild flower in the west, taller than a tulip in the central plains, and eight feet high in the east. The central plains, where I grew up, was a transitional area, dependent on the intermittent rain, which never seemed to fall twice in the same place. In dry years, needlegrass and other short grasses from the west would intrude to mix with the central prairie's June grass and wheat grass at the top of sunbaked ravines; in wetter years, big and little bluestem would creep in from the east, taking hold along moisture-laden ravine bottoms.

This stunning panorama of wild flowers and native grasses, their species described meticulously by early botanists, would probably strike the modern eye as one vast, impressionistic canvas swept by variegated colors that changed with the prairie's varied moods. How delicate this meadow must have appeared in the blue light of an early morning, as bland morning breezes bent the tips of grasses, displaying the muted colors of the blades' undersides. How vivid at midday, the sky as clear as in a Chinese painting, when through the crystal light, according to artist Thomas Mails, you could see a spot of color twenty miles away. Or after a shower when the grass was "gemmed with the reflection of innumerable pendant raindrops," according to Major Stephen Harriman Long. And how serene under the purple light of a quiescent evening, when deer might be seen stepping through the shoals which separated sand bars on a meandering river like the Platte—a "stilly scene, like shadows of phantasmagoria, or Ossian's deer made of mist," wrote Henry Marie Brackenridge.

Not only did colors shift with the various moods of each prairie day but also with each season: white in winter, green in spring, yellow in summer, and red-orange in autumn, says Mails, but that simplifies the matter too much in a land where winter may look like a mirror as a sudden drenching of February rain turns the plains into a continuous sheet of water. Or brown, as snow melts to reveal the stubborn remnants of the prairie grass, some of which live for twenty years. In early spring, the slender shoots of bright new grass may well sprout up a sharp and tender green in the winter-yellowed sward. But spring, like autumn, is when the wild flowers reach their peak of intensity, glazing the meadow with purples, pinks, red, yellow, and white. In the overplus of August's brittle light, sere stubble may suddenly mirage into an islanded lake, while through the October haze of a reddened Indian summer sun, the prairie colors are seen as though wrapped in smoke.

The beauty of the Great Plains, however, is not for everyone. The space I took for granted as a child—what the Plains Indians called the Waho, the great circle, the circle of the horizon—was more than most newcomers, whose ideas of space had been formed in hilly, tree-studded country, could bear. "The first experience of the plains, like the first sail with a 'cap' full of wind, is apt to be sickening," wrote an early viewer, Colonel Dodge. More than one traveler, in diary or letter, told of standing still and lonely, overwhelmed by the silence and vastness of the place. "Magnificent, though melancholy," wrote Henry Brackenridge in 1811, while Thomas Farnham noted, in 1839, that his eyes ached from his attempts to embrace the view. Many a writer mentioned a general feeling of emptiness or dwelt on the nauseating loneliness. Even Coronado, who must have been reminded of portions of his native Spain when he entered this dry, treeless land, expressed surprise at its scope, saying, "I came upon some plains so vast that in my travels I did not reach their end, although I marched over them for more than three hundred leagues"—nearly one thousand miles, as we measure land.

The plains were most frequently compared, by early journal writers, to an ocean, an ocean where one swell melted imperceptibly into another. Some, like expedition leader Wilson P. Hunt, used this figure of speech literally. "The limits of the visible horizon," wrote Hunt, "are as exactly defined, and the view as extensive as at sea, the undulations on the surface of the earth here bearing no greater proportion in scale than the waves of an agitated ocean." Others were more poetic. Thomas Farnham called the plains "vast savannahs, resembling molten seas of emerald sparkling with flowers, arrested while stormy and heaving, and fixed in eternal repose." Adopting a more tragic perspective Abbé Emmanuel H. Domenech wrote, in 1860, that the grasslands of west Texas were "like an ocean of dark stunted herbs, in which not a single bush or bramble obstructed the view, where nothing marked a beginning or an end, and where all was mute and motionless." Some, like the young American scientist Brackenridge, found the ocean comparison inadequate. "If the vast expanse of the ocean is considered a sublime spectacle," he wrote of the central plains in 1811, "this is even more so; for the eye has still greater scope." Or, as Hamlin Garland would put it decades later, "my eyes / Fasten on more of earth and air / Than sea-shores furnish anywhere."

Those to whom the vast open space was not oppressive found it, as I did, exhilarating. "The nerves stiffen, the senses expand, and man begins to realize the magnificence of being," wrote Colonel Dodge, once he'd recovered from his seasickness. Brackenridge, who had stepped out onto the plains from a Missouri river boat, wrote: "Instead of being closed up in a moving prison, deprived of the use of our limbs, here we may wander at will. The mind naturally expands, or contracts, to suit the sphere in which it exists — in the immeasurable immensity of the scene, the intellectual faculties are endued with an energy, a vigor, a spring, not to be described."

Exhilaration, however, could tip quickly into terror, and often did, particularly when unprepared travelers first met the Great Plains' thunder bird, that spectacular mythological creature which flies through the air with its eyes closed, its gigantic wings flapping out "peals of thunder which seemed to shake the earth to its centre," thunder which visibly enraged the buffalo bulls who pawed the earth and bellowed as the big bird rumbled overhead. When the thunder bird blinked, the Indians said, great spears of sprangling lightning would flash out of its open eyes, leaving the pack animals to huddle abjectly together, heads drooping and limbs stilled, while humans trembled for their lives.

The Great Plains is justifiably famous for its violent thunderstorms, one of the more dramatic aspects of the region's changeable, highly versatile weather. The storms, typically of short duration, often produce downpours of three to six inches or more. The rain tends to be local, drenching the earth in one spot while the surrounding area remains dry. Most thunderstorms are caused when two of the region's three major air masses collide, when the cold dry air from Canada strikes either warm moisture-laden air masses from the Gulf of Mexico or air that has swept across the Rocky Mountains, Pacific air masses which range from warm to cold, moist to dry. Most rain falls from April to July, with storms reaching their maximum in May or June, the months when most early travelers began their long treks into, or across, the plains. As a result, early journals abound with tales of travelers drenched to their skins, spending cold, sleepless, wet nights, unable to find a bit of dry bedding or clothing among all their gear. Along the Platte River, famous for drawing thunderstorms, immigrants reported almost daily downpours in the spring of 1839.

Anyone who has seen a Great Plains thunderstorm in its full splendor knows that its most spectacular feature, the thing that distinguishes it most clearly from an equally violent downpour in the city, is the simple fact that the storm can be seen coming from miles away. Indeed, the plains area is so large that a storm, from a distance, can be perceived as a single entity, its black clouds churning, its lightning jets leaping, its gray sheet of rain falling in a slant torrent even while the sun shines directly overhead. Before the storm is seen, it can be heard, its thunder rumbling gently from a great distance. And before it can be heard, it can be felt: a shift in the temperature of the air, a certain silencing of the wind. "Excepting the sound of distant thunder, which was continual," wrote John Bradbury, English naturalist, of a prairie storm in May 1810, "an awful silence prevailed, and the cloud which had already spread over one half of the visible horizon was fast shutting out the little remains of daylight." As the cloud drew overhead, he noted that it was of "a pitchy blackness, and so dense as to resemble a solid body, out of which, at short intervals, the lightning poured in a continual stream for one or two seconds. Darkness came on with a rapidity I never before witnessed." He wrapped himself in a blanket and lay down on the open land. "The lightning," wrote Farnham of a storm in 1839, "was intensely vivid," as three black clouds, one in the southeast, one in the southwest, and one in the northeast, "rose with an awful rapidity towards the zenith." As he looked up, he saw the cloud "rent in fragments, by the most terrific explosion of electricity we had ever witnessed." Peal upon peal of thunder followed, as burning bolts leapt from cloud to cloud, enveloping the land in a "lurid glare."

Hail often accompanied these storms, although the size of hailstones seems curiously to diminish with the passing of time. One of Coronado's conquistadors, Pedro de Castañeda of Náxera, reported hail in the southern plains in 1541 "as large as bowls and even larger, and as thick as raindrops, that in places they covered the ground to the depth of two and three and even more spans." The huge stones destroyed their tents, dented their armor, bruised their horses, and broke all their pottery, a problem for the Spanish army since the local Indians, who ate only fruit and meat, had no use for crockery and could supply them with none. Many years later on the plains, a report circulated of an Indian who had been knocked down by a hailstone the size of a goose egg. As for myself, although I stood on our screened-in back porch through many a summer storm with my father, a farm boy who never tired of watching it rain, and although I saw countless white stones fall from the sky and bounce across our green lawn, I cannot say that I ever saw a prairie hailstone larger than a marble, although some were as big as taws. However, the folks over at Republican City swore they'd seen hail the size of Ping-Pong balls, and they had cars with bashed-in windshields to prove it.

These violent thunderstorms stunned the senses of those who lived through them, protecting themselves as best they could against the elements. Some, of course, were killed. After an unexpected storm in the spring of 1855, a caravan of immigrants found that its four guards had been knocked down and that another man lay insensible in his tent. "A Mr. Myers," wrote Lydia Waters, one of the caravan, "who had a nice carriage, got into it to keep the blinds down to prevent the lining from getting wet, and was found sitting in the front seat dead. The lightning had struck the top of his head and run down his neck and side, escaping out of the carriage without leaving a mark, except for a very small bit of broken moulding on the top." Early the next morning, the travelers gave Mr. Myers a typical prairie burial. "He was dressed in his best clothes, wrapped first in a sheet and then in a patchwork quilt. The men dug a deep grave and cut cottonwood and laid it over him to quite a thickness to prevent the coyotes from unearthing his body—which no doubt they did anyway. We had seen numbers of graves destroyed that way." Waters kept a lock of Mr. Myers' hair, burnt off by the lightning, to give to his wife, who'd been left with a three-month-old child. "No one else had thought of cutting it for her," she wrote.

Less dramatic than the storms, but equally unnerving—at least for some—was the prairie's *trompe l'oeil.* Optical illusions, caused by the combination of a rarified, transparent atmosphere with distances so great that "only the curvature of the earth's surface limits the view," often fooled the eye of the inexperienced observer. Objects, which could be seen with remarkable clarity from a great distance, became strangely distorted. Some were magnified, so that a raven might be mistaken for an Indian or an antelope for the much larger elk. Some were diminished, so that the leafy tops of a line of timber along a distant river seemed to "wave and mingle among the grass of the wild swelling meadows." Some, objects like tufts of grass or buffalo bones, were elevated, stretching up so high that they looked like humans. The first to mention this phenomenon was one of Coronado's chroniclers, who wrote that the land where buffalo roamed was "so level and bare that whenever one looked at them, one could see the sky between their legs, so that at a distance they looked like trimmed pine tree trunks with foliage joining at the top." Sometimes, under the intense glare of a pitiless August sun, the "earth and sky seemed to blend." In its most extreme form, this illusion became a mirage, such as the one described in 1849 by Alonzo Delano: "The glare of the sun upon the distant plain resembled the waves of a sea, and there were appearances of islands and groves."

This "abnormal land" was home to me. As I was growing up, I knew no other world but the prairie's vast Waho, its thunderstorms, its wind-blown fields. This natural habitat would render agoraphobia—the fear of open spaces—as incomprehensible to me as, many years later, my claustrophobia when ringed in by mountains or trees would confuse those who judged such restrictions "natural." Like a medieval woman, I was limited by the world I knew but knew not that my world was limited. What was "abnormal" to historian Walter Webb, whose book *The Great Plains* is justly considered a classic in this field, became gradually my norm. As a result, history — after a generation or two — became increasingly a dichotomy for me, as I suspect it must for anyone who has grown up in this magnificent region. With whom, at last, does one identify? For isn't history, in the final analysis, a question of deciding who one's ancestors are? Here the dichotomy began. Which did I value more, the bond of body or the bond of earth? The enigma became a question of heredity versus environment. I was, of course, an American. But who were my people? Were they the Europeans — the Scotch, Irish, English, and Germans with whom I claimed a common gene? Or were they the Pawnee, those stargazers who, for nearly five hundred years, had hunted across the acres that my great-grandparents farmed, whose paths, worn thin by trailing tipi poles, became our roads, whose villages, like ours, dotted the bluffs along the local rivers, the Republican, the Loup, and the Platte. To identify with the Europeans meant to lay claim to an intellectual ancestry that went back to classical Greece. But to identify with the Pawnee, to embrace land as the more lasting bond, was to lay ahold of another kind of history altogether, a history that preceded antiquity, a history some sixty-three million years old.

The Place of Your Dream

David Allan Evans

My mother tells me that when I was as young as two I used to sit alone in our backyard on the Wall Street bluff above the railroad tracks, and watch trains for hours. I don't remember it but it's easy to believe because we moved to another house on that same bluff when I was seven, and I often watched trains, day or night, either from the bluff or from the creosote-stained steps running down it. A couple of nights a week a passenger train went by with its windows lighted, many of them with a profile of a face. The train clicked cleanly through the dark, and if there was a moon the wheels and rails shone like beaten nickels. Sitting there alone, I often wondered what the travelers—separate profiles in separate windows—were thinking.

The image of trains seen from a bluff has stayed with me, a gift of memory. My father died when I was 23, and for at least a decade no day went by without him dominating my thoughts. Dead, he was as real to me as he had been when living. One night in my 30s I dreamed I was a boy again, watching a night train from that same bluff. Suddenly I saw his face repeated in each lighted window, the face of a man passing from one kind of darkness into another. High above him, I waved, and it seemed like I was waving at him for the last time.

My dream didn't erase my father from my thoughts, but perhaps subconsciously it showed me that I *could* live without him — as all sons must learn so that we can be fathers.

I am speaking of heights more than of fathers, though the two tend to go together.

Getting up on a high place and enjoying a panoramic view is more than a matter of vision. Not long ago, when the Foshay Tower in Minneapolis was that city's tallest building, I was on its observation floor 55 stories up, looking out on the city. I turned around and saw an obese, blind, American Indian woman helped out of an elevator by another woman, no doubt her friend. The two made their way to the safety fence at the edge of the roof. The blind woman paused, faced the steep wind like the rest of us, smiled, and said with perfect clarity:

"I've always wanted to see Minneapolis from this height."

Of course she couldn't have meant the word "see" literally. What she meant, I believe, had something to do with being up high over a landscape, of having a perspective and vantage point she couldn't have on the ground. In a word, having some *control.*

The desire to get up high and the satisfaction we feel when we can *take in* so much beneath us must be part of our biological inheritance. Almost all vertebrates, when challenged, inflate to make themselves look bigger and taller. When they lose a fight or argument they deflate and slink around with an averted eye, and appease the winners. When they win they strut, tall and confident.

We humans are no different, but we turn the biology into words that parallel our actions. We too get our hackles and our hair up. We put lifts in our shoes to appear more formidable, get pumped up for contests, vie for the tallest trophies and the position of top dog. We look up to our parents. We shoulder responsibilities as well as heroes, dead or living. We elevate our gods to the sky, and heavens to aspire up to. We bow and scrape to superiors and overlords, those over us. Or, as high brows, we raise our supercilious eyebrows and snub low brows, inferiors and underlings. We hold summit conferences, build capitols on hills for our chiefs (heads or higher-ups), who step up to power or step down out of it. We feel down or downcast or low when things go badly, high or up when they go well.

Shakespeare expressed the biology beautifully in his portrait of the great Caesar:

Why, man, he doth bestride the narrow world
Like a Colossus, and we petty men
Walk under his huge legs and peep about
To find ourselves dishonorable graves.

A recent American writer named William Gass expressed the same thing in 20th century fashion: "I want to rise so high that when I shit I won't miss anybody."

I have something to celebrate. I was born on a bluff in a town whose origin was dreamed from a bluff. The story of Sioux City, Iowa, is the story of bluffs and hills and rivers. In the late 1840s — if one can believe his journal — a man named Bruguier, a fur trader friendly with Sioux Indians in the area, married Chief War Eagle's daughter. One night, while living up the Missouri, Bruguier was restless and couldn't sleep. He dreamed that he saw a place where three rivers came together within a few miles, and bluffs and trees — all of which he had never seen before. When he awakened, his dream troubled him, and he told his father-in-law about it. War Eagle recognized the place as Bruguier described it, and said, "I will take you there."

The two came down the river, and at the mouth of the Sioux (after which Sioux City was eventually named) War Eagle said, "This is the place of your dream. Here can be a great camp."

The third river of the dream was the Floyd River, named after Seargent Floyd, the only man to die on the Lewis and Clark Expedition. Clark wrote in his original journal:

Serjeant Floyd is taken verry bad all at once with a Biliose Chorlick we attempt to reliev him without success as yet, he gets worse and we are much allarmed at his situation, all attention to him . . . Died with a great deel of composure, before his death he said to me 'I am going away I want you to write me a letter' — We buried him on the top of the bluff ½ mile below a small river to which he gave his name, he was buried with the Honors of War much lamented, a seeder post with the Name Sergt. C. Floyd died here 20th of August 1804 was fixed at the head of his grave — This man at all times gave us proofs of his firmness and Determined resolution to doe service to his countrey and honor to himself after paying all the honor to our Deceased brother we camped in the mouth of floyd's river about 30 yards wide, a butifull evening.

In 1832 the painter George Catlin came up the river in the steamboat *Yellowstone,* paused at "Floyd's Grave" long enough to paint it (as did Karl Bodmer a year later), and wrote of the view:

I several times ascended it and sat and contemplated the solitude and stillness of this tenanted mound; and beheld from its top the windings infinite of the Missouri . . . its thousand hills and domes of green vanishing into blue in the distance . . .

In 1900, a 100-foot obelisk with a sharp, pyramidal point was erected on that same bluff. It is called Floyd's Monument.

As a boy, some friends and I made swords out of laths and climbed that bluff and others along the Missouri, pretending to be in the "Lewis and Clark Exploration." Always our goal was to get up high enough to cup a hand over our eyes and look down at the glittering river. I'm not sure if it ever occurred to us that Lewis and Clark had done their traveling in *boats* — we imagined them cutting trails through trees and over hills, doing Indians in, exploring always on foot.

My hometown — a place of hills and rivers in the grassy center of the prairie — had many heights for a growing boy to see from. (I was lucky: my parents gave me almost total freedom to run and play. Mine was such a physical boyhood that I can barely remember the inside of the three houses I lived in before my high school years.)

In my early teens I sometimes stopped at the public library on Saturday mornings on the way to the YMCA, not for books but to hear records of poetry readings. That was my first awakening to poetry (though not to other literature), and it was no accident that the very first poem that I couldn't help memorizing was "Dover Beach" by Matthew Arnold — a poem whose words are spoken from a bluff above the sea. I didn't understand every word but I caught the music from those opening lines:

The sea is calm tonight.
The tide is full, the moon lies fair
Upon the straits; on the French coast the light
Gleams and is gone; the cliffs of England stand,
Glimmering and vast, out in the tranquil bay.
Come to the window, sweet is the night-air!

These lines and images made sense to me, I know now, because I too had looked down from bluffs — had seen how moonlight strikes water or land, how "the light gleams and is gone"; had heard the roar of, if not the sea, the Missouri and the trains. I could never get enough of the poem. I can still recite it. When I began to write poems a decade or so later I used my middle name Allan because the name of the reader of "Dover Beach" was David Allen.

Neither was it an accident that the first "recent" poem by an American that got to me (not counting Carl Sandburg) was "In the Tree House at Night" by James Dickey, which begins:

And now the green household is dark,
The half-moon completely is shining
On the earth-lighted tops of the trees.

I too had had a tree house as a boy; I too had climbed the "sprained, comic rungs of the ladder," where I came out "at last over lakes / Of leaves, of fields disencumbered of earth."

On the Wall Street bluff, between our brick house and the house at the top of the hill (owned by a family named Hillsinger), was a weedy vacant lot with a tall tree in it. It was the tree that Ronnie Tolar fell out of one night and broke his left arm in the same place for the third time. My cross-eyed friend, Dale Jimeson, had been watching Ronnie from the ground with a flashlight. When I asked him what he did when Ronnie fell, he said: "I followed him down with my flashlight."

That was the same tree I used to climb just to get away. I climbed up to near the giddy top branches, clothespinned my legs in a favorite crotch so I was half-standing, half-sitting, and swayed and watched and thought. And sometimes sang. Once I swayed and boomed out the words of "On Top of Old Smokey" over and over.

And then one summer I had a lofty experience on a pile of sand.

I was playing hide-and-seek with two friends at a gravel company below the railroad bluff. It was my turn to hide, so I climbed to the top of a pyramid of sand, and was watching my friends some 30 feet below, who were looking for me. They walked by between some railroad tracks, not thinking to look up (they could have easily seen me if they had).

I closed my eyes and felt my heart, which was still racing from the climb, but more than that, going wild with a secret excitement. Just then, strangely, I saw myself as a man 20 or 30 years away. High up on that sun-baked sand, I knew that some day, in whatever distant place I was living, I would remember—exactly—*that* secret moment, *that* wild heartbeat.

For the last 15 years I've lived in a flat town in a flat part of South Dakota. I do have my second-story bedroom window to look out of, and I enjoy the way moonlight plays on the top of my apple tree in the backyard, and the way the streetlight beyond the alley blinks through the elms.

But I miss the hills and rivers, especially the glittering Missouri in the spring. Whenever I travel, my habit is to get up high and look down. Or if I'm driving on Interstate 29 to Sioux City, 150 miles away, there is one long hill near Vermillion that I need to get over so that the wide expanse of the Missouri Valley with its dark, shaggy bluffs can open up for me. The moment I get to the peak of that hill and look down is the moment I know I am home.

Saturday-Night Radio

Diane Glancy

What is it to be Indian, or part Indian, removed by generations & space from that heritage? The language dead. The culture severed. It should have little effect. But my sense of place in the Midwest is defined by that land that was — the vast prairies & our migration over them. It is also defined by a sense of language which is lost.

Sometimes there's an old voice in my head. Not a voice that enters the ear, except when he chants. But even then it's my voice that his rides upon. No, his voice is one I feel in Spirit. Have not radio waves carried into space & returned to earth years later? How much more a human Spirit? Especially one who dies from grief. Not a ghost, no, but a living voice that says his people are sick and without food. The snow is deep & cold hangs on. Maybe the Great Spirit sees them. Maybe when the moon dies, He will take them to the Hunting Grounds from the long trail they march.

I tell the old Grandfather it is over. Why is he grieving? Did not some of us survive the trail to the new territory? Did not the Cherokee translate hymns & the Bible with Sequoya's syllabary? Are not our stories & legends & myths replaced by faith in the living God of this nation?

I follow him into his grief. It's a large brown box I enter—as if an old radio—the kind that once stood in the corner of the living room like a buffalo. I hear the wireless transmissions of electric impulses converted into sound. Is it not Christ we see with our faith? Is it not Him who walks over the moving sludge of the world? Sometimes the arms reaching up to Him are snakes. But He speaks peace to them. Quaddo. Words are the body. The Spirit made visible. Not just a code. Oh, no. The word is not a mirror of the object, is not the object, but a making of the object into the shape of the tribe—Maybe even the Spirit Himself. That's what speaks & carries into the captivity of knowledge.

When we talk we jump-start the electromagnetic field of language. Moving waves of speech. How else do we keep ourselves from extinction? How else do we make room for ourselves as we're crowded out? Nothing left as we knew it after the transmutation of our world.

But I am without his words when I talk. You know the language of my ancestors didn't survive. A radio full of static. Once we had the reception of signals. I still hang on to what floats over the land like a stray herd—the sound waves of the ancestors that sewed the tribe together—but there was raveling of that gravity—a scissoring out of language like a gutted carp, the fish eggs of vapor drops from the journey. It's like being a space man floating in air—Suddenly the hose is severed—You whizz backward through space. That's what it's like to have no language. You are without the means to convey what you think.

Often I have the feeling my speech moves along one trail, while my thoughts follow another.

I remember listening to Saturday-night radio when I was a girl, my face pushed to the speakers. Inside I could see the faint lights of the tubes like red campfires of a migrating tribe. They are still locked in that darkness & part of me is in there with them. I am always aware of the Indian tribes that crossed our land—following herds or migrating to summer camp.

When I was growing up my father worked for the stockyards in Kansas City. Later he was transferred to other cities in the Midwest. He left his heritage to follow this world & I remember the vacuum it made in him. Our heritage doesn't die— It leaves an open gash in need of stitches. Riding in the back seat of our '49 Ford, I watched his black hair—his hands on the wheel. I remember feeling the universe there with us—& at the same time, I remember the hole in our heads where our heritage had once been. The large white moon shined over us like an eye in the afternoon sky & we were left with pieces of stars we couldn't yet see.

If you don't have words, you don't have your world. How do you shoot an antelope or jack rabbit without the huntingsign of the language that captures the animal & says, animal you are mine? How do you tie together your truth & the experience which goes against it? How do you make tolerable a world which is not?

Once when the back of the radio was open for repair, I lost that sense of an Indian camp. Then I saw the tubes as they were—a city of the plains as it would look to the ancestors if they could have seen the lighted buildings, the surreal grain silos & storage towers, the domes & terminals that would stand up on the prairie.

But it's Christ, remember Christ we saw under the moaning & wailing—under the agonies we know. I thump the old voice in my head. I say hey, you, old Grandfather— Sing! Sing your song.

What's left otherwise but hollow sounds? We speak our world into being with what we have. We make up the words which hold what happens. We learn to speak our meanings with these new words of English. Maybe the old ones wait for us somewhere. Otherwise we're transmitters in space sending signals no one receives.

Now I tell the old Grandfather I have to hang the washing on the line—I have to live in this world. I use the stars as clothespins— All

night my dreams ripple on the line like sheets until I take them in at
morning— But the moon—leave it there to shrivel—thinking how it
is barren because it is so white.

Remember the Flowers

Paul Gruchow

My father was a farmer with no use for fashions. He married and went into business for himself in the spring of 1946, raising laying hens, vegetables and berries on a seven-and-a-half-acre truck farm. Small-scale horticulture was his real interest. For the rest of his life he devoted as much time and care to his gardens and orchards and bee hives as to his row crops. The eggs he sold to the local candling plant, the berries and vegetables to the local groceries. It was hard labor, mostly done with his hands and a two-wheeled garden tractor, and it afforded a very meager living. By 1947 he had infant twins as well as a wife to support, and sometimes it took all the eggs in the hen house just to buy milk for the babies. In 1950, he rented 160 acres of land on shares. The move required investing in a collection of ancient farm machinery, but it also brought a barn and an above-ground house with three rooms and electricity (the family had been living in an unfinished basement). A decade later, my mother inherited 80 acres, giving our family the capital to finance the purchase of an additional 120 acres of land, about 40 acres of it in pasture and meadow, so my father became in the last years of his life (he died in 1970) a land-holding farmer, although still on a quite small scale.

The 1950s and 1960s were, of course, a time of great expansion in American agriculture, an expansion fueled by new markets in war-ravaged Europe, by rising demand at home as the post-war baby boom took effect, and by the introduction in 1947 of 2,4-D, the first apparently safe and effective herbicide. 2,4-D was developed but never used as a chemical weapon during the war; it was to become, instead, a powerful tool in the industrialization of farming, a cheap alternative to the labor of cultivation. It had predictable consequences, although they were not predicted. One was the sudden obsolescence of many farmers; more than a million of them left the land in the 1950s and crowded into cities, one of the great migrations of history. Another was overproduction; by the late 1950s, the Soil Bank and the Ever-Normal granary had become part of the language of agriculture, the measuring wheels of the inspectors from the Agricultural Stabilization and Conservation Service one of its tools, and ranks of Butler bins brimming with unmarketable grain one of its architectural monuments. We had created a fantastic new food machine, like Strega Nona's pasta pot, but nobody knew how to turn it off.

This was the era in American agriculture when farming became not a vocation but a business, not a domestic art but a branch of industrial science, when the farm became not a legacy, to be handed down from generation to generation, but a capital asset, from which one could reasonably expect an adequate return on investment, as measured in dollars and percents. What was the worth of a livelihood if it could not generate wealth?

It was also the era in which the American farm village disappeared. I lived in such a village in the 1950s. It had a school and church, to which I walked. It had a social life, organized around the Christmas Pageant, the end-of-school picnic, and the summer ice cream social. We lived within sight and sound of neighbors who had children with whom we played.

One Sunday after dinner, as we called the noon meal, we children were summoned to a rare family conference. "We have something to tell you," my mother said, looking strangely radiant, "but it is a secret, and you are not to tell anyone. Do you understand?" Yes, my sister and I said, we understand, we will tell no one. "Remember, this is a secret," she said. Yes, yes, we said. "Well," she said, "your father and I want you to know that we are going to have a baby. When winter comes, you will have a new brother or sister. But this is a secret just between us for now. Okay?" Okay, we said, dancing with glee. We could hardly wait for Mother and Father to take their Sunday nap. (We had not yet discovered the connection between Sunday naps and new babies.) The instant they had settled down, we crept out the door, rushed to the next farm and summoned the children.

"We have a secret," we said.

"Tell us! Tell us!"

What could we do, fiendishly pressed as we were? We told. "But don't tell anybody else," we said, absolving ourselves of responsibility.

By nightfall it was common knowledge in the neighborhood: "The Gruchows are expecting. Next winter."

In the 1960s, the news probably would have remained a secret. We didn't live any longer in a neighborhood, in any practical sense. There was nobody we might have told: there were no other children within walking distance of our farm. There was no school; we rode the bus to town. The church was accessible only by car. Neighborhood social events had gone the way of the buggy. The gossip was of acquisitions, not of pregnancies. By the 1960s, we lived, for the most part, alone. It was a triumph for productivity, but not for humanity.

My father disregarded the new agriculture. He did not want land he could not care for. He refused to use the new chemicals. He was certain they were dangerous in ways that we would come eventually to understand. In any case, they took money, and all a hoe cost was some labor, of which he already had an adequate supply. At a time when a farmer's manhood was expressed in the size of his machines, he bought the smallest Fordson tractor available, a machine so insignificant that even I, a child, was embarrassed to drive it. Monoculture was the thing; he diversified. He expanded the sheep herd, started a business in goat's milk for families with infants allergic to cow's milk, planted potatoes and cucumbers, began a big apple orchard, trapped muskrats and mink in the winter. When the neighbors were razing the groves of empty farmsteads to make more land, he planted pines. When they tilled their meadows and plowed them, he dug a new pond in his for wild ducks.

It was not that he was indifferent to success. He studied the bulletins from the Agricultural Extension Service as assiduously as anybody. All winter, he pored over the reports of the crop variety trials, making notes of new hybrids to try. He kept his own careful performance records in the pocket notebooks handed out by the seed companies. He had a soil testing kit and used it religiously. He meant to be the best farmer possible. It was just that he didn't see the connection between farming well and getting rich.

I had grown to adolescence and seen something of the world. He made me furious. One day I shouted at him, "You are like the soldier in the army who insists that everyone else is out of step!" I thought myself very clever.

He stared back at me, white with contempt. "Have you ever considered," he said, "the possibility that the soldier may be right?"

The reverse side of this, I suppose, is that my father was impractical. I dimly remember the search for a suitable piece of land when it became possible for him to buy one. He wanted two farms much more than the one he actually bought. One had a single building on a treeless hillside, a European-style farmhouse, very long, in which everything was attached: house, barn and henhouse all fell under a single roof, so that one could open a door and walk directly from the upstairs bedrooms into the haymow and from there down through a trapdoor into the animal quarters. We children were enthralled. There was an argument in the car on the way home. "Think how efficient it would be," Father said. "Absolutely not!" Mother said. "I will not live in a pig-sty! You buy it, and you can go live there without me." It was clear that she meant it. The other was a farm in the river-bottom. The house on it was literally falling down. It was worse, unlikely as this was, than the house we were then living in. (I, actually, did not live in it myself, preferring a chicken coop which I shared one agonizing night with a skunk that had come in through a hole in the floor.) On the way home from our inspection visit, Father sounded childishly excited, the only time I ever saw him in such a state. Mother said nothing, but halfway home she began to cry.

The first farm attracted my father because it included an enormous slough, the second because it was next to a river and consisted mainly of woodlands and rocky pastures. We were surrounded by farmers who thought that the most beautiful thing in the world was a flat field turned so thoroughly in the fall that nothing not perfectly black showed in it; who labored and conspired to turn every square inch of earth at their disposal to productive use; who tore out fences, cut down stray trees, drained marshes, plowed up farmyards and road ditches, forsook waterways in a desperate effort to wring the last dime out of a property; who saw any untilled acre as an offense against industriousness. But my father cherished the acres he couldn't farm as much as the ones he planted. He would no more have thought of buying a farm without some waste space in it than of moving to New York City and becoming a belly dancer.

We pulled into the yard at home after our trip to the farm along the river. He turned to Mother, who was staring sullenly out the window, and said, "I suppose you're right, honey. I suppose it really isn't practical." But you could tell that he said it out of resignation, not out of conviction.

Even now, when the fruits of farming as an industrial enterprise lay like so many rotting apples on the land, there are people who say that there is nothing wrong with agriculture that a better price for corn couldn't fix. They are right. If our success is to be measured in profit margins, let us guarantee the price of corn at $10 a bushel, or $100 a bushel—it hardly matters what the figure is—and get on with our lives. The rich will grow very much richer, and the poor will still fail. Land prices will soar, and so will land abuse, and so will the prices suppliers charge. Rural population will continue to dwindle. The communities that survive will continue to struggle to maintain decently vigorous local institutions. Every issue of short-term justice and long-term sanity will remain. But those few who survive will become rich and powerful beyond their wildest dreams.

We in rural America have a long list of enemies. The government did it to us. The bankers did it to us. The grain cartels did it to us. The professors of agriculture did it to us. But, the truth is, we did it to ourselves. We have had no agricultural policy that somebody in agriculture didn't press, and no lousy piece of advice ever came to ill, except as somebody agreed to take it. The question every farmer has to answer, Wendell Berry once said, is this: "Would you rather have your neighbor's land or your neighbor?" We have made the choice over and over again, and if we now have very few neighbors, we deserve to allocate some portion of the blame to ourselves.

There always was another choice. My father, for one, made it. It was his mark of excellence, the hilltop he made out of his life.

The heart of the matter is the question of economy. There are, essentially, only two ways to balance a checkbook. One is to make more, and the other is to make do with less. Of course there are—it goes without saying—limits to the second strategy. Even Thoreau kept three chairs in his house at Walden Pond. "None is so poor that he need sit on a pumpkin," he explained, although I once lived in a house where we sat on empty sauerkraut kegs and am not aware that it did me, or anyone else, any harm.

My father lived in an industrial economy which he did not entirely spurn. He acquired property, occasionally purchased goods and services, participated in government farm programs and received public support for his participation without, so far as I am aware, any tinge of regret. He believed in government and in its duty, not to mention its privilege, to manage our affairs, including his own, for the greatest general good.

We had a serious falling out over this issue during the Vietnam War. I refused to fight, believing the war immoral; my father held passionately that I was wrong, that I might seek in every legal way to change the government's policy, but, so long as it was the policy, he said, I had a moral and a Christian obligation to do what it asked. During this time I gave a speech arguing otherwise. My father listened to it on the radio, and when I went to the farm afterwards to greet him, he met me at the front door and told me sadly that I was not welcome, that traitors were never welcome at his house. He was no isolationist, no believer in a world where it is every man for himself.

He did, nevertheless, practice a personal economy that was at considerable odds with the public economy. It was, for one thing, domestic. By this I mean that he, as a matter of principle, tried to do as much for himself as possible. In part, this meant being handy. He was not much of a consumer, but he spent a good deal of time at the local implement dealerships, studying the latest innovations and borrowing whatever ideas he found useful. He made an occasional visit to the blacksmith's shop for a bit of ironwork he wasn't equipped to handle, but otherwise he was self-sufficient. He was his own mechanic, his own carpenter, his own electrician, his own soil scientist, his own feed formulator, his own miller, his own veterinarian. Perhaps he died so young because he insisted, until it was too late, on being his own doctor. When he wanted something, he made it. If he couldn't make it, he did without, or invented an alternative.

To some extent, my father's self-sufficiency was a matter of necessity, since he never had much money. But he seldom had much money mainly because he put so little value on it. I have little doubt that, had it been important to him, he could have made as much money as the next man. Self-sufficiency was also, for him, a matter of principle.

We raised our own food. It saved money, and he enjoyed it. But more than that, it seemed to him so logical, so obvious a thing to do that the rarity of it mystified him. That's what farmers do, he said: they raise food. If I am a farmer, he asked, and cannot even feed myself, what sort of farmer am I? Does a tailor hire somebody to make his own clothes? Does a cobbler send his shoes out to be fixed? So he raised livestock for meat and milk, kept bees for honey, chickens for eggs, maintained an orchard for fruit, tended vegetable and berry gardens, raised wheat and ground it himself into flour. He didn't have the imagination to do less.

I tried out on him once an idea I had picked up in a vocational agriculture class. "Farming," I said to him, "is, after all, a business like any other. The purpose of farming is to make a living." He flew into a rage. "Listen here, young man," he said, "the purpose of farming is to produce food for hungry people. It is a calling, not a living, and don't you ever forget it!"

In his economy the guiding principle was the avoidance of waste. He understood the word to mean the unnecessary expenditure of life or the resources of life. Idling acres to curb excess production, therefore, made sense to him, but dumping milk didn't. Idle land was not wasted, but merely lying fallow. It benefited the land and, in any case, it was of some use to the rest of God's creation. But to spend resources to produce food and then to throw it out merely because you couldn't make a profit on it, that to him was waste, a kind of blasphemy. In the same way, it seemed to him not merely practical but morally good to heat our house with wood. It was, after all, available to us for the labor of harvesting it. Why should we burn coal, exhaustible and needing to be dug by somebody else, when we were perfectly capable of supplying our own replenishable heat at no expense to anyone? Shouldn't the coal be reserved for those who had no better alternative? My father's goal, in economic matters, as in the rest of life, was to be as little trouble to anybody else as possible.

I think he also meant to be as little trouble to himself as possible. He simplified his economic life so that the rest of his life might also be free and simple. In this he was Thoreauvian, although I doubt that he ever read Thoreau, and his habits, I think, gave his neighbors the same sort of trouble that Thoreau's gave his neighbors.

My father worked diligently at farming, but he refused to work at it slavishly. He rose at sunrise, but never earlier, and, at least in the summertime, frequently went to bed shortly after sundown. He believed in long, leisurely meals, napped religiously after lunch and kept the Sabbath faithfully. Sometimes our neighbors, particularly during the planting and harvesting seasons, rose long before daylight and worked late into the night, the headlights of their machines piercing the midnight blackness. But when it got dark, the work on our farm stopped, no matter what the urgency of time or weather. I myself, as a teenager, rose at 4:30 in the morning in the summertime to work one job, took a break for lunch, and then frequently worked a second job until 10 or 10:30 in the evening. My father made no effort to stop me, but he made it perfectly clear that he regarded such effort as utter madness, as I myself now do.

He believed that a life of constant toil was badly led, a life God never intended for anyone. His farming was important to him, a noble and sacred calling. But other things were also important. He attended the flowering of wild plants, the singing of birds, the swarming of bees, the footprints of foxes. He cultivated his gardens. He walked in the woods. He prayed and meditated. In the winter, he helped his children to make igloos and snow tunnels. In the summer, he held them in his arms under the stars and sang cowboy songs to them in his sweet tenor voice.

For several years, we raised a couple of acres of cucumbers, an important cash crop. The project involved the entire family, and it might have been an unbearable drudgery. After the ground was plowed in the spring, everything was done by hand. The seeds were hand planted in hand-made hills, the patch was weeded with hoes, and during the harvest season we all spent three mornings a week, beginning before the dew had dried, picking the fruits, one by one, filling a peck basket, dumping it into the truck parked at the end of the field, filling another peck, and another, and another, until we were green and sticky to our elbows with the nauseating juice of cucumber vines and the sun was high in the sky and suffocatingly hot. It was backbreaking work, done on hands and knees, and excruciatingly boring, all the more because it had to be done meticulously. The cucumbers were graded by size, and the bigger they got, the less we were paid for them.

When we had gleaned the field, the cucumbers had to be hauled to the buying station in Willmar, 40 miles away. We all piled into the truck, grateful for the chance simply to sit, and went together to Willmar, and after we had sold the day's harvest, we went to the lake there and swam away the late afternoon and had a picnic in the shade and drove home at dusk, singing songs or falling happily asleep on our parents' shoulders. In my father's economy, those half days of lounging at the lake were as vital as the mornings spent in the cucumber patch, and without the one he would not have had the other.

Sometimes this attitude resulted in a casualness toward life that could seem callous, although I think it wasn't. One fall morning after we children had gone to school, the creosote in the chimney of our house caught fire and started a blaze in the attic. Father was miles away, on his parents' farm, plowing. Mother was home alone. She ran to the neighbor's, borrowed the telephone, called the fire department and then called Grandmother and asked her to fetch Father from the fields. The fire truck came, Grandmother came, several neighbors came, but not my father.

He worked, as usual, until noon and then returned for lunch, uncertain, of course, whether there was any lunch to be had. My sister and I had also walked home from school for lunch and were horrified when we rounded the grove and saw the commotion of neighbors and firemen in the yard and realized what had happened. Father arrived after us. When Mother saw him, she turned on him and yelled at him, the only time, I think, that she defied him in public. "Where have you been!" she screamed.

"I have been plowing the eighty," he said calmly.

"While our house was burning!" she shouted.

"I know that," he said, "but there was nothing I could do to stop it, was there? And I had work to do."

She was stunned into flaming silence.

He never did understand why she was so angry. As far as he was concerned, you worried about what you could change, and you accepted everything else. If a house burned, it was, after all, only a house.

Thoreau went to Walden Pond, he said, to conduct an experiment. "I went to the woods because I wanted to live deliberately, to front out only the essential facts of life, and to see if I could not learn what it had to teach, and not, when I came to die, discover that I had not lived." He was quite explicit about the nature of his experiment. It was not, he said, a model for the ideal life, not an experiment he meant anybody else to copy. "I would not have any one adopt *my* mode of living on any account; for, beside that before he has fairly learned it I may have found out another for myself, I desire that there may be as many different persons in the world as possible; but I would have each one be very careful to find out and pursue *his own* way, and not his father's or his mother's or his neighbor's instead." And what his experiment taught him did not, in fact, have anything to do with living "cheaply or meanly." The lesson was in values, not in prices.

> I learned this, at least, by my experiment: that if one advances confidently in the direction of his dreams, and endeavors to live the life which he has imagined, he will meet with a success unexpected in common hours. He will put some things behind, will pass an invisible boundary; new, universal, and more liberal laws will begin to establish themselves around and within him; or the old laws be expanded, and interpreted in his favor in a more liberal sense, and he will live with the license of a higher order of beings. In proportion as he simplifies his life, the laws of the universe will appear less complex, and solitude will not be solitude, nor poverty poverty, nor weakness weakness. . . .
> . . . Superfluous wealth can buy superfluities only. Money is not required to buy one necessary of the soul.

Thoreau's experiment has raised a nervous defensiveness in a long line of critics, beginning with Thoreau's own best friend, Emerson, who admired him and helped to establish his reputation, but also dismissed him at his funeral, in a memorable phrase, as "the captain of a huckleberry party."

We have a public conception of moral responsibility. Despite the long thread of individualism running through our culture, we tend to believe that whatever is good is good in the collective sense. We may admire Thoreau and his descendents, Ghandi and Martin Luther King, Jr., for the high-mindedness of their sentiments, but we are at the same time suspicious of a philosophy that seems so personal, so intensely directed at the individual life. To seek by public means to change the evil in our lives, that we can honor and respect. But simply to refuse, as one human being, acting alone, to participate in evil, that seems to us somehow dangerous, selfish, too piddling to make much practical difference. How could Thoreau, we want to know, busy himself, in good conscience, as the "self-appointed inspector of snowstorms" when the much greater turbulence of slavery was raging all around? It is true that he championed John Brown, spoke passionately in Concord and elsewhere in favor of abolition, and perhaps assisted a traveler or two on the underground railway to freedom in Canada, but it is also true that Thoreau was no reformer. His heart wasn't in it. He would sooner have gone walking in the woods. How dare such a man pretend to moral superiority?

There are two classes of moralists: those who seek to improve the quality of other people's lives, and those who are content to improve their own lives. There are professors of morality, and there are practitioners of it; and the categories tend to be exclusive. Nothing is so terrifying as a demonstration of principle. Emerson preached Nature; Thoreau embraced nature; it is Thoreau, of course, who ultimately strikes us as dangerous. It is one thing to decry the rat race, to utter ringing declarations against it, to write clever stories exposing its follies. That is the good and honorable work of moralists. It is quite another thing to quit the rat race, to drop out, to refuse to run any further. That is the work of the individualist. It is offensive because it is impolite; it makes the rebuke personal; the individualist calls not *their* behavior into question, but mine. The moralist believes in the necessity of enemies, the individualist in their irrelevance.

It was so with my father. He went to the same church as his neighbors, confessed the same creed, partook of the same absolution. He heard the same preaching: "Take no thought for the morrow," and "Lay not up treasures on earth, where moth and rust doth corrupt," and "It is harder for a rich man to enter into heaven than for a camel to pass through the eye of a needle." But he made people nervous because beyond professing these beliefs, he practiced them. When he heard that his house was burning, he went on with the plowing. People said of him what is always said of such people: How selfish, how impractical, what a shame for his family! Think what he might have done if he had ever tried to make something of himself!

One spring night my father went to bed, fell asleep and never awoke. He died as quietly, as uncomplainingly, as he lived. It was an awkward moment for a farmer to die, too late in the season to secure someone else to run the land. He had thought of that. In the papers he left behind were a set of instructions for Mother: diagrams of the farm, notes on what to plant where and when, instructions on the management and harvest of the crops, on the proper care of the machinery, on the arcane details of the year's farm program, everything Mother needed to know in order to operate the farm herself that summer, as she did, triumphantly.

Among the instructions he left behind was a plan for the flower beds in the yard, complete with planting charts, species names, and notes about when each variety would bloom and what color it would be Even in death the flowers mattered to him. They were a reminder, which I have sometimes betrayed, but never forgotten, of all that is genuinely important in life.

Town and Country

Those who really become part of the Midwest (either by birth or by immigration) are those people who have some sense of the land as central to the region. By "land" I mean not only the actual earth, water, and air, but the attitudes that have come to characterize the residents: a certain independence from herd thinking; a willingness—even an eagerness—to face hardships that include isolation and physical labor; and pride in our differences from metropolitan sophisticates. Each of these characteristics can be viewed as noble, or as provincial, but most attributes that one culture sees as ennobling can be sneered at by visiting experts. . . .

—Linda Hasselstrom

I am writing this at my desk on the sixth floor of an insurance company in Lincoln, Nebraska. From my window I can see the edge of town, and the prairie, exactly the color of buffalo hide, stretching away beyond the last frail saplings in the suburbs.

I have been living in towns like Lincoln all my life. Each is a loose pile of stones on the grass, that place in the field that the farmer avoids with his plowblade. I sit here on this rock-pile with the assurance that I know nearly everything that may be going on out there in the grass, from the field-mouse warily building its nest in the lumps of torn sod at the base of a power pole, to the lineman drinking a can of beer high up in the sizzle of wires.

I have lived and written in this place long enough to have mastered its language. I know the names of the plants, the animals, the insects. I know what to expect of the weather, I know what to expect of the people about me. I have learned how to address them, how to write a poem that is straight-forward and economical as a statement directed to them is expected to be. And I believe that the directness that this place and these people have taught me is good currency anywhere.

—Ted Kooser, from "Staying in My Place"

Bandstand

Jim Barnes

When I was just a boy, I crawled down
from my Red Flyer and under the old
bandstand, which was warping even then round

the edges of the floor. You could not know
what wind and wonder had moved to that dark.
I tell you there were mysteries that now

seem stranger still than all I knew to stalk
my nights. The bandstand was hideout for Huck
and Tom, pure heaven for the local pack

of budding musicians, den for dogs. No luck
is what we had: killer bees established hives,
they said. Now look at this stone block that took

an hour to pour, a bandstand with no give
underfoot, and underneath — no love. They
sold the old one to Hutterites. I believe

it's now a floor to a communal barn, hay
hiding lost bad notes and my honeyed sin
written on dark joists. So the sidemen play

and the leader sways on crumbling concrete in
all the festival we have. I say here
it's not the same: we need the darkling wind

beneath to lift the music from the fear
of remaining horns. From this stone kiosk
we cannot know the music of our sphere,

cannot know the beauty of arabesques
graved in wood, nor the tap of heels beneath
trombone and flute, nor the darker humming risk.

Death of a Hen

Marisha Chamberlain

My little brother and sister
chased a hen to death.
First, they were screaming with laughter.
Then they knelt down.
Mother looked once at their stricken faces,
picked up the twitching body,
carried her to the milkhouse
and cut her open.

Inside the red tunnel,
eggs were coming like planets.
The first one was big and almost hard,
the second and third eggs, smaller, smaller,
'til the last, the seventh,
which was small as a thumbnail,
soft as a thumb pad,
and barely white.
Little pearl of feathered life,
little pearl.

Rural Fantasia

Philip Dacey

The schoolbus drivers enter their buses
at seven o'clock in the morning.
They enter their buses to pick up
the children, who have waited all night,
alone, at the ends of driveways,
their little lunches tight in their hands.
Someone would be touched to see them,
their still, patient bodies marking
the prairie landscape under moonlight,
under morning sun, but no one sees them.
Not the parents, who dream in their neat
farmhouses that the children are their own,
like shocks of wheat, nor the bus drivers,
who, in the far town, can only imagine
the children and think of them as pilots
on a dawn airstrip, the crucial mission
assigned to their squadron, would think of
islands, the future's beautiful atolls.
Meanwhile the children wait. What else is there
to do at the roadside, dressed in good clothes,
as the stars turn away, ashamed again?
At eight o'clock, the children will enter
the buses, will know the jounce, the sway,
will be carried down the road, waving
at cars behind them. At eight o'clock,
the heart of one driver will break to think
of the children, the parents, the stars, and
himself, will flood with tears like a fuel
the lines and chambers of the bus and propel
it, dream-quick, to a place before one child.
The door will breathe open and a small foot

will lift toward the first step, at eight.
Which will never come. It is seven o'clock.
It is always seven o'clock in the morning.
The drivers enter their buses, then enter
again, perfect at beginning, as if
beginning were best, and bore repeating.
The stars knew all along the buses would
never pick up the children. The stars knew
how it almost happened, or happens, or will,
that the distance between drivers and children
is only this much, a key will enter it,
nothing else, the thinnest key to ignite
fire, thin enough to see through.
They are that close, prairie and town
collapse to an eye, an eye seeing
itself or another, all the air
between as yellow with sun as a bus.

In Front of a Small Town Radio Station

Randall Freisinger

In front of the radio station
the girls' basketball team
stands in a squall of snow
waiting for the school bus.
Last night they won
a tournament up the road.
They have told the whole town
their story. Now they
bounce and dance in the cold.
One, her green team jacket
unable to conceal her belly's
swell, stares at traffic
with eyes like voided checks.
She knows the other story:
how back at the gym the boys
brash and hard as maple boles
are shooting baskets.
She knows their loose half circle,
how the balls arc and fall
through the netted hole.
How boys dream their tomorrows
green and smooth as brook water.
How they've trained to use
the world to fierce advantage
like a blind pick and roll.
How each shot as it leaves
their hands feels just right,
like a perfect movie's
only conceivable beginning.

A Drive in the Country

Patricia Hampl

All week with the pink neon slash
of the Flamingo Motel over my door,
all week the nonexistent flamingo
of Long Prairie, Minnesota,
the only bird, only hot light.
Then someone offers dinner, a drive
in the country. And we arrive at
the laid table of these broken fields,
the chased gold of stubble, dusk
stroked through the charcoal light,
a wine never fully finished.
I graze like any animal,
I am better now, sighing
at the gauzy pink of the sky
though the sun's last shout is clear.
In a moment we will be lost
in the hungry black line
out there, the solemn horizon
that, not grasping, grasps us.

Airing Out

Twyla Hansen

On a bright day frozen
in January, Mother props open
the upstairs storm windows of
the farmhouse: airing out, she
calls it, a mid-winter chore.

> I move from room to room
> as if in a trance, touch
> each frozen dresser, each
> frozen bedpost, my breath
> a cloud before me rising
> as if soot from the belly
> of an ancient coal furnace.
> I trace each frozen flower
> on the wallpaper, each swirl
> on the linoleum; they are
> unreal today, yet solid
> as anthracite in memory.

At night, the storm windows
again secure, I huddle beneath
a hand-tied quilt, with aired-
out lungs I breathe, and dream;
the old house meanwhile wheezing
its stoked-up lungs deep into a
frozen night, puffing smoke to
the endless white countryside,
the clear, frozen landscape
of home.

Elsie's Cafe in Aurelia Iowa

Phil Hey

If it isn't a special place
there's no special place. Those boys,
those boys come in and they talk.

There's doughnuts and rolls
all laid out on the counter
and coffee, those glass pots
of coffee on the warmer
and lines of white glass cups.

And when those boys come in
their caps are heroic with words
like JOHN DEERE, DEKALB CORN
FUNK G HYBRID, NORTHRUP KING,
and their caps are silent
as they talk and take the rolls
and coffee at their ease
at the tables in the back.

Meanwhile, Elsie looks; she looks
through her green prescription
glasses, as she sits and listens
to the boys; and there's a tray,
big, round, glass, full
of dollar bills and piles of change
where the customers can pay
all by themselves before they leave
and not make Elsie move. The door
opens again and again.

Those boys. How they do come in.

Lincoln Nebraska

Greg Kuzma

The clouds above the city of Lincoln Nebraska
have grown together, and you cannot detect
the seams of their joining. And under
these clouds the day is ending.

I do not know the meaning of the clouds coming
together, or that there are no seams
where they have joined.
I am just here in my one small life,
doing what I call my job.

Mine is the excuse that is typical.
I was just here doing my job
when you called, I know nothing of clouds,
though I have seen them for years.
Somewhere beyond them I guess the sun is
raging.

The houses along the streets of Lincoln Nebraska
are getting older, some are in need of paint,
some look out across spacious yards
just now uncovering themselves.
A dead squirrel on the corner as I drive past.

It's a long road from Lincoln Nebraska to
my house, out in the country. Tonight I
will drive it slow, thinking with pleasure
of all that is before me. There will be no
stars, but still I will do my wishing.

The Water Tower Climbers

William Meissner

Their home town's name looms just
above them, more massive
than any thunderhead they've ever imagined.
They don't know those letters
will weigh down their shoulders
the rest of their lives —
they're strong, they're 16, they squeeze
cans of beer. They're in love with heights,
want to see all the tavern lights shrink
to blinking jewels, all those streets
become arrows of dust aimed at the limits.

Three steps from
the top, the wind
tries to blow
the first whiskers
from their faces.

At last they let go
the railing, and
balance, thinking
we could fit this whole town on our thumbnails.

Regent, North Dakota: Two Poems

Kathleen Norris

I. The Gift of Tears

> The Scarecrow sighed. "Of course I cannot understand it," he said. "If your heads were stuffed with straw like mine, you would probably all live in the beautiful places and then Kansas would have no people at all. It is fortunate for Kansas that you have brains."
>
> —L. Frank Baum, *The Wizard of Oz*

You will be sitting with children
in a school gym
watching dancers perform.

One will move out of view,
behind the lunch-tables set on end
to make wings, a stage.
Soon only her feet will be visible,
flexing in black leg warmers,
a little like the feet of the Wicked Witch of the East
when Dorothy's farmhouse landed on her.
You will be the only one
who sees this.

And in the middle of the night
when the tears come,
it will be because you married
after all, and moved back West,
to a place where tornadoes take people up
in a mad embrace.

"These tears are all I have," I write,
and the next day I show the children
the page I scrawled in the dark,
and read the new poem I wrote

in their dull prairie town.
"Do you see how it works?" I ask,
and they nod, unsure.

"Do you live in a country?"
a little girl asks.
I don't know how to tell her.
It's our secret country,
where evil spells are broken
by a promise of love,
and little girls can melt away
the wickedness that's in them.

II. The Wisdom of the Desert

When you can't see the butte, you have to go home.
—a saying in Regent, North Dakota

In the snowy desert
when you can't see the butte
you have to go home.
"There is no name for it,
there never was," says Arlie Remington,
the elementary principal;
"it's always just been 'the butte.'
A place for 'parking
and sparking,' " she goes on
and we all laugh
in the teachers' lounge
on a blizzardy Friday morning.
"You might be here forever,"
the school secretary says.

"It's got the TV booster,
and the Methodists have used it
for Easter sunrise service.
It's a good toboggan run"—Arlie is rolling,

like the snow outside —
"and in summer the weather people —
you know —" she says,
uncertainly . . . "Tornado spotters?" I ask.
"Yes," says Arlie, really beaming now:
"It's a multi-purpose butte."

I have waited, like Dorothy,
for the great wind,
for change, for somewhere else
to be. Now snow converts the earth
to one uncluttered blankness.
The butte is gone.

Arlie, all of you,
I have waited all my life
for Regent, North Dakota
and this blind white day.
I can't see where I'm going
but I know what to do.

Icehouse

Barton Sutter

The icehouses lie scattered
Like building blocks some kid
Has kicked across the floor. But no,
As you come closer, crunching through the snow,
You see these are the houses of the poor,
The plywood shacks of shantytown
You never visited before. Here
Fishermen survive on sandwiches,
Candy bars, and beer. Each year
The paper prints hot rumors
Of elusive icehouse whores,
But the truth is disappointing, dull:
There are no mermaids anywhere,
In this world or the other, and this is
A man's world, each black shack
A throwback to the clubhouse
That wore the words No Girls.

These huts are like the houses
Children draw, simple and efficient:
A door, a tiny window, smoke
Escaping in a scribble from the chimney.
Above the door of this one
The fisherman has written
His license, name, and his address—
Orville Sundquist, 37 Acorn Street,
Esko, Minnesota—as if his blackhouse
Were a package that contained
The man he always meant to be
And he hoped that somehow somebody
Would finally mail him home.

Inside, Orville, who is huge,
Hunches on a little stool
And jigs a mini fishing pole.
The stove that heats his house is small,
The sticks he feeds it kindling. Here
In his cramped confessional
Orville contemplates the zero
That his life has come to, skims
The crust that clouds the hole,
Reopening the wound, and meditates
On might-have-beens, evaporating dreams:
Christine, a degree in forestry,
That bass boat with the Evinrude
He'll never own. Well, maybe
Once the kids are grown.

The wind comes up, and Orville
Thinks of heading home. But then
He feels a signal from below
And hauls from out the icy hole
A shining thing, green-gold, glittering,
With fins, an alligator nose,
And eyes that glaze but cannot close.

Closing the Cabin

Thom Tammaro

I
In the yawn of dusk,
We drift home in Minnesota autumn,
Reciting the litany once more:
Dock in; boathouse latched;
Rugs rolled; plugs pulled;
Windows hinged; floors swept;
Pilots out; pipes drained;
Faucets opened; doors locked;
Hummingbird feeder taken down;
Key hanging in its secret place.

II
In the flicker of lights near the city's edge
We talk easily, gather within
All that the summer has given:
A great fish, slender and shiny,
Diving for bottom; loons calling
In the still afternoon;
Stars swirling above the rooftops.
Near home, vees of geese circle,
Circle in the shadows above us.

III
Later that night, we pause
On the stairs — winterward —
Unlock that other season
Where little puffs of winter dust
Rise when we open the door.

Poet in Residence at a Country School

Don Welch

The school greets me like a series
of sentence fragments sent out to recess.
Before I hit the front door
I'm into a game of baseball soccer.
My first kick's a foul; my second sails
over the heads of the outfielders;
rounding third base, I suck in my stomach
and dodge the throw of a small blue-eyed boy.
I enter the school, sucking apples of wind.
In the fifth-grade section of the room
I stand in the center of an old rug and ask,
Where would you go where no one could find you,
a secret place where you'd be invisible
to everyone except yourselves;
what would you do there; what would you say?
I ask them to imagine they're there,
and writing a poem. As I walk around the room,
I look at the wrists of the kids,
green and alive, careful with silence.
They are writing themselves into fallen elms,
corners of barns, washouts, and alkali flats.
I watch until a tiny boy approaches,
who says he can't think of a place,
who wonders today, at least, if
he just couldn't sit on my lap.
Tomorrow, he says, he'll write.

And so the two of us sit under a clock,
beside a gaudy picture of a butterfly,
and a sweet poem of Christina Rossetti's.
And in all that silence, neither of us
can imagine where he'd rather be.

Looking Up

Paul Zimmer

I am born of family with slight curvature
Of the spine, we rarely look up, but this year,
All year long, epiphanies above me.

In April the most astonishing sight,
I looked up into cold, light rain
And saw billions of crystals stippled
Against white sky, driving and soaring
In wind, countless, frozen points
Swirling in light before melting,
A vigorous, cosmic pointilism.

In July I stepped under brush
And looked up to see red berries
Ripe and clustered, bearing the branches
Down in graceful arcs with their fecundity,
All above me these sanguine pebbles.

Thick fog overhead in October leaves,
I watched it roll in an afternoon,
Up from the run, quickly over the meadow,
Combing itself through trees above me,
Over the roof to soften the brightness.

In a December night, my head held high,
A city man looking for stars in country fields,
Suddenly the cold moon struck my shoulders
From behind, taking my breath away.

The Tender Organizations

Carol Bly

Nature is so rife with life that tender organizations can be serenely squashed out of existence like pulp. . . .

— Henry David Thoreau

There is a natural, satisfying enmity between ecstatic people and practical people. The Marthas of the world know the Marys are goldbricks. The Marys, smiling at their gurus' knees, would never trade their numinous excitement for housewives' depression.

Where we go wrong is in supposing that it is the ecstatic people who find the practical people boring. They do, of course — but not nearly so boring as the practical people find the ecstatics. Of course anyone skilled in breadmaking and other kitchen work gets irritated by the ecstatic people's pouring oil over the mentors' feet or at the way the ecstatics wait silent until their mentors stop speaking, and then give off an odd singsong trill of admiration. All that is merely irritating: what drives the practical people to exasperation, and finally drowsiness, is the way ecstatic people can't get hold of a project and do it simply. In parish churches all over the world, not just in Clayton, Minnesota, practical people go straight to sleep while the ecstatic people cry, "Oh! Oh! How *shall* we get people to *feel* the loving-kindness in our beautiful universe!" The practical people simply drop off to sleep, right there in the Lady Chapel or the Guild Hall or the Fellowship Room.

Sally Thackers, the Episcopal rector's wife, was a methodical sort. She was twenty-eight, a healthy-faced woman who went about in a Hollofil vest in the wintertime. In the summer she was a raiser of perennials; in the winter she planned to develop beds of the sparer flowers: she planned where she would put Carpathian harebells, and how to present their slight flowering as delicate, instead of simply scant. She was pleased to spend a lot of time in the kitchen—rather more pleased to be there than participating in her husband's discussions before the rectory hearth. She had nothing striking about her looks: her hair was already turning pale, and her healthiness seemed just that: healthy, rather than decorative. Her plainness was not all bad. She found it easy to slip from the rectory living room to the kitchen, with a deprecating wave—"There is the bread to be looked after"—hiding in her persona of Jack Thackers's practical wife.

In the last week before Saint Andrew's Feast, she hovered at the kitchen window, listening to the hushed sleet tick on its panes. She half overheard the men's conversation in the living room; she half sang a nursery rhyme to her unborn child. She sang sotto voce its violent plot. She sometimes pretended that life was as it had been before these seven and a half weeks of her pregnancy. She pretended she was a freestanding person, at liberty to be lost in the universe. She wished that her husband's few, slight failings—his fear of dogs, his belief that God answered personal prayers—struck her simply as touching, the way they had before her pregnancy. Now that she was to be a mother, she saw him as the loved, honored father of her child but also as a man not one hundred percent reliable. She would have to stay on tippy toe.

She and Jack had a slightly older friend, an oncology nurse named Mercein. Mercein's brother Dick had come to the rectory this morning to share with Jack that he had laid out the fleece for God, and God had answered. Dick must be forty-two, Sally thought, old enough to know better. Dick had told God that if God wanted him to move from Clayton down to the Twin Cities, as Dick's wife wanted to do, God was to give a sign. If no sign was given on the designated day, the man would know it was all right to stay in Clayton, where life was so pleasant, with the mixed forest to hunt in and all the calm, low-paying jobs. Dick went hunting up around Route 6 all day. He checked out the little lakes near Emily, and Outing, finally standing in a blind on Lawrence Lake, but he never got a shot. When he got home he told his wife, and she agreed what it meant, even though she had wanted to be in the Twin Cities so much. Now Dick wanted Jack to know that he had spoken to God, and God had spoken back. It was O.K. to stay. Dick gave Jack and Sally a Williams-Sonoma bowl.

Sally listened a little from the kitchen, her lip curled. When she went into the room with a tea tray, she saw Jack nearly weightless on his seat, his body bent toward Dick. His face was guileless and vacuous; he prompted Dick's story nearly in a whisper. Sally had trouble even thanking Dick for the bowl. Born-again Christians would never just give you something. They never said, "Sally, here is a bowl." You had to listen to their rhetoric, as well. "Sally and Jack, I really feel as if you two are really Servants of God, you know? I feel as if I can really tell my feelings about God to you—here is a bowl."

It was hard for the Thackerses to find a whole morning, or afternoon, or even a whole evening, to be alone with each other. Two days after Dick's visit, Jack brought in an armful of the dry ash firewood from 1988 and announced that they were going to spend the morning hanging out. Since Sally felt nauseated, he would make the tea.

The wood came from an eighty just north of Carolyn's animal hospital, straight across from the regular people's hospital. Two summers ago, George, Carolyn's husband, who had the Super Valu store in town, and Carolyn, and Mercein (the hospice nurse), and Norma, the new UCC minister, had taken down eleven trees. The following January they stood in the snow, brushing against the spiny redwood bushes, and Swede-sawed up all the trunks. Now the wood was perfect.

Just as Sally and Jack settled down to waste the morning, Mercein called up to say that the Otto Schlaeger situation had become intolerable and would Jack please get on the stick and use whatever clout he had with the Schlaeger family's pastor to intervene. And also get the daughter home. The man was dying fast.

Aloud, Sally said to Jack, "You can have him over." To herself she said, Goodbye, hearth, for *this* morning.

A disadvantage of clerical life was that Jack couldn't use the statement so handy to people in the women's movement: *Sorry, I need to do something for myself*—so would you please take your problems with the Schlaeger family somewhere else? Jack's $24,000-plus package deal made him a professional, the way the president of Merrill Lynch was a professional.

"Too bad," Jack said, lingering in the kitchen doorframe. "I really thought this time we could just drink a lot of tea and get nervous and enjoy the fire. Now we have Kurt instead."

He dutifully dialed the Missouri Synod church number. Sally heard him say in a full, open-throated voice, "Sally's baking something with raisins in it that smells wonderful! How about making it over here in a half hour or so?"

Kurt would come. He was a huge, comfortable man, whose body dropped fast into any inviting space. He always took Jack's recliner when he visited the rectory. If the chairs were unevenly drawn up to the fire, he inched his forward until it was fair. He was interested in the arms buildups of all countries—not just of the big ones. He knew, for example, that Afghanistan rebels had repulsed Soviet helicopters with their mix of rifles, even old Enfields, as effectively as they would have with SAM Sevens.

Sally said, "I had better go ahead and bake something with raisins that smells delicious, then."

Jack looked apologetic, and then smiled. "How is the baby?" he asked.

They had not told anyone they were expecting a child, so it was still a mysterious happiness and pathos of their own. Sally imagined the baby somewhere on the wall of her vaulty, blood-colored womb. She imagined the egg and the seed still so newly joined they were curious to have found each other: they were binding themselves together as fast as night. She imagined the baby hanging on for dear life, now in November using only the tiniest part of the space reserved for it. The womb must feel very rangy to the baby.

She and Jack found their rectory a little rangy, too. There it stood in their town of 2,242, a fake-half-timbered-English house rough, in its sleety grapevines, in the police catchment area of Saint Cloud, in the hospice catchment area of Jack and Sally's friend Mercein, in the mental health catchment area of Mora, in the Anglophilia catchment area of the Episcopal church. Its walls were hung with British servants' hall hangings, in the way that Missouri Synod Lutheran parsonages have Dresden flower stollen plates, or barn-owl steins made in West Germany.

In Jack and Sally's house the kitchen hanging said that any servant caught feeding dogs under the table would be fined threepence halfpenny. Any servant coming to dinner without his jacket would be fined twopence. "It's not evil — it's just silly," Jack said to Sally. "Any object from a revered place feels *holy to* people. People revere England, period." He no doubt recognized the expression on her face: he said firmly, "We are *not* either just a museum piece of Anglicanism."

Now they clung together a moment. "I am singing to the baby every day now," Sally told him. "And using less bad language. Today the music is the Magnificat, half *tonus peregrinus* and half fauxbourdon, and the nursery rhyme is 'Three mice went into a cellar to spin — Puss passed by and Puss looked in.' " She added, "On with the raisins and white dough."

A half hour later, she shamelessly eavesdropped as she spread an ironed piece of old Fair Linen on a tray. Jack was explaining the Schlaeger situation to Kurt.

"There's old Otto Schlaeger in horrible pain now, from the cancer, and apparently Vi is secretly not giving him his painkillers. She *tells* Mercein she has given it each time, but when Mercein shows up, Otto is often in outright agony. Apparently Vi is skipping the every three or four hours' morphine dosing. Mercein says the idea is to give the meds at exactly the same time intervals. Vi isn't doing it."

No sounds for a moment.

Then Jack's voice again: "If you skip one of the scheduled times, the pain gets so out of control it takes a shot to bring it down. Shots are not the idea," Jack went on, obviously relating information exactly as the hospice nurse had recited it for him. "Oral meds is best. Then suppositories. Third, injection."

"Yeah? Suppositories?" Kurt's full, friendly voice.

Good, Sally thought, taking out the white-dough-and-raisins muffins. Kurt is taking an interest.

Kurt's voice again: "Suppositories, huh? I would hate to have to have a suppository."

Jack's voice: "So Mercein said to Vi, three days ago, that she absolutely must *not* fail to give Otto his meds. Vi told Mercein to get out of the house. Mercein couldn't even get back in this morning. So that's where we are with this now," Jack wound up.

Kurt said, "A difficult time of life for those two — very, very hard going, I know. I remember when my dad got his cancer. . . . Well, now — Otto and Vi Schlaeger. Much to be said on both sides, Jack . . . much to be said on both sides. That isn't a marriage that's always been easy. I don't think I am talking out of school when I say that."

Jack's voice: "Easy marriage! Easy marriage, Kurt! Holy shit, Kurt! Otto's been beating Vi for twenty-six years! The grown daughter won't even come home!"

Kurt: "These things are so darn difficult to judge from the outside. Naturally I've heard some about this, and I'm not at leave to pass all of it on. But I will say that Vi came to me twice, saying how hard he was on her."

Jack's voice: "Just twice?"

Kurt gave a small laugh. "She wanted me to look at a mouse she said he'd given her. Both times. Same thing. My feeling was then and is now that I'd want to hear both sides of these family things before I moved on it."

Jack: "So did you hear both sides?"

Kurt: "Otto never came complaining to me, so I figured they'd worked out something. I know that I sure gave them focus in my prayers, for quite a while there. Well, Jack: it does take two to tango, it really does. I know Vi is supposed to be a wonderful homemaker — all that canning and gardening and all — but there isn't any rule says a woman can't put on a spot of lipstick once in a while, or get herself done up a little."

Sally carried in a tray of the muffins and coffee. Kurt smiled happily and took two. She went over to Jack. They mentioned the sleet and how it would freeze soon and Interstate 94 would be a mess. Sally knew they would keep making small talk until she left the room.

"Schlaegers have a wonderful dog," Kurt remarked. "Airedale bitch. It'd be fun to have a really smart dog like that along for hunting. I'm not one of your hunters who has to have a dog *to work* all the time! I'd just like to have it for the companionship. A lot of people forget that hunting is supposed to be recreation and that goes for the dog, too. They treat it as if it were just work, work, work."

Sally slid back into the kitchen and regarded the sleet out the window. It lay in shining fur along all the basswood branches.

Then she heard two clear thuds in the living room. She put her head around the door. Kurt had dropped to both knees on the Belgian rug. Now Jack, not very willingly, was sinking to his knees, too.

"Almighty Father," Kurt said. "We would ask that you intervene in the hearts of Vi and Otto Schlaeger in this time of their need." His voice was solid and good-willed. "Guide Vi to set aside her angers. Guide her to know and rejoice in your love of her. . . . "

In the kitchen closet, Sally found her Hollofil vest and a sou'wester hat and let herself out the back door. She drove very carefully down Main Street and then over to Seventh Avenue, to George's Super Valu.

The frozen-foods manager told Sally that George was out back somewhere. A shelf stocker told her to try the office, all the way back, past all the crates in the warehouse part of the building. Sally barged along the huge, shadowy warehouse aisles, where the air was snappy and smelled of old ground. She knocked at George's little ply-and-bare-studs office door. Inside, it was all bright light, sudden heat from the electric strip, and George's work spread out on a desk — claimed coupons, bad credit notes, truck vouchers. He poured Sally a cup of boiling water with a beef-flavor cube in it and listened to her story. He made a telephone call. Mercein, he told her, would be there in five, and thank God someone was doing something.

George and Sally made negative, catty small talk as they waited. They and their group — Carolyn, Jack, Mercein, and Norma, the UCC minister, and even George's frozen-foods manager, who was also VFW post commander—had too high profiles to gossip in the usual places: at coffee parties on Eighth or Ninth avenue, or at the VFW, or during dishwashing at Men's Fellowship or at Guild. Therefore it was delicious for them to assess and criticize when they could. George told Sally that as far back as he knew, the Schlaegers were the worst family in town. They weren't the worst in the conventional sense—that is, they didn't live in an AFDC addition and they didn't miss church because of hangovers. They were quite respectable. In fact, Otto was the one who first proposed that everyone on Eighth Avenue mow their lawn on the same day of the week so that the grass height from lot to lot would match. Once he had gone around to Mercein's brother, Dick, and told him to set his mower height lower because it wrecked the look of the whole street. The Schlaegers were middle-class, but everyone in town was sixty percent sure he beat his wife whenever he had three beers, and for all anyone knew, the kid as well. That would be his daughter, George said, looking up, thinking: who must be something like thirty-five now. Gone away to the Cities.

Sally offered, Beaters are beaters. In the Episcopal church, the wife-beater was the guy who made sure they ran up the flag of Saint Andrew every November 30. Sally said, How is Carolyn? George told her he didn't see much of his wife this time of year, when the rich went to McAllen or Waco to get away from the Minnesota winter. They left their domestic animals in Carolyn's kennel.

Sally and George gave each other the superior look of people who stay through the winter. Then Mercein burst in, bright from the cold.

"What're you two hatching up?" she said. "I could tell from your voice on the phone." She gave Sally a fast appraisal. "How are you, Sally Thackers?" she said.

Sally instantly saw that Mercein knew she was pregnant. So much for that secret, she thought.

George said, "We have a solution for the Schlaeger problem. You move in, Mercein. Nights. Tell Vi that Otto needs round-the-clock nursing care."

"Tried that," Mercein remarked. "As soon as I saw Vi was trying on purpose to make him suffer. For revenge! I told her I would move in, but she threw me out."

Sally explained the fine points. "We force her," Sally said. "We threaten to call a psychiatric social worker from Mora if we have to. That ought to work."

Mercein heard them out. "O.K.," she said. "But I don't go over there alone. This last time she offered to set that airedale on me."

George said, "Sally and I go with you."

Sally said, "No—I go with you. George stays here. George, we save you for *heavy metal* if we need it later. And our backup plan is to haul in the whole ministerium if we have to."

Mercein said, "That's no good. The Schlaegers' pastor won't do anything. And he's a fourth of the ministerium."

George said, "That's right, and we can't use Norma, either. She's had that UCC job less than a year, and she can't get in trouble with breaking and entering, in case Vi goes to court. Speaking of clergy, Sally, are we telling Jack about this?"

Sally said, "Jack needs to not know. If Vi calls him, he can draw a complete blank. It'll have to be just us, Mercein."

Sally thought, as she and Mercein moved out through the drafty warehouse, past all the piled vegetables far from wherever they were grown: This is an untoward business for the baby. On second thought, though, she decided the baby was still so very small—only a scant eight weeks old—it couldn't be paying even the most unconscious, most inchoate attention to her projects. Still, she felt that the activist flavor was not right for in utero people. She would counteract the tone of all this with some bland song, the moment she got free.

Mercein and Sally stalled outside the Super Valu window. "We had better take both our cars," Mercein said. "I may need to stay a while, if we ever get in there today. By the way, this might get tough. If it gets tough, Sally, you do exactly what I tell you to do, and you do it right away."

"What nonsense," Sally said. "I am stronger than you, and I've seen grievouser and worse things in the world than you ever thought up in a bad dream." The moment she had said it, however, she couldn't make a mental image of one grievous thing she had seen. She felt like a faint, ridiculous child, brought up in a childish way, helping other people live childish lives, and now carrying a still fainter and more childish child inside her. It all seemed rather wonderful, if stupid.

Mercein said, "People who are expecting should stay out of fights."
Sally felt as if she were watching a flare slowly sink down above her.

Mercein said snappily, "For goodness' sake, I am a nurse. I know
you are pregnant. I can tell a birth or a death months ahead."

"How nice to be a prophet,' Sally said.

Mercein said, "You know we're stalling, don't you? We're both
scared to death. Let's go over there and get it over with."

Each got into her own car and drove through the new slush to the
Schlaegers'.

Mercein stood to one side of the storm door; Sally rang the bell.
The moment Vi Schlaeger opened the inner door to see who had
come, Mercein whipped around and put her foot in the storm door
opening. She was an old hand: she put her boot in so that when the
home owner slammed the door on it, it hit the soft part, not the an-
klebone.

Vi was a German–American immigrant's grandchild. She had the
remarkable horizontal eyebrows and forehead width of thousands of
northern faces. The eyes were gray-blue, with handsome dark eye-
lashes; the mouth was wide. The straight, abundant hair, now gray,
was drawn back. Every single feature was handsome and powerful,
yet the overall effect made your blood run chill.

"Told you before, I'm telling you again: you get out, and you're not
coming here anymore. He don't need you, and I don't need you," Vi
said to Mercein. She ignored Sally.

Mercein said, "I am moving in. Otto needs round–the-clock nursing, and that's what he's going to get."

The infuriated wife cried, "He don't need no round-the-clock nursing, period!"

Sally geared up for her lines and said them. "Mrs. Schlaeger, I am
here as a witness. If you refuse entrance to the oncology nurse, I will
act as witness. It is your legal right to know that."

Vi Schlaeger did not know much about American justice, but she
watched the American average of six and one fourth hours' television
each day. She knew that words like "witness" and "your legal right"
had grave muscle. She opened the door.

Vi's bit of living room was dark and heavy, like the inside of a cave. Sally was aware of dreary lampshades, their bulbs unlit, of at least a dozen plants with wide, drooping leaves hanging above the clay rims.

Otto Schlaeger lay curled on the sofa, legs pulled up, his whole body rocking frantically. Mercein went over to him immediately. When she said his name, he jerked his head around and he cried, "For Christ's sake!"

The nurse was on the floor by the sofa, bag open, fixing her syringe. "Better in two minutes, Otto," she said.

Sally hovered a few feet behind her. She heard Vi mutter, "Hurts, does it, huh?" When Sally swung around, Vi looked back at her, steady as a column.

Sally then paid attention to everything Mercein did, interested in the earmarks of a new trade. "Just like a hobbyist," she then told herself, "learning how people do what they do—give medicines, bake bread, run stores, decorate churches. Why don't you just live your own life?" Only a part of her mind said that, however. Another part went on watching how Mercein kept her hand on the man's forehead and kept talking to him, waiting for the morphine to take. Mercein also talked to the patient's wife, in a friendly, Scoutleader tone. "Vi? Let me show you this. Say you're going to put an afghan on a patient. That afghan on the chair. Would you bring it over?"

Mercein said a little louder, "Vi, bring over the afghan."

"He don't need an afghan. He's all sweaty anyhow."

"Sally—you bring me that afghan, would you? Now. You pull it up not just *to* the shoulders but all the way over, because that's where the chilling gets in. And Sally, would you bring my bag in? And Vi, would you tell Sally where to set my things so they will be out of your way? Bad enough to have houseguests without they don't leave their stuff around!"

Mercein kept up everything in a singsong. "We'll keep Otto on these meds, every four hours, day and night, so the pain never gets ahead of us. The three of us can manage perfectly well. And if Otto needs it, he can have a bump now and then."

"A bump!" cried Vi.

"Extra morphine," Mercein said. "Everyone knows you take pride in your work, Vi. All that canning. All your housecleaning. Well, I take pride in my work, too." She kept talking.

Presently the dying man's knees relaxed. Sally thought: He doesn't look so much like a cause now. He simply looks like an ugly person asleep, who is neither interesting nor kind when awake. There must be millions, millions, of men like Otto. Sally told the baby, It's bad luck, someone like Otto. But your luck is already better.

Suddenly Vi said, "Now you get out, you the one that's not nursing or anything."

Sally said, "I *am* going home now. But Mercein is going to stay. And if you give her any trouble I am going to call the psychiatric social worker from Mora, and you know what I'm going to do, Mrs. Schlaeger? I will tell her that you live at 314 Eighth Avenue instead of 312 Eighth Avenue, so the social worker will knock there first, and explain who she is, and ask where you live."

Vi's cheeks shook. "You get out, or I'll set Hoffer on you."

Sally now realized that a large dog lay behind the vertical leaves of the dining room table. Its head arched forward about two inches above its paws. It kept one eye squeezed shut, or perhaps the eye was missing. Sally thought: Not just a bad thing for the baby, bad for me. Although she was only half as frightened of dogs as Jack was, she was still frightened her full half-share. The airedale, however, didn't move when Mrs. Schlaeger spoke its name.

Sally said, "If you try to kick us out, we are going to call the police, Mrs. Schlaeger. Not the police which is that fellow that goes to your church, either. The real police. In Saint Cloud."

"You can't call the police," the woman said, but her voice wobbled, and Sally, with one eye on the dog, now felt that everything would be all right.

"I'll walk you to your car," Mercein said.

The translucent sleet was turning to real snow. In the quarter hour—which seemed like hours—that Mercein and Sally had been inside, the snow had been disposing itself in its own tendrils and handsome ganglia along all the ash and maple trees.

At Sally's car door, Mercein said, "Now listen to me. Here is how you look at this. You keep your mind on how really peaceful and painless old Otto looked on the couch. That's *all* you think about. You remember this, Sally: in all the rest of his life — one week, ten days — he isn't going to feel any pain ever again. You understand that?"

Mercein paused a moment. Sally thought she was about to comment on the weather, because she looked about her, at the little street full of cold lawns and trees and some cars parked. But Mercein said, "Forget Vi. All her life she has had a mean husband, and her daughter ran away and never writes home, so she's mad. But the mean husband is dying, so her problems are over. I will go back in now, and talk to her some, and also try to find out where the daughter is. I'll be in touch."

In the next ten days the weather deepened. George's Super Valu staff grease-marked the front store windows: REMEMBER LAST SUMMER? WELCOME THE MOISTURE! HAPPY HOLIDAYS! Sally recovered from morning sickness and went on a whole-grain baking binge. Outside her kitchen window the snow did the one thing we want snow to do: it turned the twentieth century back into the softer nineteenth century. In this softer, quieter landscape, the snow said, technology is nothing, industrialization is nothing; surely the hole in the far south sky will heal . . . everything can be managed.

This is your first snow, Sally told the baby, since how would it know, otherwise, hiding in there, as it did, self-centeredly growing its brain, its nervous system, its stomach, still keeping its beginnings of hands curled inward.

Jack said, "Kurt just called. Of all things, he called to say that God has answered our prayers about Vi Schlaeger."

Sally heard the "of all things" as Jack's willingness to join her in a small jeer at the Missouri Synod Lutheran pastor. She also saw that Jack leaned a little springily in the kitchen doorway, his elbows sticking out, one hand touching along the back of the other in front of his stomach. "Did you know — " he went on, "perhaps you didn't know — that Kurt and I prayed Vi would find it in her heart to let Mercein take over the care of old Otto?"

Sally felt Jack's mind alternately flaring and shrinking in front of her, wanting her to agree to this mysterious outcome, that something had come of the two men's prayers. He wanted her to agree to it, of course: worse, he wanted her to feel wafted away, as he seemed to feel. Once, in their five years of marriage, she had pretended to get more pleasure in bed than she had felt at the time. It was a February night, as clear as stars in her memory. She had gone to sleep early, exhausted from housecleaning the whole rectory. She had made herself get through all the cleaning, knowing that once bathed and in bed, she could look over the new garden catalog. She had her pen and paper and a clipboard lying alongside her, on Jack's side. She carefully drew all the flower plots and drew some brick layouts. She planned how to keep something white and something blue in bloom throughout the summer. She liked flowers that had a good deal of green, with space between the blooms, rather than crowding flowers, like daisies. She wanted Carpathian harebells.

Jack's lovemaking had not distracted her from her thoughts. Therefore she had lied a little. Now, looking toward him from the kitchen worktable, she lied again: that is, she gave him a smile, but she squinted her right eye, hoping it would make the smile into a kind of twinkling, good-natured grin.

Jack then said, "Funny fellow, Kurt. He calls me up to tell me about the Immanent God, but he gets onto deer hunting, deer hunting, deer hunting."

Nearly five hundred of Clayton's two thousand and more people sat in Saint Paul's for Otto Schlaeger's funeral. The great, bluff pastor told them that Otto Schlaeger's father had come to America so he would not have to serve in the Kaiser's army. Kurt's sermon went on, quietly, undeniably giving its own kind of consolation. It connected the little town with the great world outside. It connected the past of Germany and America with this death. If that German had not emigrated, Kurt told them, he might well have dressed in field gray, and he might have shot at our Clayton, Minnesota, men who met Germans at Château-Thierry. That man's son, whose life among us we celebrated today, might never have served as a rating on the USS *Mississippi*.

As Kurt began to maunder, Sally let her thoughts shift here and there. She told the baby she would teach it history, because learning history—it was a simple fact she had not thought of before—makes people happy. She daydreamed about that idea for all the rest of the service. It spared her getting irritated when Kurt got lost on one of his hobbies: he was listing Navy ordnance options to this funeral audience. It spared her feeling sardonic at the grave, when George's frozen-foods manager and a young guardsman stretched and yanked corners of the flag, put it roughly into its triangles, and then took it, a pad of cloth now, and marched, squaring imagined corners across the undertaker's green cloth and the snow, to Vi Schlaeger. The post commander presented the flag to Otto Schlaeger's widow on behalf of the President of the United States. Clearly the widow didn't know what expression to arrange on her face. She seemed to try two or three. In the end, she settled on the expression of people returning to their pews after they have taken Eucharist.

As they came away from the graveside, Jack put Sally's gloved hand into the crook of his elbow. "Tomorrow I am going to make a fire and we are going to sit around our house, *alone,* all day. There's no one in the hospital. No one is getting married."

"I will bake whole-wheat rolls with oat bran in them," Sally said. "On the other hand, there is something really depressing about oat bran."

"That's true," Jack said in a happy voice. "Oat bran sucks."

The next morning, however, someone banged their door knocker before ten o'clock.

It was an energetic-looking woman in her early thirties, with springing hair, glittering eyes, an expressive mouth; she was made up fully—there was something of everything: shadow, liner, mascara, blush, and lipstick—yet the woman's focus was so strong, even aggressive, that the makeup couldn't gentle it.

"Mrs. John Thackers?" she said loudly. "They said over at the church that your husband was home today."

She jammed her way in past Sally. That was close, Sally said to the baby. She felt cheery. Whoever this visitor was, Sally meant to throw her out after fifteen minutes. Sally had been a good rector's wife: she had gone to the funeral, even out to the cemetery, instead of waiting in the Saint Paul's basement with the old, the pregnant, and the greedy. Now this was her and Jack's day off. Besides, the woman had thick, strong hair. She probably had a coarse nature, Sally decided.

"I don't guess you'd know who I am," the visitor said. "I'm Francine, Vi Schlaeger's girl."

Jack came in with an L.L. Bean canvas full of fireplace wood.

"This is Jack Thackers—Ms. Schlaeger," Sally said.

"We didn't know you'd got here for your dad's funeral," Jack said.

"I wouldn't come for his funeral!" Francine said with a laugh. "I drove up from the Cities this morning. Just to pick up my mother and take her to stay with me a week or so. Just to put the dog down and get the stuff out of the refrigerator. But then, on the way up, I had an experience. A direct relationship to God."

Jack motioned toward the chair Sally usually sat in, by the fire. Sally started to ease out to the kitchen, as she always did as soon as people started talking about having a direct or personal experience of Jesus Christ. She did so not so much to spare herself the thrilled, self-congratulatory voices but because people having a religious experience always want to tell it to someone in authority—a clergyperson—not to a spouse who happens to be there.

But Francine called after her. "Don't go away! I won't be long! In fact, my mother's waiting out in the car!"

"Waiting in the car!" both Jack and Sally cried, going toward the door.

Francine raised and dropped one shoulder. "She wouldn't come in," she said. "She doesn't want to hear about the way God spoke to me! I don't know why I am surprised. She wouldn't even listen to ordinary-life things I tried to tell her as a child. And things I tried to tell her about . . . Anyway," she said. "Anyway. And I couldn't go to Pastor Kurt, because of course he's gone hunting or trapping. And anyway . . . there was some nurse that took care of Dad hanging around the house this morning, and she said to come to you."

She stopped, giving Jack a look.

"Now," she said, "I hope you don't *mind* hearing about a personal religious experience?"

You're in luck, Sally thought, looking at the woman. It's too late for *me* to get out of the room, but Jack not only does not mind personal religious feeling; he likes it very much. Sally felt like a Martha who has been told she absolutely may *not* go out to bake the loaves: she *must* stay, like Mary, and pour oil and be admiring.

Francine had driven out of Minneapolis very early in the morning, before full light, if you could call any daylight in December full light. She was half asleep on Interstate 94 when a voice said very clearly, Keep a sharp eye out for animals on the right side of the road. Now, Francine was very surprised, since she thought the only person who heard voices was Joan of Arc, a Roman Catholic. Francine didn't particularly *want* to hear voices. This voice persevered. It insisted she watch for "beautiful animals on the right." Well, all right, she told the voice, but I don't expect anything out of this. Now Francine said to Jack and Sally, "I expect very little of God and very little of people of God, too. The one time I ever went to the pastor in need, he told me I should be a good girl and not go around carrying tales about my dad."

She'd kept driving and presently whizzed past a crow, which stood right beside a fair-sized carcass, a dog or something that size. As roadkill goes, it must have been very fresh. It was a cold day, but the entrails, some of which hung from the crow's beak, were still bright red and flexible. The crow was so pleased with its find it scarcely budged as the powerful car shot by.

Francine then said to the voice, "If that is your idea of 'beautiful animals,' forget it."

The voice said monotonously, "Keep watching for beautiful animals on the right."

Another ten or fifteen minutes later, Francine's car fled across the Rum River bridge. There, far on the right, with their skinny black legs silhouetted against the white ice, stood a buck and several does. The bridge noise startled them: they pawed once, and the buck bobbed his head so Francine saw his full rack.

Now her face, under its no-nonsense permanent, was bright. "So you see? . . . You see?" she nearly shouted at Jack.

Jack said steadily, "That is a wonderful, wonderful story." He spoke in a companionable, respectful, calming tone, but Sally felt his excitement as well. And his right foot went lightly pigeon-toed and back several times.

Eventually Jack let Francine out of the doorway. Sally heard him say, " . . . something to hang on to for a lifetime."

Sally told the baby, Well, your father is an extraordinary man. He would be delighted to have such an experience himself. He always nearly comes out of his chair when someone tells such stories. But he never, at least not ever that Sally knew of, let on how much he wished *he* saw visions or heard voices or got any proofs of anything numinous.

By the time Jack had closed the door, Sally had her Hollofil vest on. "I'm off for just a half hour, " she told him. "Then I'll be back, and we will still have the whole day."

He held her shoulders. "Where are you going?"

"Out," she said ironically. "You don't want to know where."

Then he said, "Don't slip. It melted last night and then froze up again this morning."

Carolyn's animal hospital and kennel were at the north end of Clayton, past the flower shop, past the nursing home and hospital. As she drove by it, Sally gave a respectful glance at the hospital's maternity wing. A part of her fate had already moved in over there: it was much the way a part of her fate had moved into the rectory when Jack first showed it to her, before they were married.

She found Carolyn examining a cat. The vet kept one hand on its breast and reached for things behind her with the other.

Sally said, "We just got a telephone call from Francine Schlaeger, of all people. She said she'd been trying to reach you, but the line was busy."

"It wasn't," Carolyn said briefly. "I've been right here, working on this fellow."

Sally relaxed. "I suppose she had the wrong number. She asked me to tell you she has changed her mind about that airedale of her dad's and she wants you to give it to me. Along with a leash and a couple of days' food. Then she will call me and make other arrangements later."

Carolyn said, "She wanted me to put that dog down, I thought. She said it was vicious."

Sally said brightly, "Well, she's changed her mind."

"She has, huh?" Carolyn said. She molded her hands around the cat and laid it in a small cage. She went out back and reemerged with a one-eyed animal, which Sally recognized as Hoffer, the dog under the Schlaegers' dining room table. It looked huge. Could it have grown in two weeks?

Carolyn took a leash from the wall. 'Now, you want to be careful with this one, Sally. She's been knocked around some. Ill-fed, too. My guess is, if you feed her and water her a lot, right from the first, she'll make her home with you. Don't move fast around her at first. Did Francine Schlaeger tell you what to do with the nine-dollar check for the Nembutal?"

"Oh," Sally said, "she certainly did. She absolutely wanted you to keep it, in return for your trouble."

Carolyn grinned and said, "Yeah, she did, huh? Well, here's enough dog food for until Ms. Schlaeger decides to relieve you of the dog. Now . . . in case she changes her mind *again* and doesn't relieve you of the dog, bring her back in so I can give her some shots and check her over for you. Airedales are airedales. I thought you were scared of dogs, hey."

Sally thought: If I put the dog in the backseat, it might bite me in the neck as I'm driving. Also, I would see it in the rearview mirror and get scared. But if I put it beside me, as a passenger, it might leap at me. Life, she told the baby, is made up of the greater evil and the lesser evil. She put the dog beside her.

At the rectory, Jack took Sally's vest and hung it on the visitors' coat tree. He also took the leash and said, slightly in his falsetto, "Hello, Big Fellow. Welcome."

"Big Girl," Sally said. "Her name is Hoffer."

Jack dragged the fifty-pound feed bag to the kitchen. He came back with the Williams-Sonoma bowl, filled to the top with dried dog food. He made another trip and returned with a bowl of water. He set the food and the water between their two chairs before the fire. The fire reflected a little in the water. Then Jack and Sally sat down, leaving the dog at the back of the room.

"You see what a first-rate husband I am?" Jack said. "Do you hear me asking any questions? No. And after a while, when I recover from the cold sweat that animal put me in, I will go to the kitchen and make cocoa. Then we will not have any more adventures all day."

Sally and Jack heard a series of thuds. They turned to see.

Hoffer had lain down bonily, with the idea of thinking everything over. She knew that eventually she would creep forward; eventually she would do that, and eat some of that food and drink about half of the water, if that's what that was in the other bowl. She also knew she would kiss the hands of these human beings, the male one and the female one, who had left their fingers hanging off their chair arms, in full sight. She would do that, although they were nearly strangers. She had seen and scented the female only once before, and the male not at all.

Life doesn't offer perfect choices. When Hoffer lay in a pile of puppies, her mother had told them all: Look, you either *adore people* or you live your whole life in the Great Emptiness. You take what people give you, kisses or blows or both, because if you don't, you know what you'll end up with? The Great Emptiness—that's what! The puppies didn't know what that was, but it sounded execrable.

Hoffer obeyed her mother. She spent about two thirds of her life being beaten by the male of her people, sometimes by the female. Once, even, the male of her people set upon the child of her people, and Hoffer had had to make the only decision of her life: her nose had raged with the scent of the same blood on both sides as they struggled. Hoffer, in terror, elected to save the child of her people. She leapt upon the male. In return for her trouble she lost one eye. Then the child went away and Hoffer went on being beaten by both of the others, but less and less frequently. A sorry business.

Now then, these new people: Hoffer's jaws were already wet with her plan. She meant to creep forward and thoroughly kiss their hands, between all the fingers and up to the sweater cuffs. She decided on the female of them first, then the male. She had a notion, which she knew she couldn't get across, but she had the idea, anyway. It was that she would explain with her tongue how close to death she had been; she meant to explain with her tongue how life always looks much more ordinary than it really is—how its dangerousness, and its ecstasy, scarcely show.

State Fair

Garrison Keillor

It has been a quiet week in Lake Wobegon and it's a great pleasure to be here at the Minnesota State Fair. I've come every year since I was five, and that's more than twenty years. Every August my mother said, 'Well, I don't know if I care to go to the Fair this year or not.' Nobody had so much as mentioned the Fair, we were too busy canning vegetables and perishing of the heat and the steam from the pressure cooker — a burning hot day and us stripping skins off tomatoes, slaving to put up a hundred or so quarts of a vegetable we were rapidly losing our appetite for. She said, "There's too much work to do and we can't afford it, it's too crowded, and anyway it's the same as last year. I don't see how we can do it. I'm sorry."

It was her way of lending drama to the trip. So we'd come to the Fair, the roar of engines and the smell of grease, and Mother marched around the Home Activities building looking at competitive cakes and jams. One year we shook hands with Senator Ed Thye, and another time we won a roll of linoleum by guessing the number of agates in a toilet bowl. One year we wandered into the Education building and saw a demonstration of television, an interesting invention: people stood in a crowd and looked at a picture of themselves on a screen. When they moved the picture moved — interesting. Hard to see why you'd want one if you had a mirror, but it was entertaining for a few minutes.

I came with Mother and Dad, and because we were Christians we gave a wide berth to the Midway, where ladies danced and did other things at the Persian Palms and Harlem Revue tent shows. We avoided sin, but it was exciting for me to be so close to it and see flashing pink lights and hear barkers say, in a voice like a talking dog's, "See Miss Roxanne just inside the gate, just beyond that tent flap, she's waiting in there for you, she wants to show you a *good* time," and I tried to see beyond the flap, not wanting Miss Roxanne to be disappointed by my lack of interest in her. It was exciting to hear bands playing slow raunchy dance tunes and to walk past the freak show with the two-headed boy, where the gypsy ticket-seller looked at me with a haughty look that said, *I know things you'll never know, what I've seen you'd never understand.*

I loved the Fair, the good and the bad. It was good to get out of our quiet town into a loud place with bad food and stink, music and sex blaring — listen — it's gorgeous. Dad gave me three dollars and I walked around not spending it, just gaping at the sights. Once I saw a sad midget stand and smoke a cigarette, holding his dog's leash, a big dog. Once I saw a man necking with a fat lady behind the Tilt-A-Whirl. He was running the ride. People were getting tossed around like eggs in a blender, and he was putting his hands up her shirt. Once I saw the newspaper columnist Olson Younger sitting in a booth under the sign MEET OLSON YOUNGER. He was puffier than his picture in the paper and more dejected. He sat drinking coffee after coffee and scrawling his autograph on free paper visors. He led a fairy-tale life in his column, meeting stars of stage and screen, eating meals with them, and even dancing once with Rita Hayworth, and he shared these wonderful moments with us through "The Olson Younger Column." The bad part was that I had to wear fundamentalist clothes to the Fair, white rayon shirt, black pants, black shoes, narrow tie, because we had to sing in the evening at the Harbor Light gospel tent near the Midway gate. We sang "Earnestly, tenderly, Jesus is calling, calling for you and for me," and fifty feet away a man said,

"Yes, she is absolutely naked as the day she was born, and she's inside, twenty-five cents, two bits, the fourth part of a dollar." I held the hymnbook high so nobody would see me. I wanted to be cool and wear a T-shirt. In the pioneer days before polyester, a rayon shirt was like wearing waxed paper.

When the service was over, we got one ride on the ferris wheel, rising up over the bright lights into the dark night toward the stars, and falling back into our real lives. On the long ride home I slept, and when I woke up I was in a classroom that smelled of floor wax; Mrs. Mortenson was asking me to explain the Smoot-Hawley Act.

In 1955 my uncle Earl saw an ad for the $2,000 Minnesota State Fair Cake Baking Sweepstakes, sponsored by Peter Pan Flour, and he entered my aunt Myrna. He didn't mention this to her because he didn't want to upset her. She was a nervous person, easily startled by a sudden hello, and he was right, she made the greatest chocolate angel-food cake on the face of the earth. (To call it devil's food would give Satan encouragement so we didn't.) She also kept the cleanest kitchen in the Christian world. I liked to walk in, say hello, and when she recovered, she sat me down and fed me chocolate angel-food cake. As I ate it, she hovered overhead and apologized for it.

"*Oh,*" she sighed. "I don't know. I ought to throw this out for the dog. It's not very good. I don't know where my mind was—I lost track of how many eggs I put in, and I was all out of the kind of brown sugar I always use." I looked up at her in a trance, confused by the pure transcendent beauty of it, and she cut me a second, larger piece. "My mother was the one who could make a chocolate cake," she said, and then she allowed herself one taste of cake. And frowned. "It's gummy," she said. "It's like pudding."

"No," I said. "It's the best chocolate cake I ever tasted."

"Oh," she said, "your mother makes cake just as good as that."

Once my mother heard that and smiled at me, hopefully, but all my life I've tried to tell the truth, and I replied honestly, "Sometimes she does, but not often."

Aunt Myrna was one of the few truly slender women in town. She set an impossible standard for the others. "She's small-boned," they said, but the truth is that she was so critical of her cooking, which was head and shoulders above everyone else's, that food didn't satisfy her. She was supernatural that way, like an angel. Angels who visit earth don't feed on corn dogs and pizza. Heavenly creatures have low metabolism; a little bite of something perfect is more than enough. Like her cake. An angel visiting Minnesota to do research on sweet corn could go for a week on one thin sliver of Aunt Myrna's chocolate cake.

When, in early August, Uncle Earl got an invitation from the Peter Pan Flour people, none of us was surprised she was chosen, she was so good. She was mad at him when he broke the news; she said, "I can't bake in front of a hundred people. Stand up and make a cake and have them stare at me like I was some kind of carnival freak. I won't do it."

He considered that for a minute. "I was thinking of it," he said, "as an opportunity to witness for the Lord. If you win the bake-off, I'm certain that you get to make a speech. You could give that Scripture recipe, 'Take four cups of 1 Corinthians 13 and three cups of Ephesians 4:32, four quarts of Hebrews 11:1. . . . ' "

"I don't know if I would be up to it. . . . "

"I can do all things through Christ which strengtheneth me. Philippians 4:13."

She practiced for two weeks and baked about forty cakes, most of them barely edible. She was experimenting with strange ingredients, like maple syrup and peanut butter, marshmallows, cherry bits. 'You can't just stand up in front of a crowd and bake an ordinary chocolate cake,' she said, but we convinced her that hers was good enough. She baked two of them that Friday, both champs. On the big Saturday she packed her ingredients, cake pans, mixer, and utensils in a cardboard box and covered it with a cloth, and they drove to the Cities, stopping on account of car trouble in Anoka and transferring from the Dodge to the bus. The bake-off was at three o'clock.

They arrived at two-thirty. She had assumed the bake-off was in the Home Activities building and then she discovered it was here at the grandstand. Peter Pan Flour had gone all out. The bake-off was part of the afternoon grandstand program, which also included high-wire acts, a big band playing Glenn Miller tunes, and Siberian tigers jumping through hoops of fire. She and twelve other women would stand on stage and bake cakes, and while the cakes were in the oven, Joey Chitwood's Thrill Show would perform daredevil stunts on the dirt track, and Olson Younger the newspaper columnist would judge the contest and award the prize. We helped Aunt Myrna to the stage. She was weak and moist. "Good luck," we said.

I stand here and look up at the grandstand and can see how nervous she must've been. I remember sitting up there in the forty-ninth row, under the pavilion, looking down at my tiny aunt in the green dress to the left of the saxophones while Joey Chitwood's Thrill Show drivers did flips and rolls, roaring around in white Fords. She stood at a long table whipping mix in a silver bowl, my aunt Myrna making a cake. She was mine, my relative, and I was so proud.

And then the cakes came out of the oven. The State Fair orchestra put down their newspapers and picked up their horns and played something from opera, and the radio-announcer emcee said that now the moment had come, and Olson Younger pranced around. He wore a green suit and orange tie and he waved to us with both hands. It was his moment of glory, and he sashayed from one entrant to the next, kissing her, rolling his eyes, and tasting her cake. When he tasted Myrna's cake, she shrank back from his embrace. She said a few words to him and I knew she was saying, "I don't know. I just can't seem to make 'em as rich as I used to—this isn't very good at all. It's gummy." It was the greatest chocolate cake in the world but he believed her. So she came in tenth.

A woman in white pedal pushers won because, Younger said, her cake was richer and moister. He had a hard time getting the words out. You could see the grease stains from her cake, beads of grease glittered in the sun. Uncle Earl said, "That's not cake, that's pudding he gave a prize to. This is a pudding contest he's running. He wouldn't know chocolate cake if it came up and ate him." And he was right. When Younger waltzed over to give Aunt Myrna her prize, a bowl, you could see he didn't know which way was north. It wasn't fair. She was the best. We waited for her in front of the grandstand. We both felt bad.

But when we saw her coming, she was all smiles. She hugged us both. She hardly seemed like herself. She threw her head back and said, "Oh, I'm glad it's over. But it was fun. I was so scared. And then I just forgot to be."

"But it wasn't fair," I said. She said, "Oh, he was drunk. It was all whiskey cake to him. But it doesn't matter. It was so much fun." I never saw her so lighthearted and girlish.

That night an old man came forward at the Harbor Light gospel meeting. He was confused and may have been looking for the way out, but we latched onto him and prayed for him. When he left, he seemed relieved. He was our first convert and we were thrilled. A soul hanging in the balance, there in our tent. Heaven and hell his choice, and he chose heaven, with our help, and then Dad lent him busfare.

That night, I said to my mother, "This is the last time I wear a rayon shirt, I hate them." She said, "All right, that's fine." I said, "You're not mad?" She said, "No, I thought you liked them, that's all."

I went up in the ferris wheel for a last ride before being thrown into seventh grade. It went up into the stars and fell back to earth and rose again, and I had a magnificent vision, or think I did, though it's hard to remember if it was that year with the chocolate cake or the next one with the pigs getting loose. The ferris wheel is the same year after year. It's like all one ride to me: we go up and I think of people I knew who are dead and I smell fall in the air, manure, corn dogs, and we drop down into blazing light and blaring music. Every summer I'm a little bigger, but riding the ferris wheel, I feel the same as ever, I feel eternal. The combination of cotton candy, corn dogs, diesel smoke, and sawdust, in a hot dark summer night, it never changes, not an inch. The wheel carries us up high, high, high, and stops, and we sit swaying, creaking, in the dark, on the verge of death. You can see death from here. The wind blows from the northwest, from the farm school in Saint Anthony Park, a chilly wind with traces of pigs and sheep in it. This is my vision: little kids holding on to their daddy's hand, and he is me. He looks down on them with love and buys them another corn dog. They are worried they will lose him; they hang on to his leg with one hand, eat with the other. This vision is unbearably wonderful. Then the wheel brings me down to the ground. We get off and other people get on. Thank you, dear God, for this good life and forgive us if we do not love it enough.

Dear John Deere

Mark Vinz

He lived with his mother on a quiet residential street in the south side of the city. They had a nice little house with two plum trees and a front porch glider, but they didn't have a car. Every other house on the block had a car parked in its driveway or garage, but they didn't even have a driveway, much less a garage.

"Buses will get us where we need to go," his mother said. "And if I really need one, we can always call a cab. We can't afford a car — you know that, John, since your father went away."

His father died and he was big enough to know all about that, so why did she keep saying his father "went away"? It was just like not having a car, just like having to ride in cabs. He hated them because they always smelled funny inside and were dirty and dented. He knew that cab drivers really didn't care about their cars, either — they were just the place they worked, like his mother worked at Mercy Hospital and didn't really care about her job very much. But he couldn't really blame her, since Mercy Hospital looked a bit like a cab — old and dirty on the outside, and the smells on the inside were so bad that he didn't even want to visit her after school.

Buses were better, but they still weren't like cars. Still, he had to admire them, in spite of all the smelly black smoke and the crowds of people. Buses worked very hard, after all, just like camels, and nobody seemed to care. They just threw trash in the aisles and complained about being late. He used to sit on the corner and wave to the drivers on Route 32-A, which sometimes took him and his mother downtown. He'd study the broad front of each vehicle for some sign of recognition because ever since he was small he believed that buses had faces—wide, sad faces that knew all the pain of the world. But they never seemed to look back at him, as if they were just too tired, too busy. Cars were different, though. In their faces he could see many things, and it didn't seem to matter who was driving them.

Once when he was in fourth grade he wrote a composition about the faces of different cars, and his teacher, Miss Morton, who was old and tired and whose face looked a little bit like the buses on Route 32-A, got very upset with him. She even sent a note home to his mother, who got angry because she thought it was just another way to make her feel bad that they couldn't afford a car. "The boy is a hopeless daydreamer," she said—or rather her note said, as his mother read it aloud at the kitchen table. "This fantasy he has about machines is not very healthy at all." He wasn't sure what her use of the word "fantasy" meant, but he did understand "machine." He had a hard time thinking that a car was just a machine like a cement mixer or a TV set.

After the note, his mother took him to the library and made him check out books on famous people—mostly presidents and scientists—and Miss Morton brought him books from the school library like *Black Beauty* and *Lad, a Dog,* and then she made him do book reports. They were pretty good books to read, but there was a lot he couldn't understand about animals. And he really didn't like the books his mother got him, especially not the one on Herbert Hoover. He fell asleep every time he tried to read it.

The summer he was going into sixth grade his mother got very sick and he guessed it was probably something she picked up at Mercy Hospital. Her sister, Aunt Mildred, didn't live very far away, so she came to stay with them. She didn't have a car either, only an old yellow bicycle which she chained up to one of the plum trees in the front yard. One night when he couldn't sleep, he heard the two of them talking about his uncle Stan, who was his father's brother he hadn't seen in a very long time, and who lived on a farm somewhere up in North Dakota.

"That boy is going to be the death of you yet," his aunt Mildred said, and his mother was crying. "He's just not right." That's all Aunt Mildred kept saying, over and over, except for one other thing, which was, "Why not ship him off to Stanley's for the summer? A couple of months on the farm is just what he needs. Lord knows, you and I are in no shape to take care of that kid." When she said that, he knew she'd been drinking whiskey from the quart bottle she kept in the fridge, and pretty soon his mother would be drinking whiskey too, and pretty soon he knew he would be on a train to visit his uncle Stan on the farm.

From the train windows he watched the flat and endless fields go by, and every so often he saw some kind of machine at work. Some of them looked like cars, but others looked like dinosaurs with huge clanking bodies and long, long necks. He fell asleep dreaming of farm machines lumbering in a heavy dance in the fields, and when he awoke at the station in Grand Forks he half expected his uncle Stan to come for him on one of those machines. But it was only a battered GMC pickup whose face looked very much like that of a bus.

Except for a new tractor, Uncle Stan didn't have farm machines like the ones he'd seen from the train—partly because he didn't have any animals except for a few chickens, and partly because it wasn't quite time yet for the harvest. Then there would be plenty of those machines—mostly combines, as he was told—when the harvest crews came through to cut his uncle's wheat. In the meantime, Uncle Stan took him and his cousin, Stanley Junior (who was going into high school and liked to be called "Butch"), into town the next morning, to the farm implement place, to teach him all of the names—not just names like combine and baler and cornpicker, but others, strange and interesting, like Allis Chalmers and Massey-Ferguson. Even though it had been raining that morning, he spent a long time walking through the muddy implement lot, patting the machines on their wet and shiny flanks, and repeating the names to himself again and again. Stan and Butch didn't seem to mind at all. They were tall and rawboned and almost black from the sun on their arms and necks, and they smiled and called him "city cousin," and they all laughed a lot and told some jokes about Norskies and Krauts and went home to eat a huge "dinner" of baked ham and corn on the cob, even though it was only about noon.

They kept him busy on the farm doing all kinds of chores, which was a word he'd seen only in books. When he was home with his mother, he did "jobs," which amounted to just about the same thing, except that on the farm there were a lot more of them. As a kind of reward for helping out, his cousin Butch began to teach him how to drive the pickup, after supper each evening—first by simply setting the throttle and letting him steer the truck across an open stretch of yard, and then through all the intricacies of clutch and gears, out on the endless, dusty country roads. Each night he would write a few lines to his mother, mostly about Butch and the driving, and each morning before breakfast he would walk the half mile or so to the big bluff at the edge of his uncle's property and sit awhile with the old steam threshing machine that watched the farm like a kind of sentinel. Uncle Stan had told him that the thresher hadn't been run in several years and would probably never run again, but was his father's so he kept it on the hill as a kind of souvenir—a "reminder" of what it was like long ago. It was a mysterious contraption, faded and rusty, and from a distance it looked like a giant grasshopper. The hill was the most special place on the farm, and even though Aunt Ruth sometimes got irritated when he was late for breakfast, all Uncle Stan ever said was "Leave the boy alone" and "We'll make a farmer of him yet." He wasn't so sure he wanted to be a farmer, but this was certainly better than watching the buses on Route 32-A, even if Uncle Stan didn't have a car either. He thought about that a lot, and for some reason he started picking garlands of wildflowers and draping them across the thresher's long neck. Once, though he certainly knew better, he left some sandwiches and a pan of water in the shade under the machine's front end. The next morning they were gone, which didn't really surprise him at all.

It was then that he stopped visiting the hill, because Butch showed him what was in the old shed behind the grain bins—"another old relic" is what Butch called it, a faded green tractor which, though still in good working order, hadn't been used in some time, not since Uncle Stan had bought the new red International Harvester tractor, which was huge in comparison. But he didn't like the new tractor very much, even though it was fun to sit with Uncle Stan in the air-conditioned cab. It was too much like a bus—sad and distant, even though it was still quite shiny. But the old tractor was something very different, and he could just make out the lettering in the dim light of the shed—John Deere, it said, which was his name and the name of a marvelous leaping animal he had never even seen. John Deere. Now he had something else to dream about every night, and after supper and a lot of coaxing, Butch began to teach him all about the machine—how to put in gas and oil, how to start it up and work the gears, and even how they repacked the wheel bearings.

Best of all was John Deere's face—not like International Harvester's, which was somehow too proud and strong. John Deere's face was kind and tired, in a way very different from any of the other faces he had ever seen. It was a special face that knew a lot of important things, and even Uncle Stan talked about how John Deere had been a special helper.

"Remember when we took the doc through the mud to Mrs. Kite's when the roads got washed out?" Uncle Stan had asked Butch at dinner. "I didn't think we'd ever make it through."

Butch just smiled and went on smashing down his boiled potatoes.

"Maybe that's why I keep it in the shed," said Uncle Stan. "It's like an old horse. Some day, I suppose, we'll have to park it up on the hill next to that old thresher. That's where it probably belongs. There, or in some museum." Uncle Stan laughed, and Butch laughed, scooping gravy onto the pile of potatoes on his plate.

"If you want to be a farmer," Uncle Stan said, "then you've got to have the best equipment. That's one thing a farmer's got to learn."

"Like plowing," Butch said. "Riding on that old beater all day, you'd have to come in and dig the topsoil out of your eyes with a toothpick."

But it wasn't the time for plowing now; it was the time for harvesting. The wheat was ripening quickly and Uncle Stan told him that soon enough the combine crews would arrive. Already they had started work on other farms in the township to the north and west, and once they came there would be no stopping them until all the fields were harvested and all the grain was either hauled off to the elevator in town or stored in the metal bins that lined the far side of the yard. "It should be real exciting for you," Uncle Stan said. "You'll even get to help Butch shovel wheat in the boxes of those big trucks."

Uncle Stan and Butch seemed to get busier each day, and sometimes they came in so late he was already asleep. That was when he started waking up in the night and sneaking out to the shed to be with John Deere, and one morning when he fell asleep in the shed and didn't wake up in time to get back to his bed, Aunt Ruth found him curled up next to John Deere on a pile of old sacks. She seemed very upset, and he knew that she would call his mother that evening, just as soon as the long-distance rates changed.

That morning it had rained hard, but by early afternoon the clouds had begun to lift and there was only a thin drizzle. Uncle Stan and Butch had gone into town for some parts and groceries, and Aunt Ruth was doing chores somewhere in the house — sewing, probably, or cleaning up the dinner dishes. It didn't take him long to sneak up to his room, put some clean clothes into his knapsack, fill a Thermos with lemonade, and spread some peanut butter on two slabs of Aunt Ruth's bread. By the time he got to the shed, the sun was beginning to break through the clouds, and he knew there wouldn't be much time. John Deere came to life, cranky and stiff, but anxious to get out of the shed. The gears worked perfectly, just like Butch showed him, and he even remembered to tie on an extra five-gallon can of gas and a couple of quarts of oil. International Harvester would probably never miss them.

"Dear John Deere," he said as the old tractor lurched into the yard. Aunt Ruth didn't even come out to the porch; she was probably on the phone. "Dear John Deere," the clattering engine seemed to say, and its exhaust bounced the little metal flap on the pipe in front of him. He bumped along the muddy driveway ruts and then beneath him was the flat gravel of the country road. When he came to the stop sign at the intersection—the old yellow one that was full of rusted bullet holes—he turned onto the road he guessed was heading north. Even the drizzle was letting up now, and somewhere ahead of him, lay the border of Canada, the fields of ripe grain where there would be combines, and soon the vast and starry dark.

Corn Village

Meridel LeSueur
St. Paul, 1930

Like many Americans, I will never recover from my sparse childhood in Kansas. The blackness, weight and terror of childhood in mid-America strike deep into the stem of life. Like desert flowers we learned to crouch near the earth, fearful that we would die before the rains, cunning, waiting the season of good growth. Those who survived without psychic mutilation have a life cunning, to keep the stem tight and spare, withholding the deep blossom, letting it sour rather than bloom and be blighted.

Looking for nourishment, we saw the dreary villages, the frail wooden houses, the prairies ravished, everything impermanent as if it were not meant to last the span of one man's life, a husk through which human life poured, leaving nothing behind, not even memory, and every man going a lonely way in a kind of void, all shouting to each other and unheard, all frightfully alone and solitary.

And fear, fear everywhere on the streets in the gray winter of the land, and the curious death in the air, the bright surface activity of the pioneer town and the curious air-dissipating powers of fear and hate.

The Middle West is all so familiar to me and yet it is always unfamiliar, a dream, an unreality. There are Kansas, Iowa, Illinois, Nebraska. They were for a long time frontier States. There villages are yet the waste and ashes of pioneering, and the people too waste and ash, with the inner fire left out. There is still the pioneer tension as if something was still to be done, something conquered, something overcome, and there is no longer anything to conquer and no longer an enemy. I have walked around the streets of many small towns in Kansas. I have travelled over the country looking and looking. I lived my impressionable years in a Kansas corn village. In my youth as now I was looking for sustenance. I was looking for something to live on. I was trying to grow, to come alive.

In the mid-center of America a man can go blank for a long, long time. There is no community to give him life; so he can go lost as if he were in a jungle. No one will pay any attention. He can simply be as lost as if he had gone into the heart of an empty continent. A sensitive child can be lost too amidst all the emptiness and ghostliness.

I am filled with terror when I think of the emptiness and ghostliness of mid-America. The rigors of conquest have made us spiritually insulated against human values. No fund of instinct and experience has been accumulated, and each generation seems to be more impoverished than the last.

Look at the face of the Middle Westerner and you know he has been nourished in a poor soil without one day of good growing weather.

Yet there is the land abundant, in seasons. I have looked and looked at the land. The symbols of this country are winter, the departure of the year, the "death of all sweet things." It is the symbol of man's foreboding and his birth and his death. Life is not embodied. It is either just dying or being born. Who can tell? All our Americans have had this anxiety of life at the low ebb. I had it in my youth and still have it, a sickening anxiety like a disease, and all in that small town where I lived had it. It was limned on their faces like the ravages of some plague, some mysterious unmentioned disease of which we were all suffering. The sun leaving the earth and a terrible insecurity at the bottom of every man's soul, fears, dangers, hardships known and unknown as if one were never going to live to maturity, the days so tenuous in substance, a sheer fabric of horror and the town falling to pieces with its rotten wooden houses, and the gray shredded faces, and the place a horror, out of the world, doomed. I could not bear to get up in the morning after the winter solstice, as if some malignant power were in the air, the dim, dim faces, the blank interior of the continent, the winter madness coming on, the winter death, the sun leaving the great dark continent, the black, cold prairies, the shocks of corn desolate in the fields, the earth upturned in the cold sunlight, the smell of loam, the dark fields jagged and turned to the cold, the cattle wading through the black frozen mud and the wild embodied wind of the prairies like a presence among the fields.

The terrifying beauty too of the plains, the black stiff trees shadowless, the soft shadowless ice-world curving beneath the shadowless sky. Boys tracking down the valley, gophers hanging from their belts, gopher tails from their stocking caps. Men swathed in woollens watching the east-bound train. A hunter coming into the village, a rabbit hanging from his arm, the blood dropping from its eyes. The farm houses silent in the gullies, in the low curve of plain. The horses in the frozen corn. The smoke of the little brush trees in a mist of frost. The white earth sloping and still, the leaden sky, all things closed, no vista, no shaking out, no revelation. Where has life gone that there is no fire and no shadow?

I was born on these prairies while the land was lying low in this mid-winter solstice, lying low like this and dreaming. It curves now in low, long swells lying stark in the blue frost, so strong, so spare. Men come out of the wooden houses. I see their naked red arms, their hulking shoulders, their stubborn stocky heads. They run from the house to the barn, ducking their heads against the wind. These meaty men live in this delicate world, their bloody lives, and are looked upon by the rabbit, the prairie dog, and once the deer.

What does an American think about the land, what dreams come from the sight of it, what painful dreaming? Are they only money dreams, power dreams? Is that why the land lies desolate like a loved woman who has been forgotten? Has she been misused through dreams of power and conquest?

Anyhow the awful imprecations of the land lie heavily on the guilty white spirit. Remember the sadness and innate depression of Lincoln as symbolic. He was naturally a lover, but he never loved the land, though he walked miles over it, slept and lived on it, and buried the bodies of those he loved in it; and yet he was never struck with that poetry and passion that makes a man secure upon his land, there was always instead this convulsion of anxiety, this fear.

One night, in late fall, driving back from the country our car stalled. The low dusk had come down over the prairies deepening and deepening around us like water and it was rather frightening too, because the distances became illusive and that strange emptiness and fear that no one admits were in the air. We were stalled in the road in front of the Simonsons' and, sensing our nearness, the Mrs. stood in the door and he came swinging his long frame through the dusk down the lane to us. Their house was a wooden one, shambling, behind a windbreak of trees, and the barns were better than the house and the stock better than the people.

"Hello," he called, and his voice sounded far away as if it echoed and was lost in the hollowness of the prairies.

"And John," his wife called and we could not see her, "you'd better not go out without your coat." In that voice of the Yankee woman nagging her men.

Simonson came up to us and we saw his face and his tall Yankee body, the angular disjointed body Lincoln had.

"What's the matter? Stalled?" he said grinning, but he encompassed us with no warmth. He was simply curious and looked at us from a distance. I looked at his emaciated body with its hint of sickness like a stubborn, sturdy, thwarted tree, yet with a certain tenderness in it too. I remembered Lincoln's body, looking at Simonson; and again the old mystery presented itself in the underworld dusk of the phantom prairie world, the mystery of the slim, tenuous Yankee body, hard and gawky like a boy's, never getting any man suavity in it, but hard and bitter and stubborn, always lanky and ill-nourished, surviving bitterly.

"Well," he said, suddenly gentle and impersonal, "that's too bad." And there was really a sad gentleness about him, so that I couldn't help liking him despite the acrid, bitter odor of the body, the slight warped sparseness of it that repelled, and yet the gawky tenderness. Lincoln too had this — the loose frame, the slight droop, the acrid, bitter power and tenuosity, the sense of hanging on in bad seasons, of despondency from lack of nourishment, that well-known Yankee form and the mystery of it, the strong, deep, lanky chest, so powerful but so with-drawn and gnarled, and the sudden tenacious sentimental sympathies, that would start wars for quixotic idealisms, provoke assassins' bullets and leave a wife embittered and maddened a little, left out always, never wholly warmed at that breast, the flesh never really warm and hanging from the tree of life, always a little acrid and ghostly, and the tenderness not enough to warm. And the anxiety always cooling the blood, making it spectral, the Yankee anxiety about something that leaves its mark on the face, on the skeleton, in the blood.

"Well," he said, scratching his ear and looking at us from his long, sorrowful face, "you better come in, hadn't you? You can come in if you want to. . . . " The far, desolate slopes of the prairie were now invisible and the chill came down around us on the black land. Simon-son began to talk to us as we walked over the black land and the hori-zon swung in its wide circle around us, and he went on talking in that sepulchral voice, as if he were the only man in the world, a far, lone man at an outpost, just waiting to move on, to move back, to move. There was his familiarity, his heartiness and the insensitive body, and his will set on not caring, not thinking, not attending to life at all but just to tramp blankly on from minute to minute in a vacuum.

We went toward the tumbling building so temporary and lost. There were no stars now the darkness had come, no North star, no guide, and Simonson talking in a void, the last man on the frontier, a far, lone man at an outpost, waiting to move on, to move back, to move. . . .

We rarely went out of the town alone. In groups we sometimes went to some known place for picnics, usually where a stream made the prairies more gracious. But usually we went walking only a little way out of the town, as if we were besieged, surrounded by some mysterious forces. I remember feeling frightened at first stepping out of the close town onto the prairie, so wide with the wide sky opening away. . . . But I did not go out often alone.

There was an Irish family I knew who lived out a few miles from town. They were lazy and enjoyed themselves, and were considered somehow immoral by the townspeople. All the foreigners in the town were isolated by their gaiety, the festivals, easy love and birth. They were always attractive to me. The foreign girl prostitutes, the great Polish woman who kept a "house," where the college boys went and whose name we were forbidden to speak. I liked her body, so rich and loose, and her broad-hipped lazy walk. The acrid Yankee body is a hard thing to live with, always ungiven, held taut for some unknown fray with the devil or the world or the flesh. These illicit women, so menacing, were the only ones at that time who could wear bright colors.

This Irish family, Irish and goaty, came to town on Saturday, and I liked to ride out with them. They had large earthy, loose faces. We rode in a wagon through the hard, tight Kansas cold, the ruts frozen so hard our teeth rattled — no snow, just the frozen bald earth and the black scrub trees. The house was a little white house sitting on the top slope of the prairie. It was dirty and derelict. The inside would be cold and we would be cold, our hands and legs chapped and raw. Out of every window we could see the desolate cold prairie and the wind over it, the frozen stiff corn in the fields. At last there would be a fire in the stove, the lamps would be lighted. There was no evidence of any one living in the house; there were chairs, beds, adequate things, but it was like a camp, no idols, no tokens of intimate life. And then Mrs. Kelly would fry the thick fat pork and cook the potatoes in their jackets, and then we would eat in the lamplight, grinning at each other in that wild, wild way they had, and making jokes, prodding each other slyly and eating the rich pork and gravy, too rich and porky, no wine, no grace, just the greasy, porky meal with the raucous plain lopping outside to the dismal horizon and this sly human grinning at each other, the sly grin of the Irish goaty faces, bewildered too but chewing a good cud of life somehow that they had brought with them over a black sea.

I am baffled to know the meaning of people in the mid-West towns. Lewis has not been right. He has portrayed their grimaces, a seeming reality, but still only their faces in a mirror. Anderson of course has apprehended them with love, but that too has left out a great deal.

I was hungering then, a-hunger and a-thirst. So were others. The whole communal organism suffered perhaps. One individual is only an articulated sensitive point for the great herd suffering. I went about the streets looking and looking, and what I saw seemed to be without pith or meaning, dark and spectral. And every one peering through the strange air of a new continent perhaps saw the same thing, the outward busy, strenuous life and the pithless core, the black abyss. . . . Perhaps it is inevitable that in a new country communication must be muffled and silent, that there is just a babbling on the surface, a genial, meaningless babbling, and that the real reciprocation must be in silence. Frontiersmen have put themselves aside.

So the only time the reality is revealed, the terrible surface torn aside, is after some violence. Violence somehow stirs up the deadly becalmed surface, breaks open the body. There was always excitement in cyclones, — the darkness, the wind from another world, the delicious terror as if at last something would be expounded, — even death, a real death, — and then the great genii appearing on the becalmed horizon, approaching the marooned town, so that everything started to a kind of horrific reality, impressing its life through the ghostly maze — a hand lifted in terror, widened eyes, people running, screaming, embracing each other, waking from a dream, as if from a long, terrible journey, and the excitement afterward, the eye still widened, the hand uplifted, the heart accelerated, the streets swarming, trees felled, houses upended, graves revealed, bones upturned, bones of Indians, the bones of French, Spanish, those who had been dead long in the land. The talk for days, — "It took all the buttons off Sam Marvis' coat. Can you beat that? Yes, sir, he laid down in the field and the goldarned thing ripped the buttons off his coat. . . . " A visitation from a pagan world it was. But gradually the excitement would wear away, the strong cotton insulation of emotion would muffle it.

You look and look and you cannot see life anywhere apparent, only in bitterness, and sparseness sold out for that neat, hygienic and sterile success that we all must have. There are whispers that so and so is doing this or that, but violence must erupt the awful lethargy, the fading away of the soul.

Once on Saturday when the town was crowded with farmers, and their wives were marketing in the thick black mud, a man shot a woman on Main Street. The woman was a young woman with gold hair, legendary as she lay dead, and she was standing looking into

Stevens' Millinery Shop at a hat she probably coveted very much. And suddenly this man, her lover, jealous over a small thing, ran down the street brandishing a gun. Every one on the street stopped, a man fixing the bridle of his horse, a woman with an orange in her hand; and the distraught man stopped, took aim, and shot his sweetheart straight through the heart. She crumpled up, still looking at the hat, without a sound, and then while the man still stood with the bridle and the woman with the orange uplifted, he turned the gun upon himself and shot himself straight through the temple and fell in the street. For a moment no one moved. Every one stood as if bewitched. Something had happened. There it stood on Main Street, an ancient Thing. Then there was an eddying and rapid movement like dammed water let loose and the torrent broke in every breast—the townspeople broke in around the two and looked upon them in their own blood. The whole town was submerged by this torrent then. It broke in every breast and bound us all together. We turned like somnambulists looking at each other at last, not as ghosts distant and distraught, but now bound together alive, knowing ourselves alive.

There was something about it like a purging. A woman comes across the road to borrow some baking powder, and there is tenderness in her as she clicks her tongue, "The poor young things, . . . " and something in the female blood wakens to think of love being like that.

And the men gather at the street corners and talk, and the close, dark knot of human form is woven close together—they no longer straggle, stand unwoven, apart, they stand close together, welded together in the lines of their bodies, their heads leaning close, for one of their kind has felt something and let it ripen and come to expression.

The town is woven in this lovely dream. The children, round-eyed, whisper together. The women gather. The men gather. Men and women draw closer to each other in the night. Love awakens in the town. Every one is drawn into the great warp of myth.

The whole village files into the church passing the two coffins where the two lovers lie together now. Something has been said now for the whole town. It's an expurgation, a catharsis. Women embrace each other and weep for their own sorrows. Men are hearty and gentle, meeting each other on the street, and for a moment looking through the mist, apprehending each other.

The day of the joint funeral is a holiday. The air is rich with meaning, the streets look no longer harried and idiotic. They have meaning now, the black houses have meaning, the church, the steeple, the railroad station. These are now places where the human scene is enacted, where there might be great feelings, shedding of the blood even. The sun pours down and it is good to be a man and a woman. Something has happened. May it never be forgotten!

But it is forgotten. The lethargy looms again, everything closes up, the streets are as they were before, and men become again only traders, movers, buyers, sellers, farmers.

Another violence—the revival. The evangelist would be a strange man, often handsome. The young girls would stand in a bright group, twittering as he came into town, shying off yet eyeing him and he them. The boys would watch him going down Main Street. The matrons asked him to their tables. There were dreams of him in the night. Even my grandmother got excited. The opening night of the revival there was always something special on our table, the dinner was a little better, there was the hint of rite and symbol.

I never saw her so excited as upon these nights of revival, so happy, so contented. She was like an actress on her opening night. She put on her best dress. She was affectionate even, and my grandmother never kissed us. She was embarrassed by any excess of feeling and had a way of turning down her lips bitterly. She had that acrid, bitter thing too about her body, a kind of sourness as if she had abandoned it. It was like an abandoned thing; perhaps it had not been occupied. The Puritans used the body like the land as a commodity, and the land and the body resent it. She never took a bath except under her shift. Hearing her move about her room alone I always wondered what she was doing, so bodyless, with that acrid odor as if she had buried her body, murdered and buried it, and it gave off this secret odor revealing the place where it lay.

Yet she was faithful in her duties, dogged in her service to those she loved, but it seemed to be a sacrifice without joy, a love without passion, and her children, like the children of every one, seemed to have been born without contact.

Pleasure of any kind was wicked, and she never lay down in the daytime even when she was dreadfully tired. It would have been a kind of licentiousness to her to have done so.

The coldness in her and severity gave her that sense of always spying on others, and she did have that passionate curiosity that comes in people marooned in any way from life by spiritual or physical illness. But religion was her theater, her dance, her wine, her song. Every night sitting bolt upright in her strong stiff body she sang these haunting hymns, picking them out in dull chords on the untuned piano. It was a long time before I knew that they were her love songs, the only ones she and others had. With a brilliant husband and four children, still she was mysteriously marooned, unliving and ghostlike without abundance or contact, without bloom in her body, without essential growth or maturity.

The evening would come down soft and sweet, and we would set out for the revival, my grandmother very stiff and self-conscious in her best silk, walking ahead, her black bible in her gloved hands, and smiling that little smirk at her neighbors as if she knew something about them. Other people would be going sedately toward the little steepled church, and the young girls, arm in arm, and the boys together standing outside the church door, the boys standing brazenly watching the girls go in. Then they would come in a gang and sit in the balcony, looking down at the girls who would be in an agony of self-consciousness.

We would all greet each other, each thinking that the other had every cause to repent, but still more cordial than at ice-cream socials. Then every one in his best clothes in the packed brilliant church, the stir of starched clothes, the smell of violet water, and the bright faces of the choir so rosy, looking for the preacher. At last he would come out, melancholy and conscious, and sit down not knowing what to do with his hands, an unknown man to them all, a stranger from another part come into the town to stir them; and they were ready to be stirred, their close, ungiven bodies ready to be mysteriously stirred by this stranger.

When I joined the church there was a red-headed Irishman who was the evangelist, a man of monstrous amorous vitality which he threw into his sermons, a great, wild vitality wonderful to behold and a silver Irish tongue too, so that he broke all the bitterness asunder, the silvery words breaking over the land-locked, corroded people. He was a fine actor, and had a fine roll to his words and a great sonorous natural cadence that added richness to our terse Yankee speech for many days after.

Then the hymns, and still the congregation, awkward, unwelded, and the wild-bucking youth in the balcony giving a feeling of something a little dangerous.

Then he rose and put back his thick hair, just a little longer than the men in the town wore theirs, and he let his great words have their way, flow over the hungry people, and they were unafraid because they were packed so closely, because it was impersonal and the great words fell like fruit upon famine, — "This is my body. . . . I have died to save you. . . . Come unto me all ye who are heavy laden and I will give you rest," — and women who had never given one whit of love to their husbands or children let tears of love spring to their eyes and wept quite unashamed, and the young girls were hushed and the giant men sat dumb, shamefaced, and the boys with their mouths frozen in a guffaw. The close-weeping pack again welded, brought together, moving close in lovely formation.

"Let us sing the hymn of invitation. Come to your Savior now. Acknowledge him, my sisters, my brothers." Oh, the weeping now! "Come to Jesus who died for love of you."

"Oh, comfort me with apples, stay me with flagons." The breaking open at last. The choir singing, oh, sweetly, wondrously: "Jesus, lover of my soul, let me to thy bosom fly. . . . " And these people without another love song, untinged by humor. The weeping women going to the altar and the men being pushed and herded and some weeping.

Afterward, leaving the bright turmoil of the church, outside the boys lined up waiting to take the girls home and the night sweeter than a nut, at last with the stars now with meaning, the town now close and beloved, broken open with love, and all the rich juices flowing out as from some ripe sweet fruit. And the girls in ecstasy and love. And all filled with awe for those who had confessed, and the newly saved silent and tearful, and every one tender with them. And the closed houses breaking open, cracking open like nuts, and the lovely faces looking out, and Jesus with his lovely face too, and the obscure, the terrible ecstasy over the town.

But the revival ends too and the stranger leaves the town. The sinners forget they have been saved. The great midcontinent vacuum swallows everything again. Everything is quiet until the corn-husking, and that means work and competition.

O Kansas, I know all your little trees. I have watched them thaw and bud and the pools of winter frozen over, the silos and the corn-blue sky, the wagon-tracked road with the prints of hoofs, going where? And the little creeks gullying with delicate grasses and animals, the prairie dog, the rabbit, and your country with its sense of ruin and desolation like a strong, raped virgin. And the mind scurrying like a rabbit trying to get into your meaning, making things up about you, trying to get you alive with significance and myth.

I have seen the spring like an idiotic lost peasant come over your prairies scattering those incredibly tiny flowers, and the frozen earth thaw to black mud, and a mist of greening come on the thickets, and the birds coming from the South, black in the sky, and farmers coming to the village through the black mud.

I have seen your beauty and your terror and your evil.

I have come from you mysteriously wounded. I have waked from my adolescence to find a wound inflicted on the deep heart. And have seen it in others too, in disabled men and sour women made ugly by ambition, mortified in the flesh and wounded in love.

Not going to Paris or Morocco or Venice, instead staying with you, trying to be in love with you, bent upon understanding you, bringing you to life. For your life is my life and your death is mine also.

The Other Houses in Eldon, Iowa

Michael Martone

Iowans like to tell you that, once, you could go anywhere in the state and still never be more than ten miles from the nearest rail line. Today you are never very far away from a corridor of ruins.

Iowa has that tended look of a train set. The buildings of the small towns and farms were prefabricated, shipped in parts, ordered from catalogues, giving the landscape a generic, standardized look. Barn. House. Windmill. Water tower. Tree, even. Assorted animals. Townspeople. The scene is in a different scale.

The Frontier swept through here and didn't slow down until it hit the grasslands and became the timeless Frontier of further west. Iowa was settled fast and now one hundred years later has begun to take itself apart. It seems as if the tracks have been rolled up. The abandoned road beds are conduits to a past this land now has, and along the route of the Rockets, the old Rock Island Railroad's Chicago to Kansas City main line, you'll see what could not be torn down, salvaged or scrapped. Old coal bunkers. Bridge piers in the Des Moines River. Mounds of rotting ties and truckless wooden box cars used as sheds.

I followed a section of that main line, driving through the toy farms of the Amish settlement near Bloomfield, then along J 15 through Floris toward Eldon in the southwest corner of Wapello County. My great-grandfather, who farmed in Kentucky and got out of it as soon as he could, constantly schemed. One of his ideas was to buy a right of way like the one I was tracing and plant potatoes, one long row of potatoes so he would only turn the team once. Schemes.

Here and there along the road the grassy dike ducked down to the grade of the road, crossing ahead of me. I rushed over the wake of embedded rail. The state is still in court arguing who should suffer the cost of removing these little sections of track. It will come down to who was at this crossing first, who crossed who. The crossings were guarded by the X signs, a punctuation etched in my mind for stopping, looking, listening. Further on there would be a signal box, its silver paint gleaming. And then a foreshortened stand of telegraph poles sprang up in a religious grouping. When I got close enough, I saw the glass insulators had been stripped from the crossbeams by speculators. It wasn't long ago there was a market for heavy amber insulators along with the Avon bottles and Depression glass of the flea markets. No more.

I crossed into Eldon on a narrow truss bridge spanning a hearty stretch of the Des Moines River. Further downstream I could see where the rails would have crossed the climbing berm. There, on that side of the river across from the town, I could make out the smudges of the yard and shop and roundhouse foundation in with the corn. The railroad was almost everything to this town. I noticed where the two broad crossing strips of grass and cinders marked the center of Eldon. Here the other main line from Des Moines met the one from Chicago. Eldon was a division point: crews were changed, cars were classified and engines were serviced. A little station still stood at the junction, but more memorable were the huge empty places that stretched away from it. There seemed to be reluctance to encroach upon the space. The bins of the elevator to the north straddled the curving spur. The houses to the east fronted a huge playing field. Even the trucks behind the stores on main street parked at contorted angles away from the widening cinder strip as if at any moment a train of hoppers would appear again or as if the ground had been sown with salt. I was going to say that the town felt gutted, but it was more like Eldon had been filleted. The bone is all out of it.

In 1930, the artist Grant Wood traveled along these same roads with a student of his, John Sharp, who was from Eldon. The story goes that Sharp wanted to show Wood a house on the town's northern edge and took him by to see it. Wood made a sketch of the house on the back of an envelope, according to what I read on the placemat at the Jones Cafe and Gothic Room. This part I question since it seems borrowed from the details surrounding Lincoln's train ride to Gettysburg, his sketch of the speech on the back of an envelope. In any case, Wood posed his sister, Nan, and his dentist, Dr. B. H. McBeeby, a pitchfork between them, in front of the house he saw on that visit. According to the placemat, he ate at the Jones Cafe. If he sat in the corner booth as I did, near the window, he would have seen the action at the junction—a panting switch engine shunting from track to track, a crowd swelling on the platforms, a semaphore signal snapping up. Eldon as a post office WPA mural, the kind Grant Wood's students rendered in towns all over Iowa. One of those students, Lee Allen, had recently finished a painting of the house. I could buy postcard reproductions of it at the Jones Cafe. A large print of the painting hung along with posters of *Stone City* and *The Birth Place of Herbert Hoover*. But it would not be the bustling social realism in front of him that caught Wood's eye that day. Instead, his painting would comment on the small town by focusing on those two severe faces and the big blank window of the white house. *American Gothic,* one of the best-known images in the world, has always been misread. Not a farmer and his wife but a father and daughter. Not a farmer at all but a small town man. You can tell that by the shirt he wears, Wood said.

The railroad was almost everything to this town. That was the evidence I gleaned from the vertical file at the town library. Under Eldon I found rotogravure articles of last train rides, articles about boxed-lunch excursions down river. And there were articles about the painting, with the house always in the background, the capstone mention of Eldon in the formula of the inverted pyramid. While I searched the files, a painter gave estimates to the librarian. The library's spacious reading room was to be renovated. The librarian told me that this would be the first major work done on the prairie-style bungalow. She didn't want the ceiling dropped, the windows closed up. But heat was expensive. The only other patrons were a mother and son reporting on the books the boy had read this week as part of a summer contest. The librarian told me the prize was a night out in Ottumwa, movies and ice cream. Her folks had been railway people, her husband a retired conductor. She showed me the model of the *Gothic* House Kenny Norris had done, a bit squat I remember, the scale not contributing to the vertical lightness of the one in the picture. I hadn't seen the real one yet. It was cool in the library, heat only a problem in the winter. The wood was old oak and polished. The etchings and tintypes of the town fathers, the ones I read about in the centennial history, blended in with Wood's painting on the dull white walls.

"She's supposed to be the man's daughter," the librarian said.

The librarian too shared that plain, upright look of the images, the real and imagined, on the walls around her. It was hard to read her, to interpret how she felt about her town now. I saw her as the last pilot of another elaborate vehicle of the nineteenth century, still steaming on Mr. Carnegie's assumptions of the future. She was friendly, helpful, but ultimately neutral on the subject of the town she served, dispensing and collecting information.

My trip through Eldon so far had been about space. In the library's airy hall, its walls hung with images of men held rigid by braces while their images burned into metal, I thought of sacred icons. Icons are screens between holy and secular spaces. They can be thought of as a kind of transmitter between the two spheres. Through the doorway of the icon, the believer returns to the time and the place of the saints. The librarian's stare, the stare of the old tintypes, and the staring faces of *American Gothic* suggested the same kind of mirror, of window. A way back to a time of communion and community. The citizens of Toledo were able to pick out their houses in the paintings of El Greco. Perhaps what sends me restlessly along these abandoned corridors in Iowa is the wistful notion that anyplace here can be that settled, settled enough to see itself as part of a continuing story. Part of a bigger picture.

The signs are hand-painted and point to the *American Gothic* House or simply *Gothic* House. The route is also marked by the whitewashing of the curbing. I turned left into a neighborhood in the town's northeast corner. Then a right. Many of the houses share the carpenter gothic frills and ornament — the endless porches, vertical siding, idiomatic out-sized window. At first I felt I was missing something as I looked at the parade of houses, some now covered in asphalt shingling, some melting into Cape Cod additions. Then it struck me. There were no foundations. The siding sprang right from the grass. The step up to the porches a board width at best. The large windows would hit me at knee level. I could step through them. Though they were old — the Gothic House is over 100 years old — the little houses with half-stories felt temporary as though they had been dragged there. Adding to this effect was the lack of shrubbery or flower beds. No foundation to screen. Only the buzzed brown lawn. At the end of the street, I took another left and crept past the town water treatment plant. A dusty red pickup with a plastic tank in the bed was backed in to the building. The farmer was filling the tank, buying town water, while his kids ran ahead of me around the bend to the left to play in the cage of Eldon's tennis court. Wells were running dry that summer. The kids would exhaust themselves soon but find no shade in the broiling field I parked in.

Across the street the *American Gothic* House looked like its picture. In the bright sun even the shadows, cut beneath the porch roof and cast by the lip of the famous window sill, seemed generated by technique, the siding stained a permanent dark gray hue. The potted plants by the door were gone. A plaque commemorating the 50th anniversary of the painting and of the house being placed on the National Historic Registry was now attached to the front wall. The chimney had been capped, but that wasn't in the picture so it was hard to tell what was authentic. On the flat brown lawn, halfway to the quiet white house, two headless cut-out figures cast long shadows up to the porch. The palette used to paint them was too bright; no attempt had been made to shade the wrinkles in the overalls. The perspective is about right, though placing the figures in the road itself would have been closer still to the exact dimension. The heads had been removed at the collars, the elongated style of the original helping the amputation. The bodies were to the proper human scale. Below the waists the artist was on his own and it showed. The hemline was wrong, and the shoes were too big and splayed out. I couldn't imagine actually having a picture taken this way although the graceful yoke of the collars beckoned. The house had a power in its whiteness, its stark cleanness of line. That power radiated. The whole lot was empty, cleared except for the cut-outs. I wouldn't have been able to cross the road and step onto the property even if I had been with someone to take my picture in the pillory of the scene.

People still lived in the house. Wood told his sister, Nan, as she modeled the part of the spinster daughter, that he wanted to show the kind of people he thought lived there. He didn't want to disturb the real residents. Turns out Gideon and Mary Jones, grandparents of the owner of the Jones Cafe, lived in the house when Wood sketched it. Today the Hayneses, Kelly and Kelly, their two kids, her mother and a niece live in the house surviving on welfare and disability checks. The rent is $50 a month, paid to Carl Smith of Cleveland, who owns the place. When he dies, the house will be inherited by the state. The figures on the lawn were a compromise struck between the Hayneses and the people of Eldon who want immediately to turn the house into a tourist attraction. The few tourists who find their way here can snap the pictures but the cut-outs served as scarecrows too. There were no tours of the house itself, but the space of the front lawn, the rendered public domain of the picture, no longer survives as private property. So this arrangement is part and parcel of the uneasy peace of this neighborhood, a tussle over borders and the waiting for a man in Cleveland to die. Everything shimmered the afternoon I stood and looked at the house. The light was almost Mediterranean. The heat made me sleepy. The house seemed to pulsate, dropped from the heavens on a freshly cleared landing zone. Staring at the house across the road, I thought it too might be as flat as the headless figures propped in front of it. The electric blue sky became a matte, edging the iconographic outline of the house. If I looked hard enough I would be able to see through the window, see the depthlessness of the structure, see the sky on the other side.

It is a curious business, this seeing. So many small towns in Iowa seeking to diversify have fixed upon the idea of having people come see. The state estimates the cost of turning this house into a sight at

$500,000, what with the renovations inside the house, the gift shop barn, the landscaping around the sludge lagoon, and the relocation of the Hayneses. A lot of people will have to find their way to Eldon and pay to look at the house in order to recover the investment and then generate new income equal to the lost railroad payroll, the vanishing farm money. But still the scheme that will bring money in persists. The Jones Cafe, the only restaurant in town, acts as the locus of the tourist dream. There too you can buy the postcards and prints of Lee Allen's painting.

The Window: The House 57 Years Later is a picture about looking. In the WPA style, Allen pays homage to his teacher. The house has been rotated slightly. We see it over the shoulder of another couple, an older man and woman dressed simply. The man is taking a picture of the house. The woman is looking at a picture of *American Gothic*, just about to look up and away from it to the house, judging the fidelity of the painting to the house and the house to the painting as we are judging the likeness she is holding to the original in our minds. To the right, a young boy straddles his archetypal cantilever bicycle — one foot on a pedal, the other on the ground — ducks his head, looks between the couple and the house, catching both in his peripheral vision. He can even see, out of the corner of his eye, the point of view of the painter, us. We take in the intense couple, the boy on the bike, and the two racing boys tearing up the road looking only at each other, gauging who is winning .

I am attracted to the timelessness of the scene, and I understand how compelling a timeless place can be. There are few of the precious places where things haven't changed, fewer still that have been doubly blessed, recorded by art's certifying glance. I remember coming upon the Sanitary Bakery on Bleecker Street in New York, amazed it survived pretty much unchanged from the Berenice Abbott photograph from the 30's. I knew the picture before the place. Now I was in the picture. It was almost as if taking the picture a half-century before had frozen the place itself, an image now of the image.

People will come to see the house in Eldon. It is something to see. Staking a whole economy around seeing it is another matter. The rewards of seeing this house are subtle and complex. Here public and private spaces meet; art meets life. The fact that someone still lives in the house makes the experience of seeing it richer. As an attraction, it would be a shell of what it was—a western stage set or a house in Henry Ford's Greenfield Village, where the man who invented the technology that destroyed the small town collected examples of houses. The *Gothic* House, as it is now, feeds the painting that made it famous. The painting's controlled statement of well-groomed household and modest prosperity is a pentimento ironically overlaying the contemporary hard-scrabble life of the Hayneses. The painting has always been misread, misread by Iowans, farmers, townspeople mistaking what the painting said to others about them. The painting has always been cursed and adored. The act of seeing would be changed if the house became only a tourist stop. The rich confusion of art and life will be lost. In its place what the house has become—a kind of mock house, a cargo cult mock-up of a house luring in the tourist—will show through. The reasons to see the house will disappear once its only reason for being is to be seen.

When you drive the winding route to the *Gothic* House, look at the other houses along the streets. You will notice the ostentatious ornament of those houses, the windows, porches and doors, as if each house were vying for the attention of an artist's eye, begging you to consider imagining the life led behind the facades. Even in this depression, in the obvious signs of hard times, the houses should claim your attention along with the scheming inhabitants behind the windows. And on the way out of town you must let your eyes follow that blasted corridor of an abandoned connection and begin to see the layers of meaning in the landscape and entertain the necessity of living ruins in your life.

Living off the Land In Minnesota

Howard Mohr

[*Note:* My brother farms out in southwestern Minnesota, and since 1968, he has had five different tenants in an old farmhouse at a building site he owns on what he calls "Mortgage Hill." The renters were all young people who wanted to live off the land. My brother had no objection to somebody trying to live off the land. He'd been trying it himself for years.

Three of the tenants lasted less than a month. They all took off the same way: in the night and leaving nothing behind but a lot of marijuana seeds in the carpet. The fourth tenant, a young man, lasted four months — until his VW van caught fire and rolled into the creek. He stuffed his worldly possessions in his backpack and thumbed down the road.

But in 1970 my brother got a tenant who was determined to stay. We all thought he'd make it, but he didn't. After he moved out — thirteen years later — my brother found the following copy of a letter he had evidently sent, or planned to send, to his old friends back in the Twin Cities. I have left off his name. If he happens to read this guide, though, my brother says stop by sometime and tip a couple in the backyard.

It's a pretty sad deal, in a lot of ways, but he didn't lose his sense of humor, even though he lost about everything else. You might find it instructive, especially if you've been toying with the idea of subsistence living in Minnesota. We've got a bunch of abandoned farmhouses for you to choose from if you decide to make your move. —H. M.]

Dear Friend or Current Resident:

Surprise.

When I moved out to the Minnesota prairie in 1970 to start the Great Experiment on four acres of land, you and I promised to stay in touch with each other. I was supposed to be the point man, you recall, for the second big migration, and you had some notion of following me if my reports from Eden were favorable. You kept your side of the bargain by writing to me until 1979. Off and on I have felt guilty, but it always passed and so did the years. Now it's 1984.

This is my first report.

The recurring question in your later letters boiled down to this: "Did you fall in a pit or something?" I knew what you meant. If it's any consolation, I did fall in a pit, but only once, and I got out of it. It wasn't the reason I never wrote. I don't know why I never wrote.

The pit I fell in was west of the house but it didn't look like a pit, it looked like part of my lawn. In other words it looked like dandelions, quack grass, chamomile, clover, foxtail, and pigweed. Give me some credit—if it had looked like a pit I wouldn't have fallen in it. Actually, I didn't fall in, I sank in. I was walking around the house checking for a strange creaking sound in the siding, when I disappeared into the lawn up to my waist. Under the lawn was an old cistern that had been used as a large garbage can by previous tenants and then covered with dirt when it was full. I'm just thankful the previous tenants didn't operate a nuclear power plant.

I got a lot of mileage out of the cistern story in the early days, but it has worn fairly thin lately, like so much here.

I want you to know that I did reread all your letters before starting mine. Well, not all. The chickens got into the red shed (that's where the overflow from the house goes) in '76 or '77 and pecked holes in most of 1975's letters, causing large gaps of meaning. On top of that, the chickens had added some unusual punctuation. It wasn't the chickens' fault. I left the door open and they hopped in.

I never did keep the chickens in a pen because I wanted them to be free to scratch for crickets and worms and other natural foods and free to build their nests where they wanted. That made egg gathering a little tougher for me, and since the chickens tended to congregate on the front stoop during the day, it made walking barefoot tougher, too.

Which reminds me of the guy whose chewing gum fell out of his mouth in the chicken yard and he had to try five pieces before he found the right one. That joke is one of the big boxoffice grossers in this area, and depending on who tells it, the guy who loses his gum is a carpenter, a schoolteacher, a hippie, or a Norwegian. It's always a man, though, and not a woman, which makes sense to me, but I don't want to explain why I think so.

Your 1975 letters were pecked into nonsense no later than 1977 because that was the year the last hen bought the farm. At first I always kept a rooster with the hens because it was more natural to eat *fertilized* eggs, according to a brochure I picked up at the Silver Surfer Food Co-op in town. Silver Surfer sold only fertilized *brown* eggs.

The co-op was called Silver Surfer because the board didn't want anybody to confuse it with a supermarket that sold processed foods, not that they had anything to worry about. Also, Ben, the first coordinator of the co-op, had a large collection of Uncle Scrooge and Silver Surfer comics. He wanted to call the food co-op Uncle Scrooge but he compromised. Ben quit during the "Cheese Blowup." The board had decided that the co-op workers should wash their hands before they cut the bulk cheese into chunks for display. Ben said he didn't wash his hands when he cut cheese at home and he didn't see why he had to do it at the Silver Surfer. Telling people to wash their hands violated everything the co-op stood for. Next thing you know it'll be a supermarket, he said.

Ben went deeper into the wilderness after that, but when he came out in 1982, I heard he was driving a truck for Coke and taking night classes in computers. The Silver Surfer became the Friendly Food Co-op in 1980 and at present offers a full line of snack foods, some of them with preservatives. There's also orchestra music coming out of the ceiling, and once a week they have a drawing for "Bonus Bucks."

Fertilized egg doesn't sound nearly as appetizing now as it did when I got the first flock, I will say that. Anyway, the rooster always roosted on the rafters above the car in the garage. Getting up there was not easy for him, because his wings—like the wings on most domestic chickens—were not designed for flying. Modern chickens are bred for meat and eggs, not for wings, the way modern man is bred for watching TV and drinking beer. The modern chicken starts running and flapping its wings until it's airborne, in a manner of speaking, but it's about as aerodynamically sound as a St. Bernard. The rooster was overweight besides. It took ten minutes of clawing and flapping for him to reach the rafters at sunset. It was something you didn't like to watch too many times. Everything is beautiful in its own way except for a fat rooster going to roost or modern man watching "Monday Night Football" from a lounge chair.

The rooster got so it couldn't distinguish between the rising sun and the yardlight. Intelligence is not a chicken's strong suit. Four or five times a night the rooster would thud and flap onto the hood of the old Nash and go out under the yardlight and crow because he thought it was morning. I probably could have adapted to it, but that rooster's crow was not your fairy-tale "cock-a-doodle-doo." It was a cross between a plugged sump pump and a TV evangelist with tight underwear. To make a long story as short and as pleasant as possible, let me just say the rooster eventually ended up in the food freezer, after expiring suddenly one morning about 3:30 under his beloved yardlight. The hens, one by one, fell victim to the fox and the weasel.

After that I began buying unfertilized white eggs in plastic cartons. I didn't know it then, but that was the first step on the long downward trail of moral erosion.

And whatever happened to Cathy, you've asked in your letters. Our first and only winter together, we had a vicious blizzard. On the north side of the house there was a large hole under the eaves that the squirrels used as a door into their play area, but we didn't know that. The attic above the bathroom drifted full of snow. We didn't know that either, until the mid-January thaw.

The plaster ceiling of the bathroom disintegrated and collapsed. I put up some plastic sheeting and positioned peanut-butter tubs under the big drips, but still the water would plop on us when we least expected it. It was really the last good laugh Cathy and I had together. The next blizzard in early February knocked out our electrical power for ten days. The first day we snuggled and read Kurt Vonnegut to each other, but on the third day Cathy withdrew into herself. In March, she moved to Long Beach and eventually started a gift boutique with a loan from her father. We wrote back and forth for a few months. You know how it goes.

My original philosophy about living on the land came partly from the *Mother Earth News,* but most of it came from *Catch 22.* My hero was Orr, the WWII bomber pilot who always crash-landed on every mission because it was good practice in case he ever had to crash-land. And that's what I figured I was doing here on the prairies: I was living the simple life on the land because it was good practice in case I ever had to live the simple life on the land.

That philosophy has its flaws, I see that now. Take the skunks. At present, I see no reason why I had to practice removing skunks from under my house. But back then I was more idealistic. So when I came home from town one night in May after Cathy left, the house was filled with the smell of skunks (they had been mating under the house). I didn't even think about looking in the Yellow Pages. And how would I have paid Acme Skunk Eradicators anyway? With fertilized eggs?

Getting twelve skunks (the final count) out of the cellar and crawl spaces under the floors was just one more episode in the saga of self-sufficiency. For your information, this is part of what you need for skunk removal: steel traps, hamburger, command post of hay bales, red eyes from staying up all night, shovel. I would rather not go into details.

Maybe some people would say it was inevitable, but there came a point finally when I stopped practicing and decided to make a permanent crash landing. It wasn't the skunks or fertilized eggs that finally did it, and it wasn't the gophers chewing through the pump wires, or the squirrels in the ceiling. It was the garden. I never thought it would be the garden. It was like being cheated by a priest in a poker game or struck by a pacifist. You don't expect it and it's such a shock.

From the beginning the garden was the centerpiece of the experiment, the jewel in the crown. The idea was to grow everything I needed. You can't grow cheese or yogurt, so I bought milk products with the understanding that I could easily do without them. Animal protein was not a big concern for me either, but every so often that first year I would wake up with this craving for barbecued pork ribs and a pitcher of draft beer. But I knew that barbecued pork ribs were not necessary for life, and neither was Grain Belt beer. The beer I brewed in a plastic tub was plenty serviceable if you didn't drink the sludge that formed in the bottom.

By the third year my garden had expanded to half an acre and I had shifted from a spade to a gasoline-powered Rototiller (I felt bad about it). I had two compost heaps and a never-ending supply of sheep manure from a neighbor. Nothing made me happier than a wheelbarrow full of sheep manure. Those were the days.

What more could a person want? Half the year I was studying seed catalogs and the other half I was working in the garden. I grew northern jumbo peanuts, kale, Jerusalem artichokes, lima beans, four varieties of lettuce, three varieties of carrots. You name it, I planted it, cultivated it, watered it, mulched it, harvested it, stored it. Except rice. The rice paddy was a miserable flop and it took its toll.

Last year I grew only potatoes, carrots, onions, tomatoes, and lettuce. But when the seed catalogs started coming in January this year I decided I had practiced gardening long enough. I knew how to do it in case I ever had to do it. I didn't order my seeds. I've got a few jars of canned tomatoes in the cellar, but when they're gone, it's back to the grocery store, not back to the land.

My plans are to return to the Twin Cities in September. Maybe I'll see you around. I apologize again for not writing sooner, but look on the bright side, I saved you a lot of trouble.

This is my last report.

Cabin Fever

Susan Allen Toth

Sometimes when I am home, perhaps writing at my desk, or pausing at my bedroom door to decide whether to water plants or fold laundry or pick up books from the floor, or dashing to the ringing phone, I think of our cabin. I picture it, empty and silent, sunlight pouring through the large windows onto the wood floor. I let my mind walk slowly through its few rooms, noticing everything in place, swept and ready. Fresh wood lies by the stove, a clean towel hangs in the kitchen, a few magazines are neatly stacked on a low table. On the sofa is a small red cushion, plumped where I can put my head as I read. The house, I know, is waiting for me. Outside I can almost hear the wind whistling over the high-pitched roof and circling around the corners of the quiet bedroom.

In April, many Minnesotans are eager to open their cabins for the season. They have a form of 'cabin fever,' not winter claustrophobia, but an intense longing to escape to a special place of one's own. It is so powerful it can feel like missing an absent lover. When travel or unavoidable obligations have kept me away too long, I get itchy and irritable. I start crossing off items on my calendar with fierce determination; no party, concert or meeting, I tell my husband with a fiery look in my eye, will keep me in town one more week. Since Wind Whistle, our place, is winterized, I have cabin fever all year.

I cannot really call Wind Whistle a cabin. It is actually a small house, designed by my architect husband, whose feeling for modernist forms and natural wood merged with my somewhat whimsical taste in colors. The result, with its yellow-shingled siding trimmed in green, pink and lavender, is quite idiosyncratic, and in my prejudiced eyes, wonderful. (Anyone who loves a cabin believes it is wonderful; owners passionately defend what might to someone else seem odd-shaped rooms or dim lighting or primitive plumbing.) Though Wind Whistle is not large, marble or magnificent, I call it my Taj Mahal, because James created it with such exuberance and love. Fortunately, unlike the Indian mogul's wife, I am still alive to enjoy it.

But the fact that Wind Whistle is definitely a house causes me some uneasiness. We do already have a house, a fairly new and pleasant one in south Minneapolis. Not long ago, I read an interview with a local social activist, whose protests in good causes I have long admired. She was quoted as saying that, although her husband wanted to build a vacation house on some land they owned in another state, she wouldn't hear of it. It seemed wrong, she said, in a world where many people are homeless, to have two houses.

Drawn to many varieties of guilt, I tried this one on for size. It seemed, uncomfortably, to fit. So then I wondered if I would feel better if Wind Whistle were just a log cabin, with no running water, maybe not even a pump outside the door. Would that also be a moral affront? What about a cabin with a sink but no toilet? Or a toilet but no bathtub? If electric baseboards were not acceptable, was an old wood stove?

I often puzzle aloud with friends who, like me, are at the moment securely anchored in the middle class, about the moral level of consumption acceptable for a socially responsible person. I have found that most people have an intuitive but very clear set of standards about what is all right and what is too much. Those standards are wildly variable, usually depending upon income. For one friend, a $30 sweater is O.K., $50 is really stretching; for another, $75 doesn't seem unreasonable. Wandering through the Galleria or Conservatory, I can see many women who find $200 not excessive. And, of course, unloading a contribution at the Free Store at Nicollet and 31st, I am aware that for many, budgets don't allow for any new sweater at all.

Once, during the construction of Wind Whistle, I asked a friend who lives in a large, elegant house whether, though they can afford it, she ever worried about its cost. "Well," she said thoughtfully, "suppose I insisted that our family give it up? Where do you think we should live? In a two-bedroom rambler outside the city? And why wouldn't *that* be too much? Should we give up a house entirely and move into a rented apartment? Instead of an apartment, why not a single room? Where do you decide to draw the line?"

I don't know. I haven't got answers for how other people ought to live. I do know that my husband and I are very fortunate to have a retreat. Wind Whistle means so much to me now that I cannot bear to think of giving it up. It is both an escape and a destination. Like many Minnesotans, I talk about "getting away" to my cabin. We run from the hectic daily pace of our lives, the intrusive telephone and doorbell, domestic responsibilities. But what are we getting away *to?*

Most of us get away to the country. (I don't happen to know anyone who escapes to a hideaway in Duluth or Rochester or Albert Lea, and in my circle, no one owns a retreat in London or Monte Carlo.) Many go to Minnesota's lakes, some to the woods or a river or a reclaimed farmstead on the prairie. Some drive an hour, others most of the day to get to "the cabin." My husband and I head 90 minutes south, down the Mississippi to Lake Pepin, where Wind Whistle is perched high on a bluff overlooking a dazzlingly wide expanse of water.

What I notice first at Wind Whistle is the quiet. Although we do have a telephone, the concept of "long distance" inhibits most callers, and it absolutely eliminates the army of pollsters, charitable solicitors and salespeople for siding, insulation, light bulbs and rug-cleaning services who regularly invade our house in Minneapolis. Although we have neighbors on the bluff, we seldom see them. All we hear are wind, thunder, rain and sleet; an occasional train; and on summer nights, the rustlings and cracklings of mysterious small animals who prowl the woods just outside our windows.

This surrounding quiet cushions me. I lean back against it, slowly relaxing. At Wind Whistle I am able to unroll and stretch out, as if I were a thin piece of much-written-on parchment that has been bound too tightly too long and cannot easily lie flat. At Wind Whistle, I do lie flat—or curled up on the sofa. No one around me is working; my husband may sketch or make notes on a project, but he doesn't make me feel I need to get up and busy myself at my keyboard. When I want to write, I do. Mostly I read, doze, play gin rummy with James and look out the windows.

Most days, in all weather, I walk on the dusty, seldom-traveled roads and paths that connect our edge of the woods to the meadows and small farms beyond. On these walks, I find myself drifting into thoughts so light and wispy they usually get buried under the steamroller of burdened days. One early winter morning in January at Wind Whistle, when the sun was warm and the wind almost balmy, I walked for an hour down a road that leads into some undeveloped acreage in the woods. Hidden among the trees at the bluff's edge, I looked out on the frozen river through air so clear I could see the bends and curves of the opposite shoreline as if I were looking through an old-fashioned sharp-focused View-Master. High above, a bald eagle swept by, plunging and turning in the brilliant light that caught the white flash of its head and tail.

What I was thinking as I stood there I'm not sure. But suddenly two lines from an old-fashioned poem, the kind no one reads in school any more, floated into my mind and hung there, like the eagle hovering far overhead: 'A boy's will is the wind's will, / And the thoughts of youth are long, long thoughts.' When I was old enough to think myself a scholar, but still too young to have developed much understanding, I scorned such poetry as sentimental and meaningless. Now I know why it has lasted. What I seldom seem to have time for, I said to myself, is exactly that: long, long thoughts. Thoughts that start nowhere in particular, meander along like a twisting country road and pause at a wild rosebush or beside a trout stream covered with watercress. Thoughts that may not be deep, but are satisfyingly unbroken, flowing into one another like one of those streams.

In the distance, that morning on the bluff, I heard the faint whistle of a train. Trains run frequently on both sides of the river, chugging purposefully to and from Chicago with long strings of boxcars, but still singing the haunting song that used to draw me to the side of a track so I could watch the train flash by. Hearing a train whistle, I remember myself as a child, dreaming of strange cities, adventure and romance.

The sound of that whistle, slowly fading into the distance, also gives me a sense of space. The train goes on and on, past Wind Whistle, along the river, across the plains. Listening, I track it in my mind. That is another gift of a cabin: reminders of a larger world. Confined in the city, we easily forget what lies out there. I often see only the relentless spread of houses, office buildings and factories, and I picture 'development' as an armored and unappeasable dragon, eating up more and more land, belching smoke into an already hazy sky.

Speeding away from Minneapolis, beyond the encircling moats of freeways and scattered outposts of megamalls, I am always surprised how soon we are released into the country. As fields ripple past, like a softly shaken blanket outside our window, I begin to loosen as if I were being shaken too. My vision, unlocked from its narrow focus, zooms into the distance. Looking at the horizon, I am reminded how this sky sweeps north, over forests, past thousands of lakes, towards glacier and tundra. I also remember that not too far to the west, mountains break the flatness of the plains and march towards the Pacific. Following the Mississippi along the Wisconsin border, I am aware that this great river snakes its way to the gulf.

Driving past the long views across the flat lands south of the Twin Cities, then turning to wind between the soft hills near Miesville and New Trier, and finally passing beneath the bluffs of Red Wing, we see our cabin in its larger setting. The journey not only reminds me of space, it also gives me a gentle reprimand about time and mortality.

We do not make the mistake of thinking we own the land. Here on the bluff, surrounded by evidence of earlier dwellers—Indian names, a broken fence around land gone wild, an abandoned and crumbling barn—we know that we are as temporary as migrating birds who pause for a while before moving on. We also know we are city people, loving our bit of land but not belonging to it as those who work it do.

Because I love the wild beauty of our land, I want it to remain unspoiled. That is one of the ironies of cabin fever: No one wants anyone else to catch it. By building a house in the country, we are feeding the dragon.

A purist, who may well be right, would tell me that we should simply camp on our land, portaging in equipment, cleaning up after ourselves and leaving no trace of our stay. But when I think of Wind Whistle, waiting in silence for my next visit, each detail of the house is a familiar friend, often with a history. I look upwards toward the blue vaulted ceiling, watching a Japanese butterfly kite circle below the high painted beams, and I remember the day I found that kite in a museum shop. James looked it over, discussed it with me, finally approved. I think of the huge museum, the December weather outside, the noisy New York streets. I picture our master painter, Grant, carefully balancing on a tall ladder to hang the fragile paper kite.

I care intensely about what surrounds me indoors as well as out. Outdoors is wild and uncontrolled; inside, I like to feel familiar and secure. When I open the door of Wind Whistle, I am pleased that everything is in its place. I know where the unopened box of Triscuits is stashed, what half-read book is holding its place on the bedside table, exactly where the old wool shirt is hanging on a closet hook. At home, waves of clutter sweep into the house on a daily tide, stranding packages, mail, newspapers, cassettes, coupons and folders on chairs, tables and stairsteps. Here at Wind Whistle, the beach remains relatively bare.

As I write these words, I am seated at my city desk, which is heaped with papers and unanswered mail. Thinking about Wind Whistle, I get lonely for it. I look out my window at pavement and wish I were gazing into the tangle of trees outside the window at Lake Pepin. If other Minnesotans share my kind of cabin fever, enough passion is raging in all of us to melt every snow of early spring.

Gains and Losses

Contemporary Native American writers have before them a task quite different from that of non-Indian writers. In the light of enormous loss, they must tell the untold stories of contemporary survivors, while protecting and celebrating the cores of cultures left in the wake of European invasion.

And yet, in this, there always remains the land. The approximately 3% of the United States that is still held by Native American nations is cherished in each detail, still lit with old tribal myths, still known and used, in some cases, changelessly. . . .

A writer must have a place where he or she feels "Here I am, where I ought to be," a place to love and be irritated with. One must experience the blights, hear the proverbs, endure the radio commercials, go to reservation churches, roundhouses, cafés, and bingo palaces. By the close study of a place, its people and character, its crops, products, paranoias, dialects, and failures, we come closer to our reality. It is difficult to impose a story and a plot on a place. However, truly knowing a place forms the suggestive basis for every kind of linking circumstance. Location, whether it is to abandon it or draw it sharply, is where we start.

—Louise Erdrich, from "A Writer's Sense of Place"

I write on the Plains, in a small town. I'm indelibly an outsider, because I write and because I spent my formative years away. I am also an insider by virtue of family connections. . . .

I am entrusted with many memories here, and have my own to tell. What I often wonder is why others are not writing theirs. The material is certainly here: the economic upheavals of the past ten years alone might inspire a novel. . . . Instead there is silence. . . .

Perhaps it will be another generation before the story of these days can be told. . . . Perhaps, given the distance that the passage of time can provide, they will give us back the truth about ourselves. Whether or not we will listen, out here on the Plains, I cannot say.

—Kathleen Norris, from "Can You Tell the Truth in a Small Town?"

Ballade of the Dusty Old Dust

Ron Block

The corn fields of my home stretch on
further than my eye sees. They are deeper than
my seeing memory, three maybe four generations.
But their brief life may end with me: the land,
the dusty old dust my forebears orphaned—
unknowing, my parents pushed the land up in a whirl
of plows and even the land leaves the land
in the end. And there's no new world.

As we clamor to keep the land alive we've gone
to building monstrous anhydrous ammonia plants.
Have you heard of them leaking? Well, they can, and lawns
will fry, and people's lungs will burn, and plans
to evacuate these small Midwestern towns
don't exist. This ammonia's a fertilizer, but leaves curl
and brown at its heavy touch. It is toxic for humans.
At our journey's end, there is no new world.

I want to know if this is the time when our waste overcomes
our promise, when the ghost-dust of our wasted land
will blow about our ankles, broken from
the cycle of life. Our water recedes from us, the stands
of trees whither, aquifers fall away, and we stand
here waiting for foreclosure, the quick rural
ending that the creditors demand
at our journey's end, when there's no new world.

Grandfather, when your children brought you to this land
in your old age, they never planned
to plant you close by, just so you could see them
end up where there's no new world.

The Old Farm Woman Examines Her Thoughts

Grace Butcher

What comes through now
is the quarrel and twitter
of guinea hens,
the sudden noise
and the muttering
of the white ducks,
the sawing apart
of the air
by the roosters.

From the warm dark
of the barn
comes the velvety nicker
of the old horse;
the cats tease
and twist around my legs.

I have become
a good herder of chickens.
If they do not head
for the coop by dusk,
I walk behind them
quietly and skillfully
and move them towards sleep.

Powerfully
I climb the vertical ladder
to the hayloft,
toss the sweet hay
easily through the small opening.

The cats dash

between my footsteps,
but my feet go
unerringly always
to the right spot.

Now what am I to do
with all these skills?
My choice is to be here
alone, to move through
time of my own choosing,
to weave this place
around me so tightly
no one can get in.

But the fence posts rot;
the horse breaks out
whenever she wants;
the chickens are in
the neighbor's field;
the cats go down the road;
the ducks make their own lakes
every time the rain falls;
the guinea hens fly clear to the rooftop.

I might as well let some people in.
I don't really have to do chores
as often as I say I do.
And I *must* remember to listen.
Not everyone cares to know
how many eggs were laid today,
or that there's this duck
who's in love with me.

Oh, what *does* one talk about, anyhow?
There is already the sound of voices
coming up the lane.

Mine Towns

John Caddy

Much abandoned now, forced out or grown over, gone,
thrown into memory's hole. You have to dig for it.
Water-filled pits, rusted washing plants and crushers.
Tracks and spurs that just stop. The white pine cut,
the iron dug out. Not even much red left. No dust
coating cars or ground into hands. But bones mix with ore
in these empty mines, and the bones are red.

Much has always died. Towns: old Mesaba, Adriatic, Elcor.
Old pavement weedsplit. Lost customs and recipes,
causes and countries. Words: *Poyka. Sisu.* Short old women
in black babushkas clumped in front of churches.
Sayings: *May the Devil carry you off in a sack!*
Whole languages: Serb, French, Italian, stubborn Finn,
merchants who could speak them.

Much has died. Some nourishes still. Strike dreams:
1907, the Wobblies in '16, the thirties, fifties — dreams
of a living wage, justice, victory. Lost homesteads and saunas,
Finnish dovetails still wedging the squared white pine.
Logging camps: a privy, a chimney half-standing.

Some refuses death: timewarp Friday nights
on Chestnut Street, bumper to cruising bumper, sidewalks
swirling, all the bars bright, everyone calling *Hey*
to everyone, the polka lilt to the voice and the eye.
Behind town, out in the woods in old jackpine slash,
polished cones grip their seeds like gray stones,
wait lifespans for the fire to bloom.

Much is buried for the digging. The Mill Forty:
tangled concrete roots of the world's largest sawmill.
Sprinkled through fields where the company

moved the houses off, open cellars choked with raspberries.
By the back steps, rhubarb still thrusts its spear,
comfrey sprawls, mints and lilies struggle with long grass.

Abandoned now, knocked down and forced out, thrown
into memory's hole, the shaft leading to the full heart
where it all and always is embraced and laugh–angry and alive.

The Gleaning

Jared Carter

All day long they have been threshing
And something breaks: the canvas belt
That drives the separator flies off,
Parts explode through the swirl
Of smoke and chaff, and he is dead
Where he stands — drops the pitchfork
As they turn to look at him — and falls.
They carry him to the house and go on
With the work. Five wagons and their teams
Stand waiting, it is still daylight,
There will be time enough for grieving.

When the undertaker comes from town
He brings the barber, who must wait
Till the women finish washing the body.
Neighbors arrive from the next farm
To take the children. The machines
Shut down, one by one, horses
Are led away, the air grows still
And empty, then begins to fill up
With the sounds of cicada and mourning dove.
The men stand along the porch, talking
In low voices, smoking their cigarettes;
The undertaker sits in the kitchen
With the family.
           In the parlor
The barber throws back the curtains
And talks to this man, whom he has known
All his life, since they were boys
Together. As he works up a lather
And brushes it onto his cheeks,

He tells him the latest joke. He strops
The razor, tests it against his thumb,
And scolds him for not being more careful.
Then with darkness coming over the room
He lights a lamp, and begins to scrape
At the curve of the throat, tilting the head
This way and that, stretching the skin,
Flinging the soap into a basin, gradually
Leaving the face glistening and smooth.

And as though his friend had fallen asleep
And it were time now for him to stand up
And stretch his arms, and look at his face
In the mirror, and feel the closeness
Of the shave, and marvel at his dreaming—
The barber trims the lamp, and leans down,
And says, for a last time, his name.

Playing His Heart Out

Sharon Chmielarz
for my northern German uncles

We were trapped between
the godly cleanliness
of a cover of afghans
saving sofa and chairs
and the chartreuse living room walls.

We were talking about
anything except Uncle Carl—
gone, how we'd miss him—
when Uncle Gus came down
the hall and stood in

the archway, his wiry
body strapped under a black
accordian. "Haven't played,"
he said, "for a long time."
So he played a waltz and I

squirmed in my chair under
the slow flow of grief. He
played a polka and I heard
my sister clapping lightly
for the mourner and his cheek-

bones, held over the keys,
red and high as Helgoland's
cliffs on the North Sea. Gulls
whirled and screamed around
the black load on his heart.

Dear John Wayne

Louise Erdrich

August and the drive-in picture is packed.
We lounge on the hood of the Pontiac
surrounded by the slow-burning spirals they sell
at the window, to vanquish the hordes of mosquitoes.
Nothing works. They break through the smoke screen for blood.

Always the lookout spots the Indians first,
spread north to south, barring progress.
The Sioux or some other Plains bunch
in spectacular columns, ICBM missiles,
feathers bristling in the meaningful sunset.

The drum breaks. There will be no parlance.
Only the arrows whining, a death-cloud of nerves
swarming down on the settlers
who die beautifully, tumbling like dust weeds
into the history that brought us all here
together: this wide screen beneath the sign of the bear.

The sky fills, acres of blue squint and eye
that the crowd cheers. His face moves over us,
a thick cloud of vengeance, pitted
like the land that was once flesh. Each rut,
each scar makes a promise: *It is*
not over, this fight, not as long as you resist.

Everything we see belongs to us.

A few laughing Indians fall over the hood
slipping in the hot spilled butter.
The eye sees a lot, John, but the heart is so blind.
Death makes us owners of nothing.
He smiles, a horizon of teeth
the credits reel over, and then the white fields

again blowing in the true-to-life dark.
The dark films over everything.
We get into the car
scratching our mosquito bites, speechless and small
as people are when the movie is done.
We are back in our skins.

How can we help but keep hearing his voice,
the flip side of the sound track, still playing:
Come on, boys, we got them
where we want them, drunk, running.
They'll give us what we want, what we need.
Even his disease was the idea of taking everything.
Those cells, burning, doubling, splitting out of their skins.

A Broad Gauge

Jan Huesgen

I can draw a mallard with my eyes closed,
or in the dark—cleaned my first
bird at six in the narrow room
of our garage. Snow outside
the low window, sometimes all nine of us
in that small space: two or three
plucking feathers, two waxing
over a five-gallon pail—hot paraffin
hardening quick in the thin, cold air—
then singeing by candlelight, and the rest
gutting the bodies in the shadows
of a Coleman
the pickers and waxers got to have
for the light's advantage: working
near torn flesh from a hundred yard fall.

We work shoulder to shoulder for lack
of space, for the warmth a November
night does not give in North
Dakota, where our "fall hands"
are back, sore from this regular
after-supper chore in the wet.
Our knuckles are cut and recut
against splintered rib bones, trying
to pull the wind pipe from its throat.

We can take a day's hunt down
in an hour, a dozen ducks and geese,
we skin the upland game: pheasants,
partridge and dove, enough
for meals the weekend through. Sixty days
of this will see us into spring.

I think myself a naturalist now,
living on the river, where the wood ducks
nest in trees, where I still measure distance
by the outside wall of a gun, every bird
yet the first I shot at ten.
I don't like it either, but aspersion
seems the simplest response
to that means
that fed us those first winters
when the price of a gun
was almost more than we could bear.

lincoln tomb, a report

John Knoepfle

husband to wife with camera
can you get the whole tomb
no she says from the viewfinder
but Ive got mr lincoln I think

—a terrorist got him
rendered him to an insane absolute
one of our martyred presidents—

the gutzon borglum sculpture
the same on mount rushmore
robert todd marveled at it
he did not expect to see father again

husband focuses on wife
she rubs the borglum nose
a grandfather lifts two children
a small boy and his sister
it is the custom that everyone
shines mr lincolns nose

I sit on a park bench
watch the people gathering
always the families and foreign groups
the busloads of old tourists
and now a sun-bronzed woman
the nudists call a cottontail
her white behind
peeking from under her shorts
as she strolls to the tomb

palace for pharaoh
hedges of solemn yew
and burning bush

and a dogwood on each side of the entrance
camped there for blossoms in spring
no arch here
just the necessary
post and lintel

many languages spoken
I recognize spanish italian chinese
but there are others
the world cares about this man
comes here to have its picture taken
each family its several selves
poses for a group portrait
this is essential in front of the tomb
like rubbing the polished nose

while deep within
the cenotaph spells his name
and those numbers 1809–1865

a small son to his father
I saw that I saw that
was he in back of that thing

—yes ten and a half feet
behind the dark red arkansas stone
and ten feet down
safe under tons of cement

it is all right this tomb
his words hung in bronze here
gettysburg address
farewell to springfield
second inaugural the almighty
has his own purposes
blood drawn with a lash
every drop paid with a sword

I expect it to wear as well

as any thing I have produced
a truth I thought needed to be told

this terrible war
if god wills it to continue

from the side at a distance
the borglum sculpture seems enormous
a head on a judgment seat
some thing in front of the gate
we need to dare touch
it tells us who we are isnt that right
or should have been
or who we have to be

father impatient with his son
you ask me questions
I dont have any idea
how to answer

a teenage boy exits the tomb
he is alone approaching the sculpture
he rubs it vigorously
taking his solitary good-by
no magic here or sanctioned custom
his is the last fierce
affectionate touch
we reserve for the dead

and now a small child
walking to the parking lot
stops in the sunlight
she is wearing a red beanie
which supports a plastic propeller
she studies for a moment the shadow
that revolves above her shadow
and then goes on

Thoughts Stolen from Geese

Ellen Kort

If my father were still alive
he'd call them hang-gliders,
chalk marks, the season's laundry
strung across sky.
He'd tell me how geese
gather words from the river,
drum dark old songs.

Free-wheeling, he too hung his life
under the eaves of sky
wind pumping through veins
through ghostly bones.
Each autumn the heart beating
past flap of wings
looking for the lone bird
that falls out of formation
testing, returning again and again
to the lifting power of the V.

Geese honk to encourage those in front
A lead goose rotates
when he gets tired
letting another take his turn flying the point.
When a goose falls from the line
two others follow him down,
stay with him 'til he's able to fly
or until they know he's dead.

I wasn't there when my father went down
but I knew almost the precise moment
of that last wild ride.
He would have loved the way he went

slumped to the floor
robe loose and flapping
beautiful somehow
in the pure light of early morning
beautiful somehow
like geese rowing the sky
in long, shuddering strokes.

Crossing Lake Agassiz

Jay Meek

Going through our country I've found how much debris
           we have in it,
so much life already gone from our hands.
No more than ten thousand years ago,
we would have been crossing the sediment of an inland sea.

Not tonight. Tonight, travelling by bus across the plains,
we pass missile silos at ground level,
bunkers, installations,
lilacs in a dooryard and the house burned down.

It's scarcely different in cities: so much being, so much death.
Walking in New York, I have seen taxis
queued up along the park
beside the tigers in its children's zoo,

and beyond the zoo the corporate towers that cast no shadows
           on themselves,
only those glass surfaces across which the sky blazes
as if an explosion shattered one window

where a man leans heavily upon his desk
with the palms of both hands.
But I have seen the constancy of animals
come into our empty places
and bring with them a dazzling vigilance.

I have seen tigers as they leaped through a hoop of fire
in a suburban mall,
and I have seen them lying down in shadow
under the wings of a B-52,

just as tonight I know they are out there,
drinking the dark water of a slough,

or running with us a little while before cutting in ahead
               through the coach lights
as if they were calling,
calling us to come out of ourselves again.

Ideal

Carol Muske

Though my little daughter owns an Ideal farmyard
let me not direct her attention to
the bloody auction block, the rented backhoe
reversing the plow on the earth,
the iron of the farmer's hand dropped on nothingness

I know that pain has its tradition,
the slaughtering blade,
the black blood pounded into the grain.
The dreaming animals that come to drink

at this trough understand no tradition,
but I can make the cattle speak
as mildly as they have ever spoken,
the night moths appear as harmless messengers.

The woman who is standing over there
under the tree near the fenceposts,
touching the carved initials —

she is harder to invent.
In a fairy tale, she would be the familiar,
privileged trespasser: she might even be what she is,
a former owner on disputed land.

See her eyes repossess the well,
the porch, the propped-up Ford?
A man in love with speed used to drive it,

its tailpipe a red comet
down the lonely roads. My daughter
wants to know who she is, how does she fit
in the picture, the green painted pasture?

Everyone thinks they can make her put down

the rags and the can of kerosene,
maybe the dear little local paper

will crown her queen of the burning trees,
the dynamited dam. It's written in
her two-word tattoo what she will do
and it's written to you

on such a bright night, moon on the fenceposts,
the cow lowing softly, the ideal sky
split open suddenly with stars.

Picking Wildflowers in the Sandhills

Judith Sornberger
for Kris

This land is good
for loss. It won't mind
if we pick its flowers

               patridge pea
                   golden aster

won't even count its losses
as you and I count years
of work lost by our children's ages,
console ourselves with what
those years have taught us

             prickly poppy
        milk vetch

My uncle taught me
look where loss is —
blowouts where grass
let sand blow through her fingers —
for arrowheads lost or left
behind by those who hunted

                  gay feather
        lead plant

I stooped and lost track
of the sky whole afternoons
and never found a single arrow
pointing to my heart

      false boneset
          blue penstemon

First this land lost
its bison, then its hungers.
My uncle's eyes go
from quartz to slate telling
of the ranch our family lost

               fringed loosestrife

then his father's blade
across the throat
in their front garden
when he lost his county office

           puncture vine

All that's left: the house
he and his sister shared
for sixty years and now
she's gone

      Platte thistle
          cancerroot

When he moved
into an Omaha apartment
he broke the window
over his collection
and gave my sons
what I had coveted

        bastard toad-flax
   smartweed

I find the arrowheads
stuffed in their junk drawers.
They pierce me with the afternoons of hunting my sons lost,
not knowing

     fog-fruit
        motherwort

Dead flowers clutched in moist hands,
we mark our way by windmills.
Their turning bears the same
testimony as crosses:
water spirited away by sun returns

        evening primrose
          heal-all

like wind, revealing
all our losses.

Earthlings

Sylvia Griffith Wheeler

Just off Santa Fe Trail asphalt,
we are the folks presidents
talk to when times require.

Over the Midwest flyway,
strange birds quack.

Networks make-up women who will not trade
their bleaches, soaps for anything,
to look like us.

After church, we eat fried chicken
with our fingers. T.V. scans
us till bedtime.

Harry lives up the road,
Ike down. Every 40 miles there's a rest stop.
We all say "Howdy." Same inflection.
I can't hardly go on.

Dark-House Spearing

David Wojahn

In my father's red sweater
I wake to snow in the South.
His first vacation alone,
he's sleeping this week on my sofa,

says again we never owned a yellow Olds.
But I remember him
in his only suit,
leaving for the doctor in St. Paul,

1956, shoveling snow from the wheels
of the yellow car:
the memory
from which I date the world.

We have learned the balm
of trivial disagreement,
though he doesn't believe in words.
We eat breakfast

at a restaurant window,
the river murky with ice.
Because his brother,
ten years younger, died last month

in alcoholic coma,
he doesn't want talk, just company.
So even here I mention snow,
the absence of color

from the interplay
of many colors.
He tells me I will never understand
the real simplicity of things.

So I remember dark-house spearing,
Christmas in the fifties.
We walked across the bay
at Lake Mille Lacs,

the flashlight glowing
by the circle we cut.
Fish swim curious,
illegal toward the light.

Dozens come. I'm five.
Father raises his grandfather's spear,
sunfish and smallmouth swarm like bees.
Dark-house spearing,

Minnesota's sheer
December ice-mist around us.
I tell him how I woke
from the dream again last night,

of fish alive and trembling in the bag
I clutch riding home on his shoulders.
Sunrise. My uncle stands
at the window of my childhood home

and father and I are singing,
floating toward the light.
Useless to remember it, he says,
when you have the details wrong.

I have the details wrong.
Father, I wanted to evoke for you
words beyond the absence of words,
so wholly it would be enough

to cause us to begin again.
Weeping, you told me
you could not remember
your last words with your brother.

Daily, father, I wait
for the real simplicity of things.
Sometimes, when I shut my eyes,
I'm back in ashen fields,

steel-colored sky.
My hands cling to the cedar fence
you said would hold
the snow back from the world.

1956—I know already
snow will win, swirl in the living rooms,
all night drift
against the beds and windows.

And those who rise at dawn,
rubbing the night from their eyes,
none of them will understand
what they wake to or what they have lost.

What the Fall Brings

Jonis Agee

The fall here in Divinity, Iowa, always brings back such memories that I almost go running home with a sack over my head so I don't have to watch them come ghosting up high over the buildings, or leaking out of doorways like someone's washer running crazy and crazy.

Some days, I feel my body with my own hands, you know, just to make sure I'm here and not evaporating like some of the people I've known. But I've seen the way bones break, and the way they resist and grow back, so I figure they can stand a lot. I also figure that maybe they aren't so different — the folks around here — from anyplace else. I mean, we got a certain number that end up in Anamosa, the state penitentiary, not much more or less than anywhere else. We got the same regular numbers being trucked over to Independence (the mental hospital's there) by their families, or occasionally by the deputy, the squad car light whirring most of the way, just to impress everyone with the importance of his errand. And yearly, the same number more or less heads on out to the cemetery, usually carried along in the big black hearse belonging to Thompson's Mortuary, but occasionally arriving from out of town in someone else's. We get used to it. All our friends and family are there after a while.

I like to think about all of us years from now, where we'll be, how many of us will still be going to the same jobs, the same daily routines, say, twenty or thirty years from now. Since I'm just turning thirty now, hell, I could live to be a hundred, but I don't think many others will. It might be awfully lonely then. I might end up like Miss Ethel's mother — all bones and a bag of skin. What I'm afraid of, is that maybe as you get older, things start falling, out of place. Maybe a rib could detach, maybe your shoulder blades could start traveling around. It's a funny idea, I know, but after the way I've watched things start to loosen in people, it's something to think about.

Like every fall, I can't help thinking about that one time after the state fair, just when everything was beginning to color up nice, early October. I was still in high school, just my first year, I think — yes, that'd be right, because that's how I still knew him. We'd gone through grade school once I'd moved up here, and he was the second boy I kissed. The first one didn't work, so it took me a long time to work up nerve again. But Billy Bond was sure a lot nicer about it. We were in seventh grade. Billy lived on a farm outside of town, and although the school bus took him back and forth, often as not he'd walk me home, then go on and walk all the way, five miles out, just so he'd be able to spend a little more time with me. I know his daddy must have given it to him for always being late for chores, but Billy worked pretty hard, so no one could complain too much. Everyone in my family just pretended like Billy Bond wasn't there — that was their way usually. And I do recall that in the next year, the eighth grade, when Billy decided to like LuAnn Menderson instead of me, it did come as a blow. But then, LuAnn lived on the farm next to his, and I guess they could take the bus home together and see each other more, so it made sense, sort of. Better sense than walking five miles just to see me.

And they were both in 4H, I remember that. It's a big deal for kids out here, 4H and Future Farmers of America when they got a little older. They'd all walk around in their shiny satin jackets with the fancy stitching along over the front pocket — their nicknames — and in the back, the big round symbol and title — Future Farmers of America. It was like a fraternity. When they went to college, they studied agriculture and animal husbandry and came home and took over the farms, going through the usual fights with dads and older relatives about new ideas the ag school was pumping out in its monthly bulletins. Like how many cows a man without a hired help could maintain efficiently versus the farmer with help. And whether the hay was better baled and stacked, rolled in giant rounds and left in the field, or racked into long cylinders like old-fashioned curls and then bound with twine and put up in the barn. Every farmer had his pet theories, and every farmer fought with his kids from ag school about the changes.

I know, because you used to have to listen to it everywhere you went. In school the boys would get into fistfights about whose dad knew the most, and whether you want China blacks or Polands in hogs, and which wintered best—the shelled corn or the unshelled. And there was a hierarchy, too, depending on what you raised—cattle at the top, hogs in the middle and poultry at the bottom. Billy explained it once when we went to the county fair. We spent most of the day in the animal 4H exhibits, while I just wanted to ride the ferris wheel and have Billy win me a big panda bear. But Billy was a serious person; he had a big stake in doing a good job with his pig growing and didn't want to mess up by letting anything go. So we spent most of the time checking on this big old mama hog, fat as a piece of butter and smelling pretty good, with just the hint of piggy odor about her. Billy told me that he used Wella Balsam Creme Rinse on her hair to get it to lie flat and smell good. He liked the piney smell of it. Then he made me put my face down into the pen, with my nose almost touching her pink skin. He was right—piney, with just an edge of hog underneath.

God, the things he showed me to do to a pig. He'd stolen some of his mama's clear fingernail polish, and after rasping his hog's little hoofs rounded and smooth, he painted them up with the polish. Boy, did they shine. Since the animals were kept bedded in clean, sweet straw, they didn't have a chance to go out and act like pigs, get dirty again. It was like an animal palace at those fairs, the animals just lounging around, nothing to do but lie there or stand and have some person spend hours picking their ears or getting every last crumb out of their coat. Why, if you forgot these were farm animals, you'd think you were at one of those dog-grooming parlors watching fancy little poodles getting bows put in their hair or something. When I tried a joke with Billy, asking him why he'd neglected putting some eye make-up on his pig, he gave me a strange look, reddened, then opened his trunk sitting just outside the pen, and pulled out some Maybelline eyeliner and mascara. "I thought about it . . . " I didn't have the heart to laugh, so I just nodded serious-like and let it go.

I don't want you to get me wrong here though, Billy Bond wasn't the only one. These kids ate, slept, dreamed their animals. There wasn't a one of them wouldn't do what Billy was doing. It was a strange sight, believe me, to look down the rows and rows of those 4H barns and see kids with their animals, some of them sleeping in the stall, some of them outside it. Some of them bent over as they handpicked each particle of manure out, and some of them looking like little mamas, dressing their babies with a tenderness and consideration that only comes from a genuine love.

I suppose that if Billy hadn't been so careful, so meticulous about his hog raising—if he'd let something slip by, if he'd gotten interested in girls more, or horsing around with his friends when he should have been handfeeding and grooming—then things would have turned out different in the long run. But you don't get anywhere thinking like that, I guess. The facts are what they are. Like bones—there one day, and then who knows, maybe it's the skin that lets go of them somehow.

But I remember that the fall of our freshman year in high school, Billy Bond's hog, Bluebell, won the grand championship at the Iowa State Fair. She was the biggest and the best. There were pictures of Billy and his hog in newspapers all over Iowa. They were a winning couple, and besides, the pig was the biggest ever to win the 4H, and you knew that that was going to set Billy up for good as a hog grower. People remembered those things, and if Billy's pigs could turn that size and quality, then Billy wouldn't have a thing to worry about. Everyone was proud of him, I recall, his dad and brothers strutting around town like they were behind the whole thing. There was even a little parade the day Billy and Bluebell came home when the fair was done. They drove real slow down Main Street, and the high school band played some snappy songs, and the hog looked out the grates of the little trailer, sniffing suspiciously like she knew just what was going to happen next.

Because it was part of it that Bluebell had been auctioned and bought by Reese's A&P and would spend a couple of weeks on display for everyone to see right in front of the store, to honor Billy and the pig and the 4H. Half the proceeds were to go to the club in town, to build future 4Hers like Billy, and Reese could take the tax write-off and sell or donate the meat as the highest grade pork around. But Billy looked pretty miserable through the whole thing, even while he was squatting down, posing with his arm thrown around Bluebell's shoulder for the newspaper photographs. And I remember how when the picture came out a few days later, it reminded me of a boy and his girl watching a movie, the same intent distracted look on each of their faces.

I've never much liked to see animals on display, like at zoos, or at fairs and carnivals, and I think Billy's hog just reinforced that for me. It was sad to walk by her every time you wanted to get a loaf of bread at the A&P. Bluebell always came trotting up to the little portable fence, sniffing like you'd brought it a treat, like Billy probably taught it to do, then when you didn't have anything for it, she would shuffle back to the far corner and stand with her back to you, dejected. And while their mamas shopped the little kids were spending too much time tormenting her, throwing little rocks and clods of dirt to watch her stampede around, then they'd have a laughing fit seeing all that wobbly fat. I think it'd been Reese's idea to build some publicity for the hog slaughter, and put even more fat on her by keeping her confined and stuffing her good for a couple of weeks. I don't think he intended more than that. Reese is pretty harmless. He just wants to make his money and let it go at that.

Every afternoon after school, those two weeks, Billy Bond would come over, snap a little collar and lead line on the pig and take it out back to the vacant lot to eat grass and get some exercise. He was careful, though, not to let her run much since they wanted to keep the fat on and Reese had warned him about it. And I swear, the time or two I caught sight of it, Billy and that hog looked just like a boy romping with his dog at a distance.

In Divinity, the homecoming game on Saturday afternoon is the biggest celebration of the fall, and since we knew we'd win that year, everyone was real built up. You could feel it all week as you walked down the street, in and out of stores, people a bit more pumped up than usual, joshing the football players they saw, or the families of the players. As part of the celebration afterwards, Reese had decided to butcher the hog and have a big pig roast. To help things along, some of the merchants had gotten together and decided to buy a couple of kegs of beer for the adults and pop for the kids. So all morning before the game that started at one in the afternoon, the A&P had been busy with folks coming and going, buying food to fix and taking things down to the little park beside the river a couple of blocks away. The hardware store had donated some strings of lights and the men were busy with those, putting them into the trees overhead, setting up tables and chairs and cleaning up the little bandstand.

I don't think anyone thought much about the empty pen outside the store. People were used to the animals that came and went from season to season. Farm kids learned early that that was the way things were. I guess I didn't keep track either. It was the first high school homecoming I was actually going to be a part of, like I belonged instead of some dumb kid running around. And I had a date, my first, although I had to take my sister Baby along, so nothing could happen. Kenton Maxwell, the boy, told me not to worry though, he was a year older than me and knew how to get around big obstacles like Baby. Just before one that afternoon, we'd walked up to the game, the three of us from my house, where Kenton's brother had let him out. None of us but Baby were old enough to drive yet, and Baby was too big to fit behind a normal steering wheel, so she still couldn't. EuGene, as usual, wouldn't have a thing to do with any of us, and just drove off in his empty car to pick up his date. I was so excited, I guess I didn't think much about the aroma of roasting pig that drifted through that afternoon, it was all part of the excitement — the game, the picnic and dance later. And I was going to all of it. Probably no one even missed

Billy Bond, not even his family, because everything was focused on his brothers, who were on the varsity string playing that afternoon.

Of course, our small towns always choose to play the smallest, weakest team they can find for their homecoming, and I don't know who this team could play since it came from such a small community that they were barely fielding the two lines. To no one's surprise, we trounced them good and sent them brokenhearted and brokenheaded onto their buses at four, for the long ride back home, while we all came busting out of the field, running for our cars and the victory parade down Main Street afterwards.

Some of the high school clubs had fixed up floats, and the candidates for homecoming queen were all dressed up, sitting on the backs of honking convertibles. It was the sort of thing that is still going on each October in this town. But the reason I remember this one so well is Billy Bond, who had climbed on top of the four-story bank building, the tallest we have, right in the center of town while everyone was at the game, and who was, apparently, driven crazy by the sight and smell of the beloved Bluebell turning slowly over the coals in the late afternoon sun, because by the time the parade was halfway through town, he had picked up the BB gun he'd climbed up to the roof with and started shooting at things in the street below him, hollering.

I can still remember how loud his voice was. You could hear it clearly, plainly, above the marching band even. Although the range was too much for the BB gun most of the time, he managed to pop one under the skin of Reese's forearm before everyone took cover. Reese was plenty mad when that happened, and after a moment of shock, then realization that it was Billy Bond up on the bank roof taking pot shots and messing up the parade, he sneaked into the drugstore and called the sheriff's office, which was stupid, since the sheriff and his deputy were both on their posse quarter horses leading the parade like always. When Reese realized this, he went ducking and sneaking down the street to where the two men sat on their horses, taking stock of the situation, well out of range of the BB gun.

Reese demanded that they do something, "take the little bugger off of there," calling Billy every name in the book and waving his forearm with the welt from the BB rising red and angry, looking like a big spider had bit him or something. The sheriff was trying hard to hold off a smile—you could see that a mile away—and whether Reese could or not, I don't know, but he could sure tell he wasn't getting anywhere, because in a few minutes he stomped his feet and started walking straight back to his place in the parade, forgetting about Billy for a moment until a BB ticked the top of his head, ruffling the hair enough to send him cursing and sliding into the cover of the hardware store. Then he started yelling right up at Billy, saying, "Goddamn you, Billy Bond, I'm gonna get you for this. You're going to Anamosa, you goddamn juvenile delinquent," and stuff like this. Billy just answered by showering the street below with more BBs—he had a Daisy Repeating Rifle, must have gotten it when he was eight or nine years old, like most of us kids. The BBs keep bouncing around, like someone was throwing little pebbles down from the sky, most of them harmless, but an occasional one getting enough velocity that they'd stick in something. Meanwhile, folks started getting tired of holding the parade up, and began drifting away, with the deputy directing traffic down to the park.

When Billy realized that the parade was breaking up, he stood up and started calling for Reese, "the Nazi butcher," to come back. Finally, he was so mad, he started threatening everyone in sight, saying he was going home for a real gun, his dad's .22, if they didn't listen, and warning them not to eat Bluebell. His parents, everyone noticed, had kept out of sight, because on a day when their other two sons had done such a fine job, Billy had to go and embarrass everyone, so they were trying to ignore him like a whiney child, I guess. By the time the sheriff and deputy had put their horses away and gotten back, a group of local men had gathered a block away to discuss what to do with Billy. Everyone else was down at the river having a drink and savoring the smell of the nearly done, crisping pork they would soon be eating.

Some of the younger men wanted Mr. Bond and his sons to climb up there and take Billy down forcibly, and kept muttering about what a disgrace it was to have a kid making such a big fuss in front of the whole town. Mr. Bond looked pretty uncomfortable, but kept his silence. I don't think he trusted Billy not to shoot him with the BB gun as he came over the top. Besides, he was sick of Billy's moping around about the damn hog anyway. "I'll leave it up to the sheriff," was all he'd say. Then the men turned to the sheriff and asked what he intended to do.

The sheriff looked around him, hooked his thumbs in his belt and announced, "Nothing. I'm going to get a beer and some food now, and if Billy Bond wants to sit on that roof all the rest of his life, he can." Then as he moved through the group, he added, "But I bet he'll be down by the time the snow falls." And true to his word, he went to the park, got himself a beer and started flirting with the younger women, like he always did. Some of the men tried to get up energy to go get Billy after that, but the heart was gone out of it, and the town just went on and celebrated the homecoming, drinking beer and eating roast pig.

I liked Billy, but I tried not to think about him up there alone on the bank roof, probably sobbing his heart out while the rest of the folks were down there eating his Bluebell. 'Things have to go on in life,' that's what people told each other that night. "You can't take on so about a mere animal; you have to know that they're here for people to eat. This is a good experience for him," they told each other, and his dad promised he'd get a good whipping once he got off that roof. So everyone felt pretty good, and I didn't even mind so much being with my sister Baby on my first date. She got so wrapped up in the food, like I knew she would, and Kenton was careful to get someone to keep supplying her with big full plates while he and I snuck off with some of the other kids our age to the dance. All in all, it was a fine homecoming, and even Reese got to laughing about the BB in his arm by the end of the evening.

No one gave Billy Bond a thought as we drifted back home around eleven that night. The big bonfire that'd been built down on the riverbank was starting to die down, but its aroma filled the cold fall air with a wonderful burning wood smell. And I guess we just assumed he'd gotten down and walked back to the farm—that is, if we thought about him at all.

The next day, when Billy hadn't shown up by one o'clock, after church services were out, and no one had heard a word from the roof, the sheriff and his deputy did go up there to see if they could find him. He was there alright, sitting in the corner, hugging himself like he was still cold from the hard frost we'd had overnight, but when the men tried to talk him into standing up and coming home, he'd looked up at them with a face as white as milk—that's what they'd said, he was just gone. There wasn't anything left in him, so they'd carried and dragged him down the ladder to the street below and carted him off home. But it didn't do any good. A few days later, as we were going to school one morning, there goes the deputy driving by the high school with Mr. Bond beside him in the front, and Billy Bond sitting in the back still hugging himself, looking out the window with a face like an empty bowl. And when I waved, he looked at me like I was the man in the moon.

A Simple Matter of Hunger

Sharon Oard Warner

Last night Paul told me that loving Jancey will have to be my job. "I can't do it, Eleanor," he said. "Every time I go in and look at her, see how beautiful she is, how special, a cold wind rushes around inside me." We were in bed, and the room was so dark that I couldn't see his face. He was a voice speaking, and I was a body listening. Silent, I stared into the darkness, tried to see right through it, but the harder I looked, the thicker it got, until the darkness itself seemed to have texture, like the furry back of an enormous black bear.

In the thin hours of morning, I woke and heard Jancey rolling around in her crib. She wasn't crying, so I waited, thinking she might go back to sleep. Tiny as she is, she can make that crib creak. It's an old thing, plenty used when we bought it. Joel slept in it for nearly three years and now Jancey. Good thing she's so small, I told myself, but it's not a good thing at all.

In another minute, her crying wafted ghostlike down the hall, and before I could convince myself to throw off the covers, Paul nudged me with his knuckles. He's one of those people who can only go to sleep once each night, so he does what he can to keep from waking. Used to be, people would call in the middle of the night—broken pipes and such—and after saying hello, he'd stuff the receiver under the pillow and go right on sleeping. Eventually, we switched places. Now, I sleep closest to the phone.

The house was chilly, but Jancey's room glowed warmly. Two nightlights burned, one under the bed, and the other, a china cat, on her dresser. She wakes often, and I like to be able to change her, take her temperature even, without turning on an overhead light. Both of us stay sleepier that way. Her eyes were closed, but she was moaning and pitching from one side to the other, as though she were in the midst of a sea dream.

"Jancey," I whispered. At the sound of my voice, she opened her eyes and stared up at me, clearly awake. I hated to think of her like that, fully conscious but eyes closed. "Oh, Jancey," I said, picking her up. She was damp with sweat and so hot that I carried her across the room and switched on the light without thinking, blinding us both for an instant. I wanted to hurry her down the hall to Paul, press her close to him, wake him for good and all. Instead, I closed the door and did the only things I knew to do: I took off her sleeper and diaper, wrapped her in a blanket, coated the rectal thermometer with Vaseline, inserted it gently, and sang to her while we waited.

It read 105. Drawing a deep breath, I took her into the kitchen, dribbled red liquid down her throat, and made a pact with myself. If her fever wasn't down in half an hour, I would call Dr. Kesl and have Paul drive me over to the hospital, to hell with them. As I carried her back to her room, I wondered if she could feel the pounding of my heart.

Most of her clothes were piled on the floor by the washing machine, so I put her in one of Joel's old sleepers, blue of course, but heavy and warm. She kicked her legs and stared up at me while I worked. Ordinarily, her thick black hair stands out all over her head, but last night it was slick with sweat, and after I'd dressed her, I combed the wet strands and clipped them into place with a blue barrette. "There now," I said. "You're pretty enough to go out on the town." With her dark coloring, she looks better in blue than Joel ever did.

He was a pasty little bald-headed thing, no hair on his head to speak of for over a year. "Please, God, let him have hair for a few good years," my husband, Paul, had prayed at the dinner table, one of those jokes that's no laughing matter. Paul's hairline has receded to the edges of his head now, nothing left but fringe around his ears and neck. He's not a vain man, but it bothers him when my hand strays to the top of his head while we make love. I like to rub the smooth skin there; something in me responds to the warm pulse beneath my fingers. I used to rub Joel's head while he nursed, my palm cupped around his skull. Love is never a pure emotion, is it? Sometimes Paul's hug brings back that sinking sensation I used to feel in the arms of my father, and once, kissing Joel goodnight, I was surprised by the same wash of tenderness that had come over me those last days with my mother in the hospital.

Jancey and I rocked for a good hour, and slowly her temperature fell. She relaxed and settled against me, her eyes opening and closing, opening again to find my face. I kept mine on her, smiled my reassurance. Once the medicine began to work, she drifted off, but as soon as I reached for the remote control to flip on the TV, she looked up at me, alert and interested. I muted the sound, but turned the chair so she could watch. She likes television — the motion and lights, the peculiar sounds. For a five-month-old, Jancey is attentive and obliging. When smiled at, she smiles; when given a toy, she holds on, waving it about with an expression that's downright grateful. If she senses she is supposed to sleep, she closes her eyes and nuzzles against me; her breathing slows. She could fool Dr. Spock with her act. We sat together and watched a couple dance across the screen, maybe Fred Astaire and Ginger Rogers. I couldn't tell for sure because I didn't have my glasses on. Their fuzzy forms swished back and forth, so graceful in the dark silence of my living room. The movie was in black and white, and it occurred to me that the dancers were probably dead, gone now except for these bits of celluloid. I went on watching until the movie was over and Jancey was deep into sleep.

Paul's side of the bed was already cold by the time the alarm went off. Up-before-he-has-to-get-up is a bad sign. When he's worried he doesn't sleep. Sometimes I find him out in the garage sweeping the cement floor, or in the back filling the bird feeder, or leaning over the fence feeding last night's bones to the neighbor's dog. This morning I found him in Jancey's room, his hands gripping the slats of her bed.

I came up behind him and rested a hand on his shoulder. "What's wrong?" I whispered. All of his muscles were strung tight, and I knew that he'd have a headache in an hour or so. Believe it or not, taking in Jancey had been his idea. His brother David is a social worker for one of the state agencies here in Des Moines, and he told us all about these babies, how there's no one to take care of them. It hurt my heart to think of them. I've always been partial to babies. One night Paul told me he'd been thinking. "Don't you see?" he'd explained. "You'd have an income, and we could do a little good in this world." Doing-a-little-good runs in Paul's family. He's a plumber, but his father was a missionary, his brother's a social worker, and his mother, old as she is, volunteers three days a week at the nursing home. She told me last week she'd started a knitting group. Just yesterday she brought over three pairs of booties for Jancey. They resemble tiny Christmas stockings in odd shades of green and gold.

Jancey was sleeping, still covered with the receiving blanket I'd draped over her. She looked peaceful, but her hair was damp again. The fever was returning.

"She's getting worse, Eleanor," he said as we filed out and I closed her door.

"I'm taking her to the doctor this morning," I told him, then followed him down the hall, scuffing my big pink house slippers against the carpet. One toe was stained yellow from Jancey's vomit. I'd washed the shoe in the sink, but the worst things, the things you don't want to be reminded of, those never come out. While I watched my slippers take one step at a time, I thought of those dancers, the way they'd seemed to float, the woman's dress billowing, nothing in the world to hold her down.

Paul put on the coffee and kept his back to me. First thing in the morning he walks around the house in boxer shorts. The material flaps around his spindly legs, and his long pale feet slap at the floor. He's a strong man in most ways, but what drew me to him, what keeps me close now, are his weaknesses. While he waited for the water, he went down the hall to give Joel his first shaking. Five or six times each morning Paul or I pull off the covers and shake Joel's foot, each time harder than the last. Joel is six years old now, but he still hasn't discovered anything he likes better than sleeping. This morning Paul tried tickling, and it seemed to work. I could hear Joel's desperate little giggle, then a breathless "Stop, Dad, stop."

The coffee was ready by the time he got back. "A new technique?" I asked, trying to keep my voice light. He filled his cup slowly then turned to me. His skin was still baggy from sleep, and he looked old. He'd been in there tickling Joel, but there was no trace of a smile on his face. "You knew it was going to be like this, didn't you?" I asked. His hand trembled a little as he replaced the pot.

"God knows I didn't," he said simply. Then he carried his coffee away down the long hall to the bathroom.

The pediatric waiting room is divided into two unequal sections by a length of Plexiglass that juts out into the middle of the room. A table at one end keeps people from walking into the flat edge. Orange and brown upholstered chairs line both sides of this transparent wall, back to back, as though some enormous game of musical chairs is about to begin. The smaller section of the room is reserved for well patients, and a prominent sign directs the rest of us to the other side.

When I carried Jancey in this morning, I stopped in the entrance-way, momentarily confused. Some redecorating had gone on since our last visit. A large oval braided rug covered an expanse of institutional carpet in the unwell section, and a baby not much older than Jancey was seated in the big middle of it. While I watched, he crawled to the edge then back again, as though the rug were an island and he were marooned.

"Come on in," one of the receptionists called to me, waving and smiling in that way teachers and nurses and social workers do, professional encouragers.

I had Jancey in her big plastic carseat. It's shaped something like a bucket or a scoop and is perfectly portable if you're big and strong. The inside was lined with receiving blankets, and Jancey was asleep among them. She'd slept straight through her morning feeding, and when I'd lifted her from the crib into the seat she hadn't so much as stirred. More than once this morning I'd passed my hand before her face to feel her breath. When I got to the counter, I heaved the seat onto it and sighed in relief. The three receptionists who work the desk dress in nurses' uniforms, but to assert their individuality, they also wear sweater vests or buttondowns in bright primary colors. They're trim and efficient and seem always to have gotten enough sleep the night before.

The blonde curly-haired one ran a finger down a list of appointments until she found the name then glanced up at me and smiled brightly.

"Jancey Hernandez," she said, her voice much louder than it needed to be. Instantly, the other two looked up. One was on the phone, the receiver cradled on her shoulder, and the other was seated in front of the computer, watching as one screen after another clicked past. The one at the computer abandoned her post to come over.

"I never pass up a chance to coo at a baby," she explained to no one in particular. Her red hair was clipped short around her ears and neck but had been left fluffy on top; little tendrils curled prettily. On her blue sweater she wore a puffy plastic heart pin, red as Snow White's apple. Last month she'd sported a snowman with a tiny top hat, and the month before that a fat Jack O'Lantern. I'd seen her many times in the last few months, watched her fingers moving over the keys of the computer, her small perfectly shaped head bent to the task. She'd never taken notice of me or my baby.

"What a darling," she cried, peering into the bucket from a safe distance. I stared back and said nothing.

"Dr. Kesl will be with you shortly, Mrs. Wilson," the blonde told me as she, too, moved closer to get a look at my baby. I was grateful Jancey was sleeping; otherwise, I knew she would smile back at them, betraying us both. Grabbing up the bucket, I turned and made my way across the brief expanse of carpet to the first available seat. I sat down just as my arms began to shake.

Of course, a baby with AIDS is the sort of thing people talk about, but I hadn't expected it from the people at the Clinic. Up until now, we'd kept the secret fairly well, I'd thought, the doctors, Paul, and I. By some sort of unspoken agreement, we rarely use identifying terms, referring only occasionally to "the disease." Otherwise, we talked about the same illnesses that worry other parents: ear infections, staph infections, urinary infections. For Jancey though, these diseases are only symptoms, not the real thing. Sometimes, I think of AIDS as a monster, the kind that lives in closets in children's books, a horrifying creature with five heads, a scaly body, and horns growing out of his tail. The more frightened I become, the bigger and uglier he gets, until I am sure that he will burst out of the closet and kill us all.

After I'd recovered, I settled Jancey's seat into the chair next to mine and pulled the covers from around her so she wouldn't get too hot. Revived by the cool air of the waiting room, she began the slow process of waking, a series of stretches, blinks, and yawns. Like Joel, she is more at home in her dream world than in this one.

The receptionists made a pretense of returning to work, but again and again their eyes strayed to Jancey. While they watched, I raised her from the bucket and into my arms, bent my face to hers, and kissed the round apple of her cheek. When I felt the warmth of her skin against my lips, my heart shrank back. I've never been afraid of Jancey before, not even that first time I held her in the hospital, when the nurse had lifted her into my arms and said, "She's yours now. God bless you." To stop it, to reprimand us all, I spoke aloud: "She's just a baby, damn it."

Only the curly-haired receptionist seemed to hear. She looked over at me as though I were a new arrival, someone she hardly recognized. "Is Jancey here today for a routine checkup, Mrs. Wilson?" she asked, her eyes flitting to a spot on the wall just above my head and then back to my face again. Obligingly, I craned my head to read the sign: THIS SECTION RESERVED FOR WELL PATIENTS ONLY. YOUR COOPERATION IS APPRECIATED. Smiling, I turned back to her. "Yes," I lied, suddenly myself again.

Jancey and I sat and played pat-a-cake for five minutes or so, until she wet her diaper. While we were off in the restroom changing it, another mother arrived with her baby, a red and shriveled newborn. Though the room was full of empty chairs, the mother took the seat right next to mine. Perhaps she noticed Jancey's empty baby bucket and imagined we might have a chat.

No big deal, really, her sitting next to us. Such a thing might have happened anywhere else, and I wouldn't have given it a thought. Jancey couldn't give her illness to either the mother or her child—even the receptionists knew as much. Still, their foreheads furrowed with concern. "All right," their expressions said. "You've made your point. Now get back to the sick section where you belong." And I considered doing just that—gathering my things, and murmuring some sort of excuse, something about a sneeze or a cough. But I couldn't do it. People who've lost control of life are a superstitious lot: they look for signs, indulge in rituals, refuse to backtrack or take peeks into the future. They huddle in the present and hold on for dear life. It seemed a bad move to go from the well section to the sick section, hasty and unnecessary. So I stayed put and smiled graciously at the new mother, dressed just as I was in the housewife uniform of blue jeans and plain-front sweatshirt, hers powder blue and mine Christmas green.

Jancey rested on my chest, her head on my shoulder. The waving and cooing she'd done while I changed her diaper were over. She seemed spent, her limbs slack, as though she were sleeping. Periodically, though, I felt the brush of her lashes against my neck. I sighed deeply, prompting the new mother to touch my arm. "It's tough, isn't it?" she said.

Her baby was tucked into the small valley between her legs, swaddled hospital fashion. Seeing him reminded me of the day I'd brought Joel home from the hospital. Anxiously, I'd unwrapped him to check his diaper then been unable to rewrap him again. Poor thing, he'd spent an hour or more on the kitchen table wailing and kicking, so angry and frightened that he finally lay gasping for breath while I rolled him up first one way, then another. By the time I gave up, I'd been crying, too. I remembered it now as though it had happened to someone else.

"Yes, it is," I replied, and while I watched, the little being in the blue blanket began to struggle, rocking himself in his mother's lap like an upended and legless caterpillar, helpless, entirely so.

"Hungry again?" his mother asked him, as though all unhappiness were a simple matter of hunger. Already an old hand, she leaned over her diaper bag, drew forth a crocheted blanket, draped it over one shoulder, and lifting the sweatshirt beneath it, readied herself to nurse. Her baby had just opened his mouth to wail when she turned his body and gently nudged his head beneath the green and yellow crochet. I watched him latch on then relax against her.

"Are you nursing?" the new mother asked, ready now for our chat. I had already decided to say yes. After all, I had nursed Joel for nearly a year. Just watching her brought back the ache of the milk followed by the pull of the baby's mouth, pain that passed into pleasure.

"Jancey Hernandez," the nurse called out. I lurched to my feet, jerking Jancey so that her head banged against my shoulder. She responded with a one syllable scream, a sound like someone falling down a well. The new mother looked up at me, surprised. Her baby lay nestled against her, both of them in exactly the right place. For them, this visit to the doctor would be nothing more than an exchange of smiles and compliments. Afterwards, they'd go home and nap together, still nearly one.

I'd been home from the clinic for maybe fifteen minutes when I spotted Joel from the kitchen window, on his way home for lunch. He trudged slowly up the sidewalk, hands in his pockets, a red wool cap pulled low over his forehead. As I watched, he smiled to himself, and my heart lifted, but the smile faded quickly. As he approached the house, Joel seemed to grow smaller instead of larger. I turned away from the window and set his place for lunch, resisting the impulse to rush out and hug him tight. I'd whipped up a box of macaroni and cheese, opened a couple of cans — green beans and fruit cocktail. I arranged several spoons of each on a plastic plate and stored the rest in the refrigerator.

"Where's your lunch?" he asked when he came into the kitchen. Usually, we sit down to lunch together.

"Shh," I said, "Jancey's sleeping."

The doctor's office had sapped whatever energy she had left. The mere sight of someone in white terrifies her. To Dr. Kesl and the others, she's a tiny hostile being, stiff and red-faced. Her rage, though I've seen it many times, surprises even me. In the car on the way home from these visits, she wails, gathers her breath, then wails again. To calm her, I sing lullabies as I drive, my voice so loud that by the time we turn into the driveway, both of us are hoarse. Once, Paul rode along, and was shocked by the din we created. "Eleanor," he cried, "you're screaming, too." On the way home today, I gave up the pretense of singing and simply screamed along with her. At a red light, I paused for breath, and turning my head, looked out the window. In the car next to me an elderly woman sat watching, one hand over her mouth. Snapping my own mouth closed, I tried to compose my features, to reassure her with a smile, but she wouldn't look my way again. She sat stiffly in her bucket seat, staring through her windshield. When the light changed, she pulled away fast, as though leaving the scene of a crime.

"What did the doctor say?" Joel asked. He sat down and picked up his fork.

"Oh, not much new," I sighed, striking that delicate balance between near-truth and outright lie. Joel knows a little about Jancey, but not as much as he should know.

"Jancey's sick, you know," I said, sitting down next to him.

He turned to me with those gentle eyes of his, my mother's eyes. "Don't worry, Momma," he said, patting my knee. "She'll get better." My words, he consoled me with them now.

"Do you think so?" I asked. Then, I got up to fix him a glass of milk.

"Be prepared," Dr. Kesl had told me. "She may take a turn for the worse." He'd examined her slowly—pressing, tapping, prodding—his big hands passing over her again and again. I stood by silently, my eyes on his face, trying to guess his thoughts. No point in asking questions. Jancey's piercing cry drowned out everything, even the ringing telephone. The nurse, who slipped in and out of the room while Dr. Kesl worked, stuck her hand in the door at one point and waved a slip of paper. ANSWER THE PHONE, it said in large red letters.

Dr. Kesl had seemed distracted in a way I couldn't interpret. Something was worrying him, but it might have been something other than Jancey. "Everything doesn't have to do with you," my mother used to remind me.

"Listen," I said when he'd finished the exam, shouted his directions, and passed on a new sheaf of prescriptions. He was stripping off the gloves while his nurse ripped the paper from the examining table. Both of them wore masks and paper gowns; I felt like a naked person on a spaceship. Dr. Kesl glanced over at me and moved to the sink, thrust his hands beneath the faucet, and began to wash in that way they all learn in medical school. "Don't adoptive mothers nurse sometimes?" I asked him. I was dressing Jancey, pushing her thin brown arms into the sleeves of a yellow playsuit. Because Dr. Kesl no longer loomed over her, she screamed intermittently. We talked in the silent spaces she left us.

"They do, yes," he replied, half-turned away, clean and ready to go. Dr. Kesl is a tall man with permanently hunched shoulders and a small bald patch on the back of the head that should make him look older but somehow doesn't. Seeing it made me think of the little bald spot newborns get from rubbing their heads against the sheet. I used to like Dr. Kesl very much. "Don't know much about it, though," he finished and went out the door. As soon as he was gone, Jancey quieted, a momentary lull. I could feel her eyes on my face, but I didn't look back at her just yet. Instead, my gaze slipped from the dark wood of the closed door over to a matted and framed photo of a waterfall that hung between the door and one corner of the wall. Dr. Kesl had snapped it himself while vacationing in Hawaii. I remembered the day he'd pointed it out to me, a better day for both of us. "You ought to go sometime," he'd suggested, his smile warm on me. I'd nodded and cradled newborn Jancey, who still trusted doctors and lay quietly in my arms.

This afternoon, the photograph seemed changed; I no longer recognized its contours. I blinked and stared, blinked and stared, but what I saw made no sense to me. It might have been abstract art. Backing up to a chair, I sank into it and turned my eyes to Jancey. She waited for me in her bucket, intent on a mobile that hung over the examining table. Little lambs, pigs, and rabbits turned slowly above our heads. When the nurse looked in, we were both watching the animals. "Are you all right, Eleanor?" she asked. I noticed for the first time that she, too, was wearing a puffy heart pin. Coincidence, I told myself, though I no longer believe in it.

After Joel returned to school, I flipped on the TV and sat down to watch my soap. I remember nothing of what I saw, though I stared at the screen, my hands folded in my lap. Halfway through the program, I got up and hurried back to the bedroom to Paul's desk. One of the drawers is reserved for my things — old letters, Joel's baby book, a box so full of Mother's costume jewelry that I keep it closed with rubber bands. In the manila folder marked JANCEY I found the letter I received a few weeks ago. The envelope is lavender, postmarked San Antonio, Texas. Holding it, I thought of pictures I've seen of the Alamo, a small fort surrounded by palm trees, the hot sun beating down on people wearing big straw hats.

Jancey's mother is a young woman, hardly more than a teenager. If the picture she sent favors, she is pretty. Her dark hair waves over her shoulders, full and soft looking, but her bangs are teased and sprayed, so that she looks as if she's just come in out of the wind. Her features are arranged neatly on her face; nothing calls attention to itself. The photo she sent, which was taken in one of those arcade booths, is actually a series of three photos. She must have sat very still while the camera clicked because all three look remarkably the same. On the back, she scrawled, TO ELEANOR, WITH LOVE FROM MARY ELIZABETH. You'd think I were her aunt or some school friend. Actually, Mary Elizabeth and I have never met. In some ways, she is no more real to me than the characters on my show. None of them has AIDS, but several have drug problems. They prick their arms with needles and take hideous chances in dark corners. Like her, these characters are young and carry their problems home to their parents. When Mary Elizabeth got sick, she moved back to her mother's house in San Antonio. In her letter, she described cramped quarters and her mother's habit of cooking more food than the two of them can possibly eat. "P.S.," she wrote, "Please call me sometime," but she didn't include her phone number.

"She doesn't really want you to call," Paul told me when I wondered about it out loud.

"Maybe she just forgot," I said.

She had printed her address in the upper left-hand corner of the envelope, so it was a simple matter of calling directory assistance. Someone answered on the fourth ring.

"Hello," I chirped, my voice falsely cheerful, like some salesperson's. "This is Eleanor Wilson. Is Mary Elizabeth there?"

"No, she's not." A mixture of accents gave the words a rich, rounded sound, but I heard the hesitancy behind them. This was Mary Elizabeth's mother, Jancey's grandmother. I tried to think what she might look like. Dark hair and dark eyes was as far as I could get.

"Mrs. Hernandez," I went on. "I'm Eleanor Wilson, Jancey's foster mother. Mary Elizabeth sent me a letter a few weeks ago. She asked me to call."

All I heard was her breath, then mine, then hers again. "My baby Jancey?" she finally murmured.

"Yes," I said.

"Do you know I've never seen her, Mrs. Wilson? Only photos and those are months old."

"Well, I could send . . . "

"No, don't," she interrupted. "It's good of you, but sometimes it's easier not to believe in her, not to believe in any of it."

"She's real, Mrs. Hernandez," I said quietly.

"To you she's real," the rich voice came back. "To me, Mary Elizabeth is real. When you called, I was putting on my sweater, going out the door. She's in the hospital. They don't say when she might come out."

"Oh," I sighed.

"I pray for you every day," Mrs. Hernandez told me. Her voice was suddenly thin. It hardly reached my ear before it was gone.

I thanked her. In the other room, the crib creaked as Jancey shifted and stretched. In another minute or so, I knew she would begin to sob.

"Do you believe in God, Mrs. Wilson?" Mary Elizabeth's mother asked. My own mother had asked the same question of me the day before she died.

"I try." It was the answer I'd given Mother, though not the one she'd hoped for. The last time I'd bent to kiss her, she'd thrown her arms around me, clutched at me as though she expected us to be separated for eternity. "Listen," I said, then stretched my arm overhead, holding the receiver into the air. Jancey was wailing; her indignant scream grew louder each time she took a breath.

"Oh, my little baby," I heard Mrs. Hernandez say.

By the time I hung up, Jancey had soaked herself, her blankets, the sheet. While I cleaned up the mess, I spoke to her in that funny, high-pitched voice she likes.

"Guess who was on the phone?" I asked. She gazed up at me intently. As usual, I had her undivided attention. "Your grandmother," I went on. "You didn't even know you had a grandmother, did you? And she loves you. We all love you."

When she was clean, I carried Jancey into my bedroom, sat down with her in the rocker by the window and put her to my breast. She seemed to know what to do. She sucked for a moment, looked up at me, then returned to the task. She will get nothing today, I know, but if we keep it up, my body may respond.

The view from this window is the best in the house. From my chair, I can see a line of farmland—tan in winter and green in summer—and above that, a wide swatch of sky. Birds glide by, soaring then dipping out of sight. When I was a little girl someone told me that birds house the souls of the dead. I don't know who would tell a child a thing like that, but the idea has stuck with me. I remember being eight years old and standing stock still in the fields, shading my eyes with one hand so I could watch those birds move back and forth between heaven and earth. It seemed to me then that they couldn't quite decide which place they liked best. Sometimes, I tried to sneak up on them while they pecked at the ground. "It's all right," I'd whisper when I got close. "I just want to know your name." Of course, the sound of my voice sent them straight back to the skies. Startled souls, they have always been just out of my reach.

Dispersal

Will Weaver

To get to the Matson sale I had to drive through town. On the edge of town I passed the red brick high school where my wife, Ellen, teaches English in the upper grades. Through the school windows I could see students moving about in front of colored posters. I knew that if Ellen weren't teaching I could not be thinking about buying that New Holland hay mower listed on Matson's sale bill. My forty Holsteins are a fine bunch of cows, but if it weren't for Ellen's town job, things on the farm would be tough.

Which made me think of Matson and his family. I didn't really know them — they were strangers to me — but I could tell from their sale bill what had gone wrong. Too much machinery, not enough wheat. Too many bankers, not enough rain. Tough luck all around.

But bad luck draws a crowd like blood pulls flies. Several pickups followed mine as I turned at the red auction flags. Soon up ahead I could see the shiny aluminum tops of Matson's grain bins. Below stood his newer white house and, beside it, lines of pickups stretched from his yard down his driveway and along the shoulders of the highway.

I parked, leaving myself room to turn around, and began to walk quickly toward the crowd. Sales do that to you. Anything can happen at a sale. In Matson's yard cars and trucks had parked on his lawn.

Their tires rutted the soggy April grass and water welled up in the zig-zag tread marks. Closer to his house, a pickup had backed over a small trimmed spruce tree. The tree remained bent over in a green horseshoe beneath the tire. I slowed my walk. For a moment I thought of turning back, of going home. If everybody left, there could be no sale. But even as I thought, several farmers passed me. I kept walking.

Ahead, the crowd surrounded the auctioneer, who stood atop a hayrack. He wore a wide black cowboy hat, and his tanned, wrinkled throat bobbed like a rooster's craw as he cried the small stuff. Cans of nails. Some rusty barbed wire. Three fence posts. Some half-cans of herbicide. A broken shovel. Beyond the auctioneer, in even lines, was the machinery, mostly John Deere green and Massey-Ferguson red. Beyond everything were Matson's long, unplowed fields.

I registered for a bidder's number, then stood in the sunlight with a cup of coffee and looked over the crowd. You shouldn't get in a hurry at a sale. You ought to get the feel of things. The crowd was mostly farmers with a few bankers and real estate men thrown in. The younger bankers wore flannel shirts and seed-corn caps, but I could pick them out right away. Like the real estate guys, their faces were white and smooth and they squinted a lot, as if they were moles who just today had crawled out of the ground into the sunlight. Moles or skunks.

Off to the side I noticed an older farmer picking through a box of odds and ends. He fished out a rat-tail file from the box and drew it across his thumbnail. He glanced briefly around, then laid the file alongside the box and continued digging.

"Gonna spend some of the wife's money?" somebody said to me. I turned. It was Jim Hartley, who milked cows just down the road from my farm. I knew he already had a good mower.

"Not if she can help it," I said.

He grinned. But then his forehead wrinkled and his blue eyes turned serious. "Hell of a deal, a bank sale like this. Imagine if you had to sell out. Had all these people come onto your farm and start picking through your stuff like crows on road kill."

I looked back at the old man with the file. But both he and it were gone.

"Be tough," I said. That old bastard.

Hartley looked around at the crowd. "Haven't seen Matson any-where. And I can't blame him for that. Good day to get drunk."

"I don't really know the man," I said. "He's a stranger to me."

"He's got some pretty fair equipment," Hartley said. "The combine looks good. And that New Holland mower—it's damn near brand new." He narrowed his eyes. "You could use a good mower."

"Maybe I'll take a look," I said. I raised my coffee cup, took a sip.

Soon enough Hartley went off toward the combine, and I found the mower. From a distance it looked good. The yellow and red colors were still bright, which meant it had always been shedded. Up close I checked the cutting sickle. All the knives were in place and still showed serration, which was like buying good used tires still show-ing the little rubber teats on the face of their tread. Next I turned the hay pickup reel to watch the sickle move. The knives slid easily be-tween their guards with a sound that reminded me of Ellen's good pinking shears. Then I saw the toolbox and the mower's maintenance manual. The thin book was tattered and spotted with grease and with Matson's fingerprints, tiny whirlwinds painted in oil. Its pages fell open to the lubrication section. There Matson had circled and num-bered every one of the grease fittings. I was sold.

I stashed the manual and walked away. I didn't want to linger near the mower and attract other bidders. I bought another cup of coffee and then stood off to the side where I could watch the mower and see who stopped by it. Two men paused by the mower, but they wore wheat seed-caps and smoked, which said they were grain men. Soon they moved on to the combine. One stocky farmer slowed by the mower, but he wore high rubber boots and a Purina "Pig-Power" jacket. I was feeling lucky until a man and his son walked toward the mower like it was a magnet and they were nails. Their cuffs were spotted with manure splash. They wore loose bib overalls for easy bending. And they wore caps cocked to one side, a habit dairymen have from leaning their foreheads against the flanks of their cows.

The son turned the pickup reel while the old man held his ear to the main bearing case. After the old man nodded, the two of them crawled underneath the mower and didn't come out for a long time.

What the hell did they see under there? Finally they came out and stood off to the side. They stared at the mower and nodded and whispered. I wondered how many cows they milked.

By now the auctioneer was in the back of his pickup and was barking his way along the hay wagons and rakes, headed this way. I went over my figures again. I knew in town that mower would sell for $5,500, give or take a couple of hundred. I had set my limit at $5,000. As long as I stuck to that figure I couldn't go wrong.

"Now here's a mighty clean mower—" the auctioneer called. The hook and pull of his arms drew the crowd forward. "Boys, if this mower were a car, we'd call her 'cherry.' You know what this mower would sell for in town, boys, so somebody give me six thousand to start!"

The crowd was silent.

"Five thousand, then!"

Still there was silence.

"Boys, boys—four thousand to start!"

In the silence somewhere a dog barked. The auctioneer's eyes flickered to the clerk and then to the banker. The banker, ever so slightly, shrugged. He was worried about the big tractors and combines, about the house and the land.

"Boys, this ain't a rummage sale, but somebody give a thousand dollars."

I saw the younger dairyman nod, and the bidding was on. At $1,600, it was between the dairyman and me. The young fellow began to look at his father before each bid. At $1,750 I saw the old man fold his arms and squint. At $1,850 he pursed his lips and shook his head. His son mouthed a silent curse and looked down.

"Eighteen hundred three times—gone!" the auctioneer said and pointed to me. I held up my bidder's number for the clerk to record as the crowd dissolved away to the next implement.

I couldn't believe my luck. Eighteen hundred was a steal, no two ways about that. My ears burned. I felt shaky. I sat down on the mower's long drawbar. I ran my hand along its cold steel. I wondered for a moment if the mower had felt any change, if it knew I was up there. Soon enough that shaky feeling gave way to a stronger idea

—that I had to get that mower out of here and home as soon as possible.

I found the clerk's booth and wrote out my check. Then I brought around my truck and got ready to hook on to the mower. Trouble was, Matson had parked the mower in field-cutting position, which meant its mouth was too wide for highway travel. I knew that the drawbar released to swing to a narrower stance. But for the life of me I could not see how. I knew I still wasn't completely over that shaky feeling because if I had been home on my own farm and just sat there a few minutes, I could have figured things out. Not here, though.

I asked another farmer if he knew, but the man was in a hurry to join the crowd around the combine. So there was only one thing to do—find someone who knew for sure. And that was Matson.

I walked up to his house. The drapes were all drawn. I rapped on the door and waited. Inside, I could hear a baby crying. Along the sidewalk was a flower bed. Somebody last fall had done a lot of work planting tulip bulbs, but now their first green spears were drowned in quack grass.

A woman answered the door. She was about Ellen's age, late thirties. She had a bone-white face that said she seldom went outside.

"Is Mr. Matson home?" I asked.

"Yes," she said. She just stood there, looking beyond me to the auction. From deeper in the house I could smell cigarette smoke.

"I bought . . . an implement," I said.

Her pale eyes returned to mine. "Tom—" she called back to the dusk of the hallway.

We waited. There was no answer. No one came forward. She shrugged. "He's back there in the living room," she said, leaning toward the now louder crying of the baby. "Why don't you go on in?"

I walked down the dim hallway into the living room. In the room the TV was a colored bull's-eye. The Phil Donahue show was on, but the picture kept wavering, then skipping ahead several frames. I didn't see Matson anywhere.

"Tom," his wife said loudly from behind me. "Some man's got a question."

Matson slowly sat up. He'd been lying on the couch, on his back.

He was fully dressed in coveralls, leather boots, a cap, even his work gloves. He did not take his eyes off the TV.

"And why should we believe you?" Donahue was saying to a man seated on the stage.

"Tom—" his wife said even louder this time.

"I heard," he said.

"The mower," I began. "I bought the mower and . . . "

Matson nodded and walked past me toward the door. I followed. Outside we walked in silence toward the mower. The auctioneer was standing on the platform of the combine. "Boys, I'll buy this combine myself," he was saying. "Then I'll put it on a truck and I'll haul it to North Dakota and I'll make myself ten thousand dollars in one day. Any one of you could do the same thing, you know that, boys."

Matson did not look at the auctioneer. He walked toward the mower like there was a perfectly straight but invisible line drawn in the dirt. I explained my trouble with the drawbar. He nodded and slid underneath. I saw him remove three cotter keys. He handed them to me, then swung the drawbar.

"Now why didn't I see that?" I said.

But Matson still didn't speak. He just stared at the mower.

"It looks like a good mower," I said, then wished I hadn't. I was sure he would ask me how much I had paid.

He was silent. Then, without looking up from the mower, he said, "I'll hook you on."

"You bet," I answered. I got in my pickup. He waved me backwards, then held up his hands. I felt him slide the iron pin through the mower's tongue and my bumper hitch, felt the clank in my spine. You know when you're hooked on.

I got out of the pickup again but there was not much to say.

"I appreciate the help," I said.

But Matson didn't reply. He just stared at the iron pin that joined his mower to my truck.

I drove off very slowly, watching the mower and Matson in the rearview mirror. It was like they were on TV. The mower stayed the same size, but Matson got smaller and smaller as the camera pulled away from him.

Suddenly Matson's legs began to move. They moved faster and faster, and Matson grew in size in my mirror. Then he was running alongside my truck, pounding on the side with his fist. Ahead of me was the highway, and I thought of speeding up and leaving him behind. But I stopped. I rolled my window halfway down.

Matson's face was completely white. He paused as if he had forgotten why he had run after me. Then he said, "It was a good mower." His right eye twitched as he spoke.

"I believe that," I said.

"It never let me down," he said.

"That's because you took good care of it," I said. "That's plain to see."

"I did," Matson said. "I worked hard. Nobody can take that away from me," he said. His voice was softer now. I could hardly hear him.

"Nobody I know ever said otherwise," I answered. "When your name came up people said, 'Matson—with a little more luck, some more rain, better wheat prices, he'd have made it.' That's what I heard other people say."

"This is not my fault," he said, swinging his arm at the pickups, at the whole auction. "—It wasn't me."

For one long moment I thought of getting out of my pickup and putting my arms around Matson. But you just can't do things like that. We waited there. Finally he turned away.

Out on the highway, I kept the truck at twenty-five. The mower started to sway side to side if I drove any faster. Ahead of me the sun was shining on the dark field where other farmers were planting. I couldn't stop thinking about Matson. About that run-over spruce tree. His white-faced wife, her tulip bed run to weeds.

I thought about Ellen, about how sometimes in the evenings when there's nothing on TV she reads me poems, poems she likes and uses in her English classes. I thought of one poem in particular, by W. H. Auden. His poem was about a painting in a museum, a painting of Icarus and Daedalus. Even I remembered that story from school. Icarus and Daedalus were prisoners on this island, and they made wings from feathers and wax, strapped on the wings, and flew away. Icarus, however, flew too close to the sun, and the heat melted the wax from his feathers and he fell into the ocean and drowned. In the painting there was a plowman in a nearby field. The plowman saw Icarus fall but he just kept plowing. There was a passing ship, too, but it had somewhere to get to and so it just kept sailing.

Suddenly my truck yawed and shuddered. Behind me the mower was whipping violently side to side — I was driving way over fifty. I hit the brakes hard. Back at twenty-five, the mower trailed straight again. I let out a breath and watched my speedometer from then on.

But I hated driving that slowly. What I most wanted to do was get the mower home, park it in the machine shed, and close the door on it. Then I wanted to eat lunch, sweep up in the barn, feed silage, milk, eat supper, watch the weather report, and go to bed. Because once I had done all those things, this day would be over.

Birth

Linda Hasselstrom

The barn is dark, except for sunlight that slants through the vertical bars of the gate. Outside, meadowlarks and redwing blackbirds sing in branches bare of everything but snow. The lariat is snug around a cow's neck, wrapped twice around a post. The rope isn't tied, because the cow might fall and strangle before I could untie or cut it. Instead, I'm holding the end, braced in case she throws her head, but ready to turn her loose if she stops breathing. My father is behind the cow, arm thrust deep inside her. The cow's eyes are glazed; she's calm from exhaustion. She started trying to have this calf sometime during the night. This morning she's given up.

When a cow is having a calf normally, we see front feet emerge, then a tongue and the calf's nose before the water breaks. This time we saw nothing. But the cow's exhaustion, her straining sides and labored breathing and the ragged ground around her feet told us she had been working hard. If my father can get two front feet pointed at the exit, we may be able to pull the calf. If it's dead, we may still save the cow. Even two hind feet would give us something to fasten the calf puller to. If we can't get hold of any part of the calf's body solid enough to pull on, we'll call the veterinarian to do a Caesarian.

Bent over and breathing hard, my father pushes his hand down the birth channel, wet silk over bone, into the universe beyond, the world before birth. He can trace the shape of the calf's body, feel damp hair waiting to be licked clean by the rough mother tongue. He finds one foot. I hand him the smooth chains I took from the nail where they hang all year; they are still warm from being dipped in the bucket of hot water, so the frost of the night won't burn tender flesh, cow's or man's. My father puts his arm inside the other world again, loops chain over the calf's ankle, and reaches in, searching for the other leg.

II

My father has gone back, retreated into that unknown silence before birth, our shadowy history — narrow and dark as a grave, warm and wet as an ancient sea. From warm oblivion we're squeezed into life; the door to death is narrow and uninviting. Egyptians pulled the brain out through the nostrils. The calf is dead. Suddenly my father is reaching ahead, into the other wonder — the time that baffles us all our lives. He searches, grasps, tries to pull the calf through to life. He's spent his days doing this work. It is only in my mind that he's close to death, because he's 80 and I'm 46. He's begun to remark on the deaths of men and women younger than he, but yesterday he pitched two loads of hay off the wagon to his cows.

III

"Which vet shall we call?" He can't get the other leg; he knows the cow will die if we don't get help. Time is over for the calf, ended before it began. My father comes back to the living, and goes to call the vet, who takes the calf out of the cow's side, explaining uterine torsion to us. For two days, because we are busy with the living, the dead calf lies shrinking in the lee of the barn, sticky with birth fluids that seem to shrivel his skin. His eyes never opened; his tongue was never sucked back behind his teeth. His mother never bawls for him; perhaps the struggle was too much, perhaps she knew he was dead. Later we skin the calf, tie the skin loosely over a calf whose mother isn't feeding him enough. After several days, the cow whose calf died in her womb accepts the new calf as hers, licks the hide of her dead baby clean. She has forgotten; only the great scar in her side reminds us of my father's reaching into life, reaching into death.

Beginning

Tim O'Brien

The summer of 1968, the summer I turned into a soldier, was a good time for talking about war and peace. Eugene McCarthy was bringing quiet thought to the subject. He was winning votes in the primaries. College students were listening to him, and some of us tried to help out. Lyndon Johnson was almost forgotten, no longer forbidding or feared; Robert Kennedy was dead but not quite forgotten; Richard Nixon looked like a loser. With all the tragedy and change that summer, it was fine weather for discussion.

And, with all of this, there was an induction notice tucked into a corner of my billfold.

So with friends and acquaintances and townspeople, I spent the summer in Fred's antiseptic cafe, drinking coffee and mapping out arguments on Fred's napkins. Or I sat in Chic's tavern, drinking beer with kids from the farms. I played some golf and tore up the pool table down at the bowling alley, keeping an eye open for likely-looking high school girls.

Late at night, the town deserted, two or three of us would drive a car around and around the town's lake, talking about the war, very seriously, moving with care from one argument to the next, trying to make it a dialogue and not a debate. We covered all the big questions:

justice, tyranny, self-determination, conscience and the state, God and war and love.

College friends came to visit: "Too bad, I hear you're drafted. What will you do?"

I said I didn't know, that I'd let time decide. Maybe something would change, maybe the war would end. Then we'd turn to discuss the matter, talking long, trying out the questions, sleeping late in the mornings.

The summer conversations, spiked with plenty of references to the philosophers and academicians of war, were thoughtful and long and complex and careful. But, in the end, careful and precise argumentation hurt me. It was painful to tread deliberately over all the axioms and assumptions and corollaries when the people on the town's draft board were calling me to duty, smiling so nicely.

"It won't be bad at all," they said. "Stop in and see us when it's over."

So to bring the conversations to a focus and also to try out in real words my secret fears, I argued for running away.

I was persuaded then, and I remain persuaded now, that the war was wrong. And since it was wrong and since people were dying as a result of it, it was evil. Doubts, of course, hedged all this: I had neither the expertise nor the wisdom to synthesize answers; the facts were clouded; there was no certainty as to the kind of government that would follow a North Vietnamese victory or, for that matter, an American victory, and the specifics of the conflict were hidden away — partly in men's minds, partly in the archives of government, and partly in buried, irretrievable history. The war, I thought, was wrongly conceived and poorly justified. But perhaps I was mistaken, and who really knew, anyway?

Piled on top of this was the town, my family, my teachers, a whole history of the prairie. Like magnets, these things pulled in one direction or the other, almost physical forces weighting the problem, so that, in the end, it was less reason and more gravity that was the final influence.

My family was careful that summer. The decision was mine and it was not talked about. The town lay there, spread out in the corn and watching me, the mouths of old women and Country Club men poised in readiness to find fault. It was not a town, not a Minneapolis or New York, where the son of a father can sometimes escape scrutiny. More, I owed the prairie something. For twenty-one years I'd lived under its laws, accepted its education, eaten its food, wasted and guzzled its water, slept well at night, driven across its highways, dirtied and breathed its air, wallowed in its luxuries. I'd played on its Little League teams. I remembered Plato's *Crito,* when Socrates, facing certain death — execution, not war — had the chance to escape. But he reminded himself that he had seventy years in which he could have left the country, if he were not satisfied or felt the agreements he'd made with it were unfair. He had not chosen Sparta or Crete. And, I reminded myself, I hadn't thought much about Canada until that summer.

The summer passed this way. Golden afternoons on the golf course, an illusive hopefulness that the war would grant me a last-minute reprieve, nights in the pool hall or drug store, talking with towns-folk, turning the questions over and over, being a philosopher.

Near the end of that summer the time came to go to the war. The family indulged in a cautious sort of Last Supper together, and afterward my father, who is brave, said it was time to report at the bus depot. I moped down to my bedroom and looked the place over, feeling quite stupid, thinking that my mother would come in there in a day or two and probably cry a little. I trudged back up to the kitchen and put my satchel down. Everyone gathered around, saying so long and good health and write and let us know if you want anything. My father took up the induction papers, checking on times and dates and all the last-minute things, and when I pecked my mother's face and grabbed the satchel for comfort, he told me to put it down, that I wasn't supposed to report until tomorrow. I'd misread the induction date.

After laughing about the mistake, after a flush of red color and a flood of ribbing and a wave of relief had come and gone, I took a long drive around the lake. Sunset Park, with its picnic table and little beach and a brown wood shelter and some families swimming. The Crippled Children's School. Slater Park, more kids. A long string of split level houses, painted every color.

The war and my person seemed like twins as I went around the town's lake. Twins grafted together and forever together, as if a separation would kill them both.

The thought made me angry.

In the basement of my house I found some scraps of cardboard. I printed obscene words on them. I declared my intention to have no part of Vietnam. With delightful viciousness, a secret will, I declared the war evil, the draft board evil, the town evil in its lethargic acceptance of it all. For many minutes, making up the signs, making up my mind, I was outside the town. I was outside the law. I imagined myself strutting up and down the sidewalks outside the depot, the bus waiting and the driver blaring his horn, the *Daily Globe* photographer trying to push me into line with the other draftees, the frantic telephones calls, my head buzzing at the deed.

On the cardboard, my strokes of bright red were big and ferocious looking. The language was clear and certain and burned with a hard, defiant, criminal, blasphemous sound. I tried reading it aloud. I was scared. I was sad.

Later in the evening I tore the signs into pieces and put the shreds in the garbage can outside. I went back into the basement. I slipped the crayons into their box, the same stubs of color I'd used a long time before to chalk in reds and greens on Roy Rogers' cowboy boots.

I'd never been a demonstrator, except in the loose sense. True, I'd taken a stand in the school newspaper on the war, trying to show why it seemed wrong. But, mostly, I'd just listened.

"No war is worth losing your life for," a college acquaintance used to argue. "The issue isn't a moral one. It's a matter of efficiency: What's the most efficient way to stay alive when your nation is at war? That's the issue."

But others argued that no war is worth losing your country for, and when asked about the case when a country fights a wrong war, those people just shrugged.

Most of my college friends found easy paths away from the problem, all to their credit. Deferments for this and that. Letters from doctors or chaplains. It was hard to find people who had to think much about the problem. Counsel came from two main quarters, pacifists and veterans of foreign wars, but neither camp had much to offer. It wasn't a matter of peace, as the pacifists argued, but rather a matter of when and when not to join others in making war. And it wasn't a matter of listening to an ex-lieutenant colonel talk about serving in a right war, when the question was whether to serve in what seemed a wrong one.

On August 13, I went to the bus depot. A Worthington *Daily Globe* photographer took my picture standing by a rail fence with four other draftees.

Then the bus took us through corn fields, to little towns along the way—Rushmore and Adrian—where other recruits came aboard. With the tough guys drinking beer and howling in the back seats, brandishing their empty cans and calling one another "scum" and "trainee" and "GI Joe," with all this noise and hearty farewelling, we went to Sioux Falls. We spent the night in a YMCA. I went out alone for a beer, drank it in a corner booth, then I bought a book and read it in my room.

At noon the next day our hands were in the air, even the tough guys. We recited the oath—some of us loudly and daringly, others in bewilderment. It was a brightly lighted room, wood paneled. A flag gave the place the right colors. There was smoke in the air. We said the words, and we were soldiers.

I'd never been much of a fighter. I was afraid of bullies: frustrated anger. Still, I deferred to no one. Positively lorded myself over inferiors. And on top of that was the matter of conscience and conviction, uncertain and surface-deep but pure nonetheless. I was a confirmed liberal. Not a pacifist, but I would have cast my ballot to end the Vietnam war, I would have voted for Eugene McCarthy, hoping he would make peace. I was not soldier material, that was certain.

But I submitted. All the soul searchings and midnight conversations and books and beliefs were voided by abstention, extinguished by forfeiture, for lack of oxygen, by a sort of sleepwalking default. It was no decision, no chain of ideas or reasons, that steered me into the war.

It was an intellectual and physical stand-off, and I did not have the energy to see it to an end. I did not want to be a soldier, not even an observer of war. But neither did I want to upset a peculiar balance between the order I knew, the people I knew, and my own private world. It was not just that I valued that order. I also feared its opposite — inevitable chaos, censure, embarrassment, the end of everything that had happened in my life, the end of it all.

And the stand-off is still there. I would wish this book could take the form of a plea for everlasting peace, a plea from one who knows, from one who's been there and come back, an old soldier looking back at a dying war.

That would be good. It would be fine to integrate it all to persuade my younger brother and perhaps some others to say no to wrong wars.

Or it would be fine to confirm the old beliefs about war: It's horrible, but it's a crucible of men and events and, in the end, it makes more of a man out of you.

But, still, none of this seems right.

Now, war ended, all I am left with are simple, unprofound scraps of truth. Men die. Fear hurts and humiliates. It is hard to be brave. It is hard to know what bravery *is*. Dead human beings are heavy and awkward to carry, things smell different in Vietnam, soldiers are dreamers, drill sergeants are boors, some men thought the war was proper and others didn't and most didn't care. Is that the stuff for a morality lesson, even for a theme?

Do dreams offer lessons? Do nightmares have themes, do we awaken and analyze them and live our lives and advise others as a result? Can the foot soldiers teach anything important about war, merely for having been there? I think not. He can tell war stories.

The View from a Monastery

Benet Tvedten, O.S.B.

In the part of South Dakota where I live, there are two attractions to which sightseers are drawn: a cheese factory and a monastery. A sign at a roadside park on U.S. Highway 12 indicates that the monastery is one of the nearby points of interest, and motorists, who are passing through, frequently swing by for a look. On Sunday afternoons people like to drive out to see the monastery. Sometimes during the week a busload of people will arrive. Usually, the bus brings a homemakers' club or school children or a group of senior citizens. Most of the time they have come directly to the monastery from the cheese plant.

I have lived in the monastery for over thirty years, and I have witnessed this unending stream of tourists. On occasion I have had the responsibility of showing the monastery to people who have arranged a tour. Many of them appear to be genuinely impressed by what they see. Others are obviously baffled. This is understandable because monasticism will always be a mystery for most people. Some tourists are concerned only about the physical structure. They compliment us monks for having constructed the monastery ourselves. They seldom ask about our prayer life.

On one tour, I thought I had given a good practical explanation for our vow of celibacy. My failure was apparent when I was asked, "Do monks go to dances?"

There are many false notions about monasticism. Pious people think that monks are holy. People who don't know much about religion think we are peculiar. The truth of the matter is that we are neither. I will concede, though, that I have known individual monks who were both. Most of us, however, are ordinary men who find that it is easier for us to be holier here than in some other place.

Brother Patrick was holy. His holiness was not the kind that is commonly associated with sanctity, but he was my kind of saint. He came to the monastery when he was in his fifties and he lived with us for fifteen years. On his deathbed, he admitted that the happiest years of his life had been spent in the monastery. Earlier he had worked on a General Motors assembly line in Flint, Michigan, and before that he had fought in the Battle of the Bulge. If we had been naive, we would have been convinced that he had won the Battle of the Bulge single-handedly.

Brother Paddy worked in our laundry for a while. By the time we had grown accustomed to pranks like having our underwear starched, he was transferred to the monastery kitchen. His menus were posted so that we could always be prepared. We learned not to expect much for lunch on a "T. T. and R." day. No one was ever able to establish if "Turkey Turds and Rainwater" was an army term or if Brother Patrick had invented it himself. The other veterans in the monastery claimed to have never heard the expression. Maybe they didn't want the rest of us to know that they could remember.

Paddy had been on the winning side in the Battle of the Bulge and in more recent years he had won his own personal battle with alcoholism. Now he knew that cancer would win the last battle. He'd had two skirmishes with it. This time it was inoperable. A week before his death, he was as eager as ever to entertain all of his "brethren" who gathered at his bedside. Sitting on the edge of his bed and chain smoking cigarettes ("Why not? I don't have lung cancer."), he regaled us with war stories and recollections of his youth in an upstate New York town where he could buy a bucket of beer for a nickel.

When Brother James was alone with him one day, Paddy told him, "Jim, when you see that I'm gone, grab this watch off my wrist. Don't let any of the brethren get to it first. It's a good watch and it'll keep time for you for the rest of your life."

A day or so before he lost consciousness, he told those of us who were in his smoke-filled room, "I hope you bastards have to bury me on the coldest day of the winter." We could have pleaded with him to wait for spring, but he was ready to leave and he seemed assured of his destination. We carried Brother Patrick to the monastery cemetery not on the coldest day of that winter but on a day with a chill factor that would nevertheless have pleased him.

Perhaps there is some misunderstanding about where monks come from. That we were somehow conditioned from childhood to enter a monastery. That our previous circumstances in life were different from other people's. This is not so. We had other alternatives. One monk gave up a navy career. Another abandoned his studies for a doctorate. Others had to dispose of a farm or a business.

Some of us came to the monastery from cities — Milwaukee, Seattle, Indianapolis, Minneapolis — and others came from farms and small towns in the Dakotas. Why did we come to this place?

I know why when I look down into the valley at night. The monastery is built on a rise from where the flat farmland of the Whetstone Valley can be seen. In the dark the fields are not visible but the lights are. The lights from Ortonville, thirty miles away in Minnesota, and the lights from Milbank, half that distance, and the lights of the smaller towns — Wilmot, Corona, Twin Brooks, Stockholm — all these lights and the yard lights in the farms create an illusion. I look at the valley and I think that I see an enormous city. It is distant and I am removed from it. This is the way it should be, I tell myself. This is the way it was in the third and fourth centuries when throngs of Christians fled from the cities of Egypt and Greece and went to live in the desert. They believed that the *parousia* (the second coming of Christ) was imminent. They wanted to be ready. In the desert, apart from the rest of mankind, they could prepare themselves by prayer and penance. They were hermits. The word "monk" comes from the Greek *monos,* alone, a solitary. Gradually these hermits evolved into communities. The *parousia* didn't occur, but monasticism became firmly rooted in Christendom. Near the end of the fifth century, St. Benedict, the Father of Western Monasticism, abandoned his studies in the city of Rome and went to live in a cave.

I can understand why St. Benedict left the city. Sometimes when I look at the lights in the valley, I think of the things I'd like to do in that imaginary city. Most of the time, though, I am satisfied to be where I am. And at dawn when we are on our way to morning prayer, the lights in the valley are going off and the sun is rising, and then I can see the reality — hay bales and fields of corn and alfalfa. It is much better for a monk to live in the country.

Agrarians can understand our need to work the land, to grow much of our own food, to provide bread for both the table and altar. People who are into Zen and transcendental meditation can appreciate our need for contemplation. Communitarians know how important it is for us to depend on the resources of those with whom we share our lot. We hold all things in common and the whole community benefits, directly or indirectly, from the abilities of the individual monks — the teacher, the carpenter, the potter, the beekeeper, the weaver, the priest. People who come here to make a retreat, to absorb the atmosphere of the monastery, know what we are about. Still, there are countless others for whom we remain an enigma.

Between the monastery church and the Whetstone Valley is the cemetery. The trees surrounding the cemetery are obscured by the night. In moonlight I cannot distinguish a Russian olive from a spruce, but I know the trees are there and I know that they enclose the graves of monks. There is no illusion here. This is where our bodies wait for their resurrection. You see, monks still believe that the *parousia* will happen. This is why we came to the monastery and, perhaps, this is why we will always remain an enigma to many people.

July 1947: Many Point Scout Camp

Gerald Vizenor

"I am my past and if I were not, my past would not exist any longer either for me or for anybody. It would no longer have any relation with the present," wrote Jean-Paul Sartre in *Being and Nothingness.* "That certainly does not mean that it would not be but only that its being would be undiscoverable. I am the one by whom my past arrives in this world."

The White Earth Reservation returned to my past in a most unusual manner. I arrived as a tenderfoot in the Viking Council of the Boy Scouts of America in time to connect with a summer adventure at the Many Point Scout Camp in northern Minnesota. Much to my surprise, the camp was located on wilderness reservation land north of Ice Cracking Lake on the eastern border of the Tamarac National Wildlife Refuge.

I had no idea that the camp was on the White Earth Reservation. Park Rapids darkened, and Fish Hook Lake passed in the last light. The bus moaned on the turns, the narrow road near Two Inlets, and crossed the reservation border near Indian Creek. White pines marched on the pale horizon. The bus rumbled on gravel roads for more than an hour through the White Earth State Forest to Many Point Lake. The camp was new and we lived two scouts to a tent. Nils, my tent mate, was from the same elementary school in the city;

he was lonesome, and the older boys abused him because he was stout and devoured canned sardines. The smell of fish in the tent reminded me of cod liver oil, the preventive medicine of the depression and the war.

Mary Norman Haase is responsible, in a sense, for my best experiences in Cub Scouts and then as a tenderfoot in the Boy Scouts. She urged me with love and cookies to be part of her den, the primal coterie of the Cub Scouts. She was generous and spontaneous, a wise mother who cared for more than a dozen boys, most of them on familial margins. Walter, her husband, was a scout master, and her son was an Eagle Scout.

Mary would invite me to her house on my way home from school; she never tested me or teased rumors from me about my mother, stepfather, or my troubles. Rather, she praised me as a parent would, and so she praised my best ash coffee table, with a rubbed blond finish, that I made in a wood-working class. Now, my sadness inhibits the truth behind the table. My mother told me she would be home, that she would wait for me to return with my surprise from school. LaVerne lied, she was not there; no note, no reason, no humor, no honor. I worried over my table and then decided that she would never see it; she never even remembered.

Mary was at rest on the porch; she invited me in with my dog and the table. She loved me, my creation, my dog, that warm afternoon, and she loved the light she saw in children. I would be a writer a decade later, a crossblood at the scratch line, and she presented me with my first desk. I am moved and heartened in these memories; she was a humane and honest den mother, closer to being a saint than a mother dared to be with children on the loose. I dedicated *Raising the Moon Vines* to her, my first book of haiku.

The Boy Scouts of America earn the honors and merits that are bestowed on them by earnest adults in the troop, in the best of times at summer camp; however, the behavior is material, political, and dubious ceremonies are borrowed from tribal cultures. That a merit badge, or the Order of the Arrow, represents the measure of a mature course is ostentatious and insincere. The badge is a cultural tribute that has value to other scouts and masters.

Many Point Lake was wild and clean with red pine and roses, with moccasin blooms and water lilies. We were in line early for breakfast, touched by the moist air. I was invited that morning, with another, a tenderfoot, to earn my merit badge in compass reading. We were driven down a dirt road several miles to a remote area south of the lake, but not far from the shore. There, we were provided with one compass, pencil, paper, and packed lunches for our first merit badge test. We had our knives and full canteens. The scout master instructed us to read our compass and find our way back to the camp. We were bored by the instructions because any fool could follow the dirt road and tire tracks back, no compass test there. Six years later, at a night compass course in military basic training, I told that scout story, the crossblood on the trail. We used the compass then because we had to mark the maps, but the real milestones were truck tire tracks.

When the truck disappeared in a cloud of dust, we decided to have a real adventure, liberation from the regimentation of the day. We followed the shoreline to the west and then north, easy enough, and ate our lunch on the far side of the lake from the camp. We could hear the distant sound of scouts in canoes; this was tribal land. The lakeshore was wild then, there were no cabins. We saw beaver, deer, bald eagles in nests near the north end of the lake, and other animals and birds. Ten hours later we walked back into camp, in the dark. We were tired, but pleased with our adventure. We waited for some salute, but we heard no praise.

Walter Haase and the other scout masters were in a panic because they were convinced that we were lost; they had organized several search parties. So, we had at least caused some adventure for other scouts. Several scouts passed the word in the camp that we had been found; we were described as scared and hungry, but unharmed.

"How could anybody get lost with a compass?" asked a senior scout at a marshmallow roast that night. He said we were stupid and gave other scouts a bad name. "All you had to do was follow the road back."

At first we both protested his censure, but later we chose silence. We were wise not to run down the compass test then, or to boast about our real adventures. Our wisdom cost us a merit badge and some humiliation, but when we told our stories about eagles and beavers, we were esteemed by the other tenderfoot scouts, if not for our adventure, then at least for our imagination. Stories are a better past than merit badges.

At the end of the two-week encampment the scout masters produced the Order of the Arrow, an adventitious comic opera with racialism, wild dancers, shamanic simulations, and a bearded man who ate fire.

We listened to wild rumors and waited near our tents until dark; no flashlights were permitted. The senior scouts, those who had been at other summer camps, would not reveal what happened at the Order of the Arrow ceremonies. At last we were led to a humid clearing in the forest and told to sit in a circle around a fire pit. Our silence was unnatural, once or twice a nervous laugh, and then there were animal sounds and a wild shout from the trees behind our circle. Silence once more, and then a ball of fire flew down from a red pine into the circle and hit the pit. The fire spread over the oil soaked firewood. At the same time the stranger with the beard ran to the pit and spit gasoline on the fire from the four cardinal points. Later, he spit fire in the main lodge. We were amazed, a high-risk performance by some of the most conservative scout masters at the camp. Later, we pursued the fire eater and learned that he had been hired to enhance the Order of the Arrow. The shamanic ball of fire was guided by a thin wire between the tree and the pit.

The bonfire created wild shadows in the circle. A dancer leapt from behind the trees, dressed in breechclout and dubious tribal vestments. The dancer pounded the earth around the fire, between the scouts in the circle. He came closer to me, wailed and circled me, and then moved to circle another tenderfoot. I watched his stomach bounce; the scout paint he used to tone his pink body was streaked with sweat. He was the scout master who shamed me for being lost. He told me, "A real scout is never lost." He would not believe that we were in agreement. I was twelve then, overawed at the circle, but later, I wondered who these white men thought they were, playing Indian on stolen tribal land.

The purpose of this comic opera on the White Earth Reservation was to scare the tenderfoot scouts, and to initiate certain proud and proper senior scouts into the Order of the Arrow. The pretend warriors raised the novice by the hair and decorated his face with paint. Then the comic warriors presented a marked arrow to the scout; he was touched on the shoulders, a modern chivalric code on a reservation. These men of the arrow were not horsemen, or gallant gentlemen of the woodland; they were pretenders to the land, abusers of gasoline, and artless readers of the compass.

Sunday mornings, in connection with religious services at the camp, we were told to write to our parents. I pretended to write to my mother: You never told me when I left for camp that they were sending me back to the reservation. You should have said something. My father grew up here you know, everybody knows that, we are on the White Earth Reservation.

There are animals and birds everywhere, but I don't like the people very much here. Everybody is always telling me what to do all the time. They think they own this place. I can't even swim when I feel like it, everything is on time, go here and go there, and I am hungry all the time.

I am living in a tent with another scout and he eats sardines all the time and leaves the cans in the tent. He said he can do it because he's a Norwegian. He smells like a fish in the tent. He never gave me any either.

One of the scout leaders started a fire in the big fireplace in the main lodge with his mouth. I was fooled at first but then I saw the gasoline he drank and spit at a match he was holding in front of the logs. But don't worry because he told us never to drink gasoline.

Yesterday they killed a whole pig and roasted it over a fire outside. I didn't eat any because it smelled awful.

Everybody tells us to work all the time. We wanted to explore around the lake but nobody would let us. One kid has all the merit badges they make. He's an eagle scout and everything, but he looks dumb with his thick glasses. He walks like Black Foot, you know, my dumb friend across the alley.

We learned about canoeing and life saving and fire building. In the morning they give us cold toast and cold eggs. They gave us time after church today to write to you.

My mother never cared much about me as a scout; she remembered my crimes, my punishments, but not my victory gardens, or my time at summer camp. I pretended to write a second letter to my mother: You won't believe this but they took us away from the camp yesterday to find our way back with a compass, but we went for a walk around the lake and they said we were lost. The kid with the thick glasses said he hoped we would get lost for the day on purpose. We had a great time. Nobody told us what to do all day. We circled the camp and walked around the lake until dark. We saw a nest of bald eagles. We knew where we were and didn't need a compass. Nobody could get lost walking around a lake anyway. It was really wild.

When we came back they thought we were lost so now we have to stay here all the time. The kid with the thick glasses laughs at us all the time. Nobody believes we were not lost. Another dumb thing here is the order of the arrow when all the scouts pretend they are Indians. Tell the Frog I will be home next weekend.

The Many Point Scout Camp is operated by the Viking Council of the Boy Scouts of America on more than twenty thousand acres of valuable tribal land on the White Earth Reservation. Not many loyal and trustworthy scouts are aware that the land was stolen from tribal people by the federal government.

Contributors

Jonis Agee lives in St. Paul, Minnesota, where she teaches creative writing at the College of St. Catherine. She is the author of two novels, *Sweet Eyes* and *Strange Angels,* and two collections of stories, *Pretend We've Never Met* and *Bend This Heart.*

Jim Barnes is editor of *Chariton Review* and professor of comparative literature at Northeast Missouri State University. He lives in Macon, Missouri. Among his many collections of poems are *The Sawdust War* and *La Plata Cantata.*

Candace Black lives in Mankato, Minnesota, where she teaches English at Mankato State University and at nearby Gustavus Adolphus College in St. Peter, Minnesota. Her poems have appeared in many magazines and anthologies, including *The Decade Dance.*

Ron Block was born and raised in Gothenburg, Nebraska, taught for several years at North Dakota State University in Fargo, and currently teaches at Marquette University in Milwaukee. He is the author of *Dismal River: A Narrative Poem.*

Carol Bly — author and lecturer — lives in St. Paul, Minnesota, and is the author of *Letters from the Country, Backbone, The Passionate, Accurate Story,* and *The Tomcat's Wife and Other Stories.*

Robert Bly, poet, translator, and editor, was born and raised in Minnesota, where he splits his time between his home in Minneapolis and his cabin in northern Minnesota. Among his many books are, most recently, *What Have I Ever Lost by Dying? Selected Prose Poems, Remembering James Wright, Iron John,* and *American Poetry: Wildness and Domesticity,* a collection of his essays on poetry.

Grace Butcher lives in Chardon, Ohio, and is associate professor of English at Kent State University—Geauga Campus. She is a former United States champion distance runner. Her books of poems include *Rumors of Ecstasy, Rumors of Death, Before I Go out on the Road,* and *Child, House, World.*

John Caddy lives in rural Forest Lake Township in Minnesota and works as a self-employed writer and poet. He is the author of two collections of poems: *Eating the Sting* and *The Color of Mesabi Bones.*

Jared Carter's books of poems include *Work, for the Night Is Coming* and *After the Rain.*

Marisha Chamberlain lives in St. Paul, Minnesota, and is adjunct professor of playwriting and scriptwriting at the University of Minnesota and Augsburg College. Her award-winning play *Scheherazade* was produced in London.

Sharon Chmielarz, author of the collection of poems *But I Won't Go out in a Boat,* lives in Minneapolis, Minnesota, and works as a teacher and writer.

David Citino is the author of seven books of poems, including *The Discipline: New and Selected Poems, 1980–1992.* He directs the creative writing program at Ohio State University and is president of the board of trustees of Thurber House, a writer's center located in the restored boyhood home of James Thurber in Columbus, Ohio.

Marilyn Coffey teaches in the creative writing program at Fort Hays State University in Hays, Kansas. Her essays about the Great Plains have appeared in numerous newspapers and magazines. She is the author of *Great Plains Patchwork,* a memoir, and a novel, *Marcella.*

A native of St. Louis, Philip Dacey has lived and worked in southwestern Minnesota for many years, where he is professor of English at Southwest State University in Marshall, Minnesota. His collections of poems include *Night Shift at the Crucifix Factory, The Man with Red Suspenders,* and *How I Escaped from the Labyrinth.*

Robert Dana lives in Coralville, Iowa, and is poet-in-residence and professor of English at Cornell College in Mt. Vernon, Iowa. He is the author of several collections of poetry, including *What I Think I Know: New and Selected Poems.*

Leo Dangel lives in Marshall, Minnesota, where he is professor of English at Southwest State University. He is the author of two collections of poems, *Old Man Bruner Country* and *Hogs and Personals.*

Alan Davis is associate editor of *American Fiction,* the annual anthology of short fiction, and the author of a collection of stories, *Rumors from the Lost World.* Davis teaches fiction writing and chairs the English department at Moorhead State University in Moorhead, Minnesota.

Susan Strayer Deal lives and writes in Lincoln, Nebraska. Her collections of poems include *Trees and Flowers, Sometimes So Easy, The Dark Is a Door,* and *No Moving Parts.*

After a distinguished career of teaching English and writing at the University of Michigan, Stephen Dunning retired to full-time writing and lecturing. He is the author of six chapbooks of poetry, most recently *Good Words,* and a collection of stories, *To the Beautiful Women.* With William Stafford, he has written *Writing Poems: Getting the Knack,* an innovative textbook on creative writing.

Louise Erdrich grew up in North Dakota and is the author of two collections of poetry, *Jacklight* and *Baptism of Desire,* and four novels, *Love Medicine, The Beet Queen, Tracks,* and *Crown of Columbus,* written with Michael Dorris.

Dave Etter lives in Elburn, Illinois, and is the author of twenty-one collections of poetry, among them *Home State, Live at the Silver Dollar, Electric Avenue, Selected Poems,* and his latest, *Carnival.* Poems from his *Alliance, Illinois* have been performed on stage by four theater groups.

David Allan Evans is the author of *Hanging out with the Crows,* a collection of poems, and *Remembering the Soos,* a collection of autobiographical essays. He lives in Brookings, South Dakota, where he is professor of English at South Dakota State University. In 1992 he was awarded a Fulbright Scholarship to Nanjing University in China.

Roland Flint was born and raised in Park River, North Dakota. Among his many collections of poems are *Resuming Green, Pigeon,* and *Stubborn.* He lives in Silver Spring, Maryland, and is professor of English at Georgetown University in Washington, D.C. A result of his study and travels in Bulgaria is a collection of translations of the work of Boris Xristov, *The Wings of the Messenger.*

Randall Freisinger lives in Houghton, Michigan, where he is professor of creative writing and literature at Michigan Technical University. He is the author of two collections of poems, *Running Patterns* and *Hand Shadows.*

Alice Friman lives in Indianapolis, Indiana, where she is professor of English and creative writing at the University of Indianapolis. She is the author of four collections of poetry, including *Reporting from Corinth.*

Diane Glancy is the author of five collections of poetry, including *Long Dog's Winter Count;* a collection of autobiographical essays, *Claiming Breath;* and two collections of short stories, most recently *Firesticks.* She teaches creative writing and Native American literature at Macalester College in St. Paul, Minnesota.

Paul Gruchow worked for many years as a journalist and editor for the Worthington, Minnesota, newspaper before turning to teaching at St. Olaf College. His essays on the natural landscapes of the prairies and plains have appeared in many periodicals. He is the author of *Travels in Canoe Country, Minnesota: Images of Home, The Necessity of Empty Places,* and *Journal of a Prairie Year.*

Patricia Hampl lives in St. Paul, Minnesota, and is professor of English at the University of Minnesota. She is the author of two collections of poetry, *Woman Before an Aquarium* and *Resort and Other Poems,* and three collections of prose, *Virgin Time, A Romantic Education,* and *Spillville.*

Twyla Hansen lives in Lincoln, Nebraska, and works as a horticulturist at Nebraska Wesleyan University. Her poems have appeared in many periodicals and in one collection, *How to Live in the Heartland.*

Joanne Hart lives off in the woods near the Pigeon River on the Grand Portage Chippewa Indian Reservation in Grand Portage, Minnesota. Her poems in *Witch Tree,* a collaboration with Minnesota artist Hazel Belvo, reflect life on the Minnesota-Canadian border.

Margaret Hasse lives in St. Paul, Minnesota, and is the author of two collections of poems, *In a Sheep's Eye, Darling,* and *Stars Above, Stars Below.* In addition to her work as a free-lance consultant, she teaches writing at The Loft in Minneapolis and at Hennepin County Adult Corrections.

Linda Hasselstrom's writing about the land and land-related issues has appeared in her collections of poems *Caught by One Wing* and *Roadkill* and in her collections of essays, *Going over East, Windbreak,* and *Land Circle: Writings Collected from the Land.* She writes and ranches near Hermosa, South Dakota.

Jon Hassler is writer-in-residence at St. John's University in Collegeville, Minnesota. He is the author of six novels, including *Staggerford, North of Hope,* and *Dear James.* He has also written two novels for young adults.

Phil Hey lives in Sioux City, Iowa, and teaches writing at Briar Cliff College. He is the author of *A Change of Clothes,* a collection of poems.

Jim Heynen lives in St. Paul, Minnesota, and teaches writing at St. Olaf College in Northfield, Minnesota. Among his many books are *One Hundred over 100,* a collection of interviews with people more than 100 years old; *Notes from Custer, A Suitable Church,* and *The Man Who Kept Cigars in His Cap,* collections of poems; and a collection of short stories.

Bill Holm is the author of the highly acclaimed *Coming Home Crazy,* a collection of essays about his travels and teaching in China. He is the author of two collections of poems, *Boxelder Bug Variations* and *The Dead Get by with Everything,* and a collection of essays, *The Music of Failure.* He makes his home in Minneota, Minnesota.

Lois Phillips Hudson was born in Jamestown, North Dakota, and since 1969 has been professor of English at the University of Washington. Her fiction and essays have appeared in many journals, and she is the author of *Reapers of the Dust* and *The Bones of Plenty,* called "the farm novel of the Depression 'Thirties" by the *New York Times.*

Jan Huesgen grew up in Devils Lake, North Dakota, where her family settled four generations ago. She lives in Fargo, North Dakota, and is the author of a chapbook of poems, *Those Who Follow.*

Garrison Keillor created and hosted "A Prairie Home Companion," a radio program that was produced by Minnesota Public Radio and broadcast nationally on the American Public Radio network. His current public radio program is "American Radio Company." Keillor was born and raised in Anoka, Minnesota, and is the author of *Leaving Home, WLT: A Radio Romance, Happy to Be Here, Lake Wobegon Days,* and *We Are Still Married.*

William Kloefkorn lives in Lincoln, Nebraska, and is professor of English at Nebraska Wesleyan University. He is the author of more than fifteen collections of poetry, including *Alvin Turner as Farmer, Cottonwood County* (with Ted Kooser), and, most recently, *Dragging Sand Creek for Minnows.*

Before retiring from the English department at Sangamon State University in Illinois, John Knoepfle taught English and writing for many years. He is the author and translator of several books of poems, among them *Poems from the Sangamon, Selected Poems,* and *Rivers into Islands.*

Ted Kooser lives in Garland, Nebraska, and is associate vice president of Lincoln Benefit Life Company in Lincoln, Nebraska. He is the author of many collections of poetry, including *Sure Signs: New and Selected Poems* and *One World at a Time.*

Ellen Kort lives in Appleton, Wisconsin, where she works as a full-time writer and writing consultant. She is the author of seven books and a play and the winner of *Nimrod* magazine's Pablo Neruda Prize for Poetry. She travels extensively, teaching writing workshops throughout the United States, New Zealand, Australia, and the Bahamas.

Greg Kuzma lives in Crete, Nebraska, and is professor of English at the University of Nebraska-Lincoln. For many years he was editor of the magazine *Pebble* and the small but influential Best Cellar Press. Among his many collections of poems are *Good News, A Turning,* and *Verticals.*

Joseph Langland was born in Spring Grove, Minnesota, and grew up on his family's farm seven miles south in northeastern Iowa. He is the author of many collections of poems and translations, among them *The Wheel of Summer, The Sacrifice Poems, Any Body's Song, Poems from the Russian Underground* (coeditor and translator), and *Selected Poems.* He lives in Amherst, Massachusetts, where he is professor emeritus of English at the University of Massachusetts.

Meridel LeSueur, a legendary figure in midwestern literature and populist politics, is the author of such works as *Salute to Spring, Harvest,* and *A Song for Our Time* (short stories), *North Star Country* (nonfiction), and *The Girl* (novel). As exemplified by "Corn Village," the substance and style of her work continue to remain both innovative and timely.

Orval Lund lives in Winona, Minnesota, and is associate professor of English at Winona State University. He is the author of a chapbook of poems, *Take Paradise,* and serves as editor of the literary journal *Great River Review.*

Thomas McGrath was born and raised in North Dakota and was that state's first Rhodes Scholar. After working as a documentary film writer and labor organizer, McGrath entered university teaching, finishing his career at Moorhead State University from 1969 to 1983. Among his many collections of poems published before his death in 1990 are *The Movie at the End of the World, Passages Toward the Dark,* and *Selected Poems 1938–1988.* His book-length poem *Letter to an Imaginary Friend* is considered by many to be an American classic.

Frederick Manfred lives in Luverne, Minnesota, in "Roundwind," a home built from native rock. He is the author of many novels, including *Conquering Horse, Green Earth,* and *Of Lizards and Angels: A Saga of Siouxland,* as well as collections of poems and essays.

Michael Martone was born and raised in Fort Wayne, Indiana, and is currently associate professor of English at Syracuse University. He is the editor of *A Place of Sense* and *Townships,* both collections of essays, and the author of *Fort Wayne Is Seventh on Hitler's List,* a collection of short fiction.

Jay Meek is poetry editor of *North Dakota Quarterly* and the author of five collections of poetry, most recently *Stations* and *Windows.* He also coedited *After the Storm: Poems on the Persian Gulf War.* He lives in Grand Forks, North Dakota, where he is professor of English and director of the creative writing program at the University of North Dakota.

William Meissner directs the program in creative writing at St. Cloud State University in St. Cloud, Minnesota. Among his numerous publications are the collections of poems *Learning to Breathe Underwater, The Sleepwalker's Son,* and *Twin Sons of Different Mirrors,* a collection of collaborative poems with Jack Driscoll. *Hitting into the Wind,* a collection of his baseball fiction and poetry, is forthcoming.

Prior to turning his attention to full-time writing, Howard Mohr taught in the English department at Southwest State University in Marshall, Minnesota. He lives in rural Cottonwood, Minnesota, and is the author of *How to Tell a Tornado,* a collection of poems, and two books of humor, *How to Talk Minnesotan* and *A Minnesota Book of Days (and a Few Nights).*

Michael Moos lives in St. Paul, Minnesota, and teaches literature and writing at the Breck School and at The Loft in Minneapolis. His collections of poems include *Morning Windows* and *A Long Way to See,* a collaboration with landscape photographer Wayne Gudmundson.

Carol Muske was born and raised in North Dakota and is currently professor of English and creative writing at the University of Southern California. Her books of poems include *Red Trousseau, Applause, Wyndmere,* and *Camouflage. Saving St. Germ,* a novel, is forthcoming.

Kathleen Norris of Lemmon, South Dakota, works as artist-in-residence for the North Dakota Council on the Arts and is on the faculty of the Great Plains Institute of Theology. She is the author of *The Middle of the World,* a collection of poems, and *Dakota: A Spiritual Geography,* a collection of essays.

Dan O'Brien ranches near Black Hills, South Dakota. He is the author of *Eminent Domain*, a collection of stories, and two novels, *Spirit of the Hills* and *In the Center of the Nation*, as well as *Rites of Autumn*, a nonfiction account of his work with peregrine falcons.

Tim O'Brien grew up in Worthington, Minnesota. His memoirs and novels include *If I Die in a Combat Zone, Northern Lights, Going after Cacciato, The Nuclear Age*, and *The Things They Carried*. He lives and writes in Boxford, Massachusetts.

Roger Pfingston lives and works as a teacher, writer, and photographer in Bloomington, Indiana. Among his collections of poetry are *Something Iridescent: Poems and Stories, Grady's Lunch, The Circus of Unreasonable Acts, Hazards of Photography*, and, with poet Ralph Burns, a photographic collaboration, *Windy Tuesday Nights*.

David Ray is the author of twelve books of poetry, the most recent being *Not Far from the River* (translations of ancient Indian love poems), *The Maharahani's New Wall*, and *Sam's Book*. He is professor of English at the University of Missouri-Kansas City.

Gail Rixen is a self-employed carpenter and substitute teacher from rural Chokio, Minnesota, and the author of a collection of poems, *Pictures of Three Seasons*.

George Roberts lives in Minneapolis, Minnesota, where he teaches English and writing for the Minneapolis Public Schools. He is the author of two collections of poems, *The Blessing of Winter Rain* and *scrut*.

CarolAnn Russell was born in North Dakota and raised in Minnesota. She is currently associate professor of English and director of the women's studies program at Bemidji State University in Bemidji, Minnesota. Her collections of poems include *The Red Envelope* and *The Tao of Women*.

Robert Schuler lives in Menomonie, Wisconsin, and is professor of English at the University of Wisconsin-Stout. For many years he edited the magazine *Uzzano*. *Kick out the Windows: New and Selected Poems* is forthcoming.

Herbert Scott lives in Kalamazoo, Michigan, where he is professor of English at Western Michigan University. He is the author of *Disguises, Groceries, Durations*, and *The Death and Resurrection of Jesse James*, all collections of poetry.

Judith Sornberger is assistant professor of English and director of the women's studies program at Mansfield University of Pennsylvania, after living for many years in Nebraska. *Open Heart*, a collection of her poems, is forthcoming.

William Stafford was born and raised in Kansas and taught writing and literature at Lewis and Clark College in Portland, Oregon, before retiring. His many collections of poetry have been appearing steadily since 1960, including *Traveling through the Dark, Stories That Could Be True: New and Collected Poems, Passwords,* and *An Oregon Message.* His *Writing the Australian Crawl: Views of the Writer's Vocation* has become a contemporary classic on the art and craft of writing.

Lucien Stryk, editor, translator, and writer, lives and writes in De Kalb, Illinois. He taught in the department of English at Northern Illinois University before turning to full-time writing and translating. Stryk's *Heartland: Poets of the Midwest* and *Heartland II* anthologies are considered by many to be among the most influential anthologies since 1960. Among his fourteen books of poems and translations are *The Penguin Book of Zen Poetry, Collected Poems,* and *The Dumpling Fields: Haiku of Issa.*

Barton Sutter lives in Duluth, Minnesota, where he is a free-lance writer and part-time teacher at the University of Minnesota-Duluth. He is the author of *My Father's War and Other Stories* and the one-act verse play *Small Town Triumphs,* produced by the Great American History Theatre of St. Paul. His collections of poems include *Cedarhome* and *Pine Creek Parish Hall and Other Poems.*

Thom Tammaro lives in Moorhead, Minnesota, where he is professor of multidisciplinary studies at Moorhead State University. He is the author of *Minnesota Suite,* a chapbook of poems, and the editor of *Roving across Fields: A Conversation with William Stafford and Uncollected Poems 1942–1982.*

Susan Allen Toth lives in Minneapolis, Minnesota, and is adjunct professor of English at Macalester College in St. Paul. Among her many books are *My Love Affair with England, Reading Rooms,* edited with John Coughlan, *A House of One's Own,* coauthored with James Stageberg, and the trilogy *Blooming, Ivy Days,* and *How to Prepare for Your High School Reunion.*

Brother Benet Tvedten lives and works in the Benedictine community of Blue Cloud Abbey near Marvin, South Dakota. He is the author of a novella called *All Manner of Monks* and *A Share in the Kingdom,* a commentary on the Rule of Saint Benedict.

Mark Vinz lives in Moorhead, Minnesota, where he is professor of English at Moorhead State University. He is the author of several collections of poems, such as *Mixed Blessings, Late Night Calls,* and *Minnesota Gothic* (in collaboration with photographer Wayne Gudmundson). His short stories have appeared in several magazines and newspapers.

Gerald Vizenor grew up in Minnesota and is currently professor of Native American literature at the University of California, Berkeley. He is the editor and author of several collections of narrative histories, short stories, novels, poems, and literary criticism, among them *Narrative Chance: Postmodern Discourse on Native American Literature, Griever: An American Monkey King in China,* and *Interior Landscapes: Autobiographical Myths and Metaphors.*

Sharon Oard Warner is the author of *Learning to Dance and Other Stories.* She lives in Ames, Iowa, and is visiting assistant professor of English at Drake University in Des Moines.

Cary Waterman lives in McGregor, Minnesota, and teaches writing at Augsburg College, Metropolitan State University, and at The Loft in Minneapolis. She is the author of *The Salamander Migration and Other Poems* and *When I Looked Back You Were Gone.*

Will Weaver lives in Bemidji, Minnesota, where he teaches fiction at Bemidji State University. His novel *Red Earth, White Earth* was produced as a CBS Television movie in 1989. His second book is *A Gravestone Made of Wheat and Other Stories.* A novel for young adults is forthcoming.

Don Welch, author of *The Rarer Game,* a collection of poems, lives in Kearney, Nebraska, where he is Reynolds Professor of Poetry at the University of Nebraska at Kearney.

Sylvia Griffith Wheeler lives in Vermillion, South Dakota, where she is associate professor of English at the University of South Dakota. Her collections of poetry include *Counting Back* and *Dancing Alone.* She is also the author of a play, *This Fool History: An Oral History.*

Roberta Hill Whiteman, a member of the Oneida tribe, grew up in Wisconsin and currently teaches at the University of Wisconsin–Madison. She is the author of a collection of poems, *Star Quilt.*

Larry Woiwode's *Beyond the Bedroom Wall* is considered by many to be among the most important American novels since 1945. His most recent books are *The Neumiller Stories* and *Indian Affairs,* a novel. A native North Dakotan, he lived and taught for many years in the East, eventually returning to a farm near Mott, North Dakota.

David Wojahn was born in St. Paul, Minnesota. His books of poetry include *Glassworks, Icehouse Lights,* and *Mystery Train.* He lives in Bloomington, Indiana, and teaches in the writing programs of Indiana University and Vermont College.

Paul Zimmer is the founding editor of the poetry series at the university presses at Pittsburgh, Georgia, and Iowa. He is currently director and editor of the University of Iowa Press. His collections of poems include *The Great Bird of Love* and *Family Reunion: Selected and New Poems*.

Patricia Zontelli grew up on the Cuyuna Range in northern Minnesota, and currently lives in Menomonie, Wisconsin, where she teaches at the University of Wisconsin-Stout. She is the author of a collection of poems, *Edith Jacobson Begins to Fly*.

Permissions

335